"The Congress of Black Writers marks one of the most important gatherings of radical intellectuals in the twentieth century ... Where else can you find the likes of C. L. R. James, Walter Rodney, Richard B. Moore, James Forman, Stokely Carmichael, Robert Hill and others, talking revolution to an engaged and sometimes combative crowd? I couldn't put the book down."
—ROBIN D. G. KELLEY, author of *Freedom Dreams: The Black Radical Imagination*

"*Moving Against the System* is a carefully constructed montage of the leadership, dynamics, and substance of what became an international 'Movement.' It is a revelatory portrait of the past that is no less revealing of the political dynamics and potential of today's Black Live Matter, #MeToo, and other activist efforts. A must read."
—HARRY EDWARDS, Ph.D., Prof. Emeritus, Univ. of California, Berkeley; Consultant: NFL, NBA

"Austin provides a wonderful contextual and critical Introduction making the contributions of C. L. R. James, Robert Hill, Walter Rodney, James Forman, Stokely Carmichael and many others not only relevant to but also very much alive for contemporary movement theory and practice. A must read for all those concerned with anti-racist revolutionary social transformation today."
—GARY KINSMAN, gay liberation and anti-capitalist activist, co-author of *The Canadian War on Queers: National Security as Sexual Regulation*

"*Moving Against the System* powerfully reminds us of the depth and breadth of the Black radical tradition and its profound, enduring contributions to anti-imperialist thought and action. But more than this, at a time when such acute insights are badly needed, Austin suggests critical ways to engage with these ideas and histories, to educate and inform today's struggles to change the system."
—AZIZ CHOUDRY, Canada Research Chair in Social Movement Learning and Knowledge Production, McGill University

"Like Stokely Carmichael and so many others who participated in the 1968 Congress of Black Writers in Montreal, David Austin seeks to transform the paradigm ... With this book, Austin further establishes himself as a leading light within that tradition."
—STEVEN HIGH, Department of History, Concordia University

"It is simply extraordinary to read, 50 years later, this collection from the Congress of Black Writers in Montreal in 1968. Not only has David Austin gathered and expertly introduced the interventions of some of the twentieth century's most important intellectuals and militants, these texts remind us of a time when the struggles against racism, capitalism, and imperialism converged on a global scale and advanced a project for liberation . . . a project which remains central and necessary today."

—ASAD HAIDER, author of *Mistaken Identity: Race and Class in the Age of Trump*

"This remarkable collection gathers electric essays from a critical site of the making of a 'global 1968.' Masterfully introduced, it includes the work of leading pan-African thinkers and freedom fighters gathered at the most important North American intellectual event of that critical year. The histories and dilemmas that they dissect are ones with which we still very much live."

—DAVID ROEDIGER, author of *Class, Race, and Marxism*

"This collection is a treasure chest of Canadian, Caribbean, and African diasporic history. And David Austin is a remarkable archivist, curator, detective and analyst of this decisive moment."

—KAREN DUBINSKY, Professor, Global Development Studies and History
Queen's University

"David Austin has done a tremendous service by bringing together this brilliant and inspiring collection from the Congress of Black Writers . . . With white supremacy on the rise once again, the insights contained here provide a vital guide to the waging of revolutionary anti-racist praxis on a global scale."

—SUNERA THOBANI, Department of Asian Studies, University of British Columbia; author of *Exalted Subjects: Studies in the Making of Race and Nation in Canada*

"Reading *Moving Against the System* as an activist and organizer is to experience time folding in on itself . . . much of our struggles today are informed in part by some of the men whose speeches and arguments appear here . . . the documentation of this incredibly important Congress in an accessible book format is sure to remain relevant and instructive for years to come"

—SANDRA HUDSON, co-founder of Black Lives Matter—Toronto

MOVING
AGAINST
THE
SYSTEM

MOVING AGAINST THE SYSTEM

The 1968 Congress
of Black Writers
and the Making of
Global Consciousness

Edited and with
an Introduction by
David Austin

PLUTO PRESS

First published in Canada in 2018 by Between the Lines, Toronto, Canada
www.btlbooks.com

First published in the UK 2018 by Pluto Press
345 Archway Road, London N6 5AA

www.plutobooks.com

British Library Cataloguing in Publication Data
A catalogue record for this book is available from the British Library

ISBN   978 0 7453 3866 8   Hardback
ISBN   978 0 7453 3865 1   Paperback
ISBN   978 1 7868 0378 8   PDF eBook
ISBN   978 1 7868 0380 1   Kindle eBook
ISBN   978 1 7868 0379 5   EPUB eBook

Typeset by Stanford DTP Services, Northampton, England
Printed and bound by CPI Group (UK) Ltd, Croydon, CR0 4YY

In memory of Franklyn Harvey

CONTENTS

ACKNOWLEDGEMENTS

There are far too many people who are part of this book in one form or another to mention, and I am bound to forget some of you. Please know that I appreciate the many big and small ways that you have been helpful.

I would like to thank Between the Lines' Managing Editor, Amanda Crocker, for her support and patience when I proposed the publication of this book—for this year, at the eleventh hour. I would also like to thank Marg Anne Morrison for her sensitive editing of the entire book; Jennifer Tiberio, BTL's Art Director and Production Manager; and the rest of the team at BTL who carried *Moving Against the System* through the various stages of production. I would also like to thank the McGill University Archives for granting permission to use images of Stokely Carmichael on the book's cover, as well as interior images of James Forman, Ted Joans, and Harry Edwards.

There are a number of women and men who have been generous with their time and have reminded me of the importance of the Congress of Black Writers and the significance of that entire historical period: Viola Daniel, Celia Daniel, Gene Depradine, Ramesh Rambaran, Bukka Rennie, and Bertram Boldon; Raymond Watts, who initiated the congress and granted me an extensive interview some years ago; Lynette Edwards, Sam Boskey, Laurette Solomon, and Brenda Paris; Yvonne Greer; and Marguerite Alfred who, in addition to her time, generously shared recordings of the congress proceedings with me. Norman Cook's insights on the relationship between Caribbean migrants and black Canadians during this period were also of great value.

They are no longer with us today, but the late Bridget Joseph, Tim Hector, Rosie Douglas, Leroy Butcher, and Franklyn Harvey shared their time and insights over the years. Franklyn deserves special mention. Not only was he a dear friend, but I also benefited from his considerable wisdom. That he and so many others have passed away in recent years serves as a reminder of the importance of recording their stories.

Robert Hill, Franklyn's old friend and comrade, not only participated in the congress and the various events that precipitated it but is an historian's historian and philosophical thinker whose insights have been invaluable to me over the years. Adeline Magloire Chancy has also been generous with her time and granted me access to her personal notes and reflections on the year 1968 in Montreal and the Congress of Black Writers. Her wonderful spirit is matched only by her acute political insight, convictions, and ongoing commitment to social change in general, and in Haiti in particular. I would also like to thank Partricia Thébaud for permitting me to reproduce images of the Congress of Black Writers, including pictures of her late husband, Elder Thébaud, co-chair of the conference.

Burnley "Rocky" Jones is a central figure in Canada's Black Power story who played a crucial role in black Canadian politics from the sixties up until his recent death. He kindly consented to the use of pictures from his personal archive. Kari Polanyi-Levitt has shared her insights on the congress and the New World group over the years, and the late Martin Glaberman was kind enough to send me C. L. R. James' speech on the Haitian Revolution some years ago. Rosalind Boyd's vivid memory, diaries, and personal archive have helped to fill in some of the many gaps in the historical record.

I would also like to acknowledge Alissa Trotz, Amarkai Laryea, Hillina Seife, Verda Cook, Adelle Blackett, Samule Furé, Kristen Young, Roberto Zurbano, Kagiso Molope, Mariame Kaba, Astrid Jacques, Melanie Newton, Beverley Mullings, Rosalind Hampton, Patricia Harewood, and Adrian Harewood; and Isaac Saney, for sharing his thoughts on Joan Jones and the Halifax parallels. Not only was Désirée Rochat particularly helpful in securing images for the book, but she also embodies the best of the spirit, politics, and convictions of the generation of Haitian women political exiles in Montreal in the 1960s.

This book would not have seen the light of day without the support, love, and patience of my family—Méshama and Alama, and my partner, friend, and comrade, Laneydi Martinez Alfonso. Thank you does not say enough.

Sometime in 1995, the late Alfie Roberts handed me several reels that included speeches delivered by C. L. R. James in Montreal in the late sixties and the proceedings of the Congress of Black Writers. I still recall being overcome with a surreal feeling as I listened to those recordings for the first time in my Côte-des-Neiges apartment on rue Édouard-Montpetit in Montreal, transfixed and transposed as if I had stepped back in time and was participating in the congress. Patricia and Alfie Roberts were dear friends, and when Alfie died in 1996, followed by Pat a few years later, it was left to me to publish both James' lectures and the proceedings from the Congress of Black Writers. The James lectures were published some years ago, and with the publication of the congress speeches I am fulfilling a long-time commitment. *Moving Against the System* has come much later than expected, but it nonetheless arrives at a timely anniversary and moment in global politics as it recalls a period when people discussed the dynamics of social change with a sense of urgency, as if their lives depended on it, as they imagined the creation of a better world.

Introduction

THE DIALECT OF LIBERATION

The Congress of Black Writers at 50 — and Beyond

DAVID AUSTIN

For the black man in Canada, it was a stimulating and edifying experience. His only hope now lies in a new era of black militance and a new humanism. To quote Frantz Fanon, ". . . man is a *yes* . . . *Yes* to life. *Yes* to love. *Yes* to generosity. But man is also a *no*. *No* to scorn of man. *No* to degradation of man. *No* to the exploitation of man. *No* to the butchery of what is most human in man: freedom."

— Barbara Jones, "A Black Woman Speaks Out"

It is interesting to note the cross section of persons and organizations represented at the conference. This would tend to provide additional credence of the ties existing between the main subversive elements both here and in the United States as well. . . . It was not in fact a presentation of literature by Black Writers. It is believed that the outcome of this caucus was programmed well in advance and in fact was a deliberate attempt to further motivate dissension and subversion within the population.

— *Canadian state security (RCMP) Congress of Black Writers file*

IFTY YEARS is not a long period in terms of historical time, but a great deal of history has unfolded since the epochal year 1968. Time, to use an obvious and perhaps outmoded cliché, is relative, and many of the central issues of that period still preoccupy us, and occupy a prominent place in contemporary geopolitics. The Congress of Black Writers was convened in 1968 in Montreal and was one of the most important black international gatherings of the post-Second World War period. But given the significance of black radical politics and movements for that era, the congress must also be understood as an important gathering in terms of left politics in general, and one whose impact was important for, but not limited to, people of African descent, not least because people of African descent live and act in this world. The world has changed significantly since that time, and the congress (and the year it occurred) is of great importance for our time.

Part of the event's relevance today lies in the fact that—in keeping with the dialectic of progression and regression—the circumstances and issues that brought the congress into being have not only survived into the present but are perhaps even more pronounced and acute today than they were fifty years ago. Because of this, the proceedings of the Congress of Black Writers, along with the tensions and contradictions that brought it into being, are important when thinking through the same political and socio-economic issues today.

The year 1968, it has been argued, represents the highpoint of a decade that was associated with several signature events: the Tet Offensive in South Vietnam and the general strike in France, which drew inspiration from the Vietnamese liberation struggle, and almost toppled the government of Charles de Gaulle[1]; the combination of anti-war protest and the Black Power movement, which fractured US society, just as the Cuban Revolution undermined US hegemony in the Americas. There were uprisings followed by suppressions in Poland and Czechoslovakia, and the popular movement that would eventually topple the military government of Ayub Khan in Pakistan; the Biafra civil war that tore at the core of a fragile Nigerian nation as, from Algiers to Cape Town, the ghost of Frantz Fanon haunted the African continent; and there was the anti-colonial struggle to free Guinea-Bissau from Portuguese colonialism, which, it was hoped, would help pave the way for a new day on the continent, even as the scourge of white supremacy in South Africa, Zimbabwe, Angola, and Mozambique persisted.

Martin Luther King Jr. and Robert Kennedy were assassinated in this infamous year, two deaths that, for many, demonstrated the folly of American democracy and the impossibility of achieving genuine freedom through conventional means. By this time the Civil Rights movement had transitioned to Black Power as the dominant, or at least most vociferous, form of black struggle in the US, Canada, and the UK. Black athletes protested against racism during the Mexico Olympics (in the lead up to the Olympics, hundreds of students were killed by the Mexican authorities during the Tlatelolco Massacre). While Black Panther Party members patrolled the streets of Oakland in order to protect black civilians from police incursions, Quebec, and the city of Montreal in particular, became a hotbed of radical socialist and nationalist politics, in part inspired by Black Power and African liberation struggles.

As French Quebec grappled with 200 years of British and anglophone domination and struggled for economic, cultural, linguistic, and political self-determination, the ideas of Simone de Beauvoir, Jean-Paul Sartre, and anti-colonial theorists such as Albert Memmi, Aimé Césaire, and, perhaps most important of all, Frantz Fanon circulated among the left in Montreal.[2] Indeed, Fanon's ideas entered North America via Quebec, where *Les damnés de la terre*, the French original of *The Wretched of the Earth*, found a home long before the first English translation. The emergence of Black Power in the United States profoundly influenced Quebec's independence movement, and particularly touched members of the Front de libération du Québec (FLQ), the militant separatist group that was responsible for a series of bomb attacks and other acts of violent protest in Quebec in the long 1960s. Two of the FLQ's leading figures sought to develop ties with Black Power figures in the United States, such as Stokely Carmichael,[3] and drew upon the ideas of Malcolm X who, allegedly made a brief visit to Montreal in January 1965 (we know with certainty that he made an appearance in Toronto on CBC's *Front Page Challenge* with Pierre Berton in the same month).[4]

In 1966, FLQ members Pierre Vallières and Charles Gagnon traveled to the US in order to make contact with Black Power and Puerto Rican militants with the goal of forming a nationalist front against colonial oppression.[5] They distributed a declaration in the United Nations headquarters concerning incarcerated FLQ members in Montreal and Quebec's decolonization movement.[6] They were eventually arrested by American authorities in New York and jailed in the Manhattan Detention Center for disturbing the peace,[7] but it was during his detention that Vallières wrote his most celebrated work, *Nègres blancs d'Amérique—The White Niggers of America*.[8] I have discussed this peculiarly Quebec conception of *nègres* in *Fear of a Black Nation*,[9] but in response to this problematic appropriation of black identity, the Congress of Black Writers co-chair Elder Thébaud retorted that, while it had become fashionable for French Quebecers to refer to themselves as Canada's *nègres blancs*, blacks were, to use a tautology, the real *nègres* in Canada and in the world at large.[10] The US Black Power movement was central to Vallières' thinking, and yet, one could read in the FLQ theorist's book that "In Quebec the French Canadians are not subject to this irrational racism that has done so much wrong to the workers, white and black, of the United States. They can take no credit for that, since in Quebec there is no 'black problem.'"[11] As I have suggested elsewhere, we might rightly ask, if the "high priests" of the left-wing Quebec separatist movement, which owed so much to US Black Power, did not recognize racism right under their very noses—not to mention the almost total elision of the colonial condition of Indigenous peoples—what hope was there for the rest of Canada? But to his credit, Vallières later revised his views on the existence of racial discrimination in French Canada, including the plight of Canada's first peoples, who were colonized by both the French and the English.[12]

Black Montrealers were a component part of this politically charged atmosphere,[13] and while the congress co-chairs argued that the event could have been convened anywhere,[14] there were particular circumstances that conspired to bring it to Montreal. Vallières' remarks came at the very moment that Montreal's black population began to swell, initially as a result of the influx of women and men from the anglophone Caribbean, although Haitians would soon become the largest of the immigrant groups of African and Caribbean descent, as well as a population that consisted of women and men from the African continent and, to a lesser extent, the US in the form of African-American draft dodgers.[15] Each one of these groups sought a new life, and each brought with them their own peculiar cultural and political luggage as they settled alongside the pre-existing community of black Canadians that extended back to the period of slavery in Canada. This community had once included Louise Langdon Norton, or simply Louise Langdon, who emigrated from the Caribbean (St. Andrews, Grenada) to Montreal in the early twentieth century, where she met Earl Little, who had migrated from Georgia to Montreal in 1917.[16] Both were members of the Montreal chapter of the Universal Negro Improvement Association and African Communities League (UNIA-ACL), a mass global black uplift organization founded by the Jamaican Marcus Garvey, with an international following in North America, the African continent, the Caribbean, and Latin America (Cuba alone had some fifty chapters of the organization). The Montreal chapter of the UNIA was established informally in 1917 and then officially in 1919,[17] and as the Guyanese writer Jan Carew, who himself played an active role in the Congress of Black Writers, has written, "Louise Langdon, her husband Earl Little, as Garveyite devotees and new converts, laid the foundation on which all the succeeding Black Power movements in Canada and the United

States were built."[18] What at first sight might sound a touch hyperbolic in fact resonates with reality when we consider that Langdon and Little were the parents of Malcolm X, the single most significant influence on the Black Power movement in the 1960s. For Max Elbaum, writing in *Revolution in the Air: Sixties Radicals Turn to Lenin, Mao and Che*, Malcolm's 1965 *Autobiography* was "without question the single most widely read and influential book among young people of all racial backgrounds who went to their first demonstration sometime between 1965 and1968."[19] Malcolm X was one of the most influential figures—and not only black figures—of the post-Second World War period and, other than Garvey himself, arguably no other twentieth-century black figure had a greater impact on the world stage than Malcolm, the son of Garveyite parents.

In the 1960s, the island of Montreal was Canada's economic and cosmopolitan cultural centre that still boasted a hopping jazz music scene (Montreal was the home of the great pianist Oscar Peterson). It attracted people from all over the world, including visitors to the International and Universal Exposition that was hosted by Montreal in 1967, otherwise known as Expo '67. These were heightened political times, and Caribbean and African-American cultural-political figures such as Harry Belafonte, Stokely Carmichael, Dick Gregory,[20] Lloyd Best, Richard B. Moore, C. L. R. James, Jan Carew, Mighty Sparrow, Austin Clarke, George Lamming, Orlando Patterson, Édouard Glissant, and Aimé Césaire, among others, visited the city on one occasion or more. This was the historical moment in which the Congress of Black Writers (October 11–14) was convened at McGill University, organized by a combination of Caribbean and black Canadian students from McGill and Sir George Williams universities (now Concordia University) and members of Montreal's wider black community. The four-day gathering was largely conducted in English, but it nonetheless brought Creole, French, and English speakers together in an attempt to address the impact of colonization and slavery and the rupture, fragmentation, dislocation, criminalization, and, of course, racialization of black lives. The congress thus represented an effort to purge the demons of the past—a kind of exercise in exorcism—and to chart a course that would transcend the social, political, and economic contradictions of the living present. In this spirit, the event's success lay in the fact that, on a local level, it fostered a renewed sense of community and purpose among blacks in Montreal, and to a lesser extent in Toronto and other Canadian cities, and served as an international locus that connected black political figures and movements in three continents.

For Yvonne Greer, who became active within Montreal's black community in the aftermath of the congress and the Sir George Williams University protest, the event was "like going to a rock concert," philosophically adding that she cannot "think of anything positive that it wasn't" or "negative that it was."[21] The event might also be described as a kind of revival meeting organized to spur black Canadians into political action, or an exorcism of the pent up anguish and frustration that had accumulated after centuries of slavery, colonialism, and racial discrimination and exploitation. Nova Scotia's Burnley "Rocky" Jones described the event as "the most exciting time for black people in Canada" and the wider society was shocked at the presence of black political intellectuals in Canada and the expression of internationalism that connected blacks from around the world.[22] The shock was combined with a sense of dread, which resulted in co-ordinated state security measures to suppress the movement that this public display of black politics symbolized.

Genesis

The idea to organize a Congress of Black Writers was first proposed by Raymond Watts, a Trinidadian autodidact Marxist and musician who moved to Montreal from London to work as a train porter in order to support his family. Watts and fellow Trinidadian Wally Look Lai had been members of a study group that met in the London home of C. L. R and Selma James in the early sixties, a group that included young Caribbean intellectuals such as Jamaica's Joan French, Orlando Patterson, Richard Small, and briefly Robert Hill, and Walter Rodney of Guyana. But lacking the formal education of his peers, Watts often felt marginalized within the London group. He and Look Lai were later part of the Conference Committee on West Indian Affairs, otherwise known as the Caribbean Conference Committee (CCC), an important Montreal-based group that organized a series of conferences about the Caribbean between 1965 and 1967 that included the participation of several prominent Caribbean writers, artists, economists, and political figures, such as Jan Carew, Norman Girvan, Austin Clarke, Orlando Patterson, Lloyd Best, Richard B. Moore, and calypso singer Mighty Sparrow. Referring to the CCC during his keynote address at the inaugural conference, "The Shaping of the Future of the West Indies," the Barbadian novelist George Lamming praised the CCC for its work: "I would like ... to let you know that what you are doing here tonight has many echoes in London and for many of your compatriots who work in various activities throughout Africa. You are in a sense operating on a world scale."[23] Lamming went on to declare: "I want also, I think, to congratulate you on what I believe is the first conference of this kind."[24]

C. L. R. James in the home of Alfie Roberts.
Alfie Roberts Collection

C. L. R. James served as a mentor to several CCC members who formed its Marxist-oriented affiliate, the C. L. R. James Study Circle (CLRJSC), established by Robert Hill, one of the CCC's founding members. At the time, Hill was a young Jamaican student, first at Carleton University in Ottawa and then the University of Toronto, and as a member of the CLRJSC and the Detroit-based Facing Reality group he took the initiative to publish James' study of the Hegelian logic and socialism, *Notes on Dialectics*, for the first time. Hill and the group's other core members—Alfie Roberts, Anne Cools, Tim Hector, Franklyn Harvey, and to a degree, Rosie Douglas—adopted James as a mentor, which resulted in a series of small classes on Marxism and politics that have since been published under the title *You Don't Play with Revolution: The Montreal Lectures of C. L. R. James.*[25] The group also organized a lecture tour for James that connected him to a new generation of students and young radicals in Canada and the US, including

George Lamming and Rosie Douglas (seated) at Caribbean Conference Committee event, 1965. Alfie Roberts Collection

CCC-CLRJSC members Franklyn Harvey, Robert Hill, Alfie Roberts, Tim Hector, in Montreal, ca. 1967. Alfie Roberts Collection

Stokely Carmichael and other figures within the Black Power and Black Studies movements.

The CCC-CLRJSC's work and relationship with James situated the group within a Caribbean radical and political-intellectual tradition. While a detailed outline of the significance of this point is beyond our scope here, it is important to note that, in many ways, the work of these "maroon intellectuals"—small political-intellectual groupings situated within the tradition of rebellious slaves who established autonomous settlements in the Caribbean and other parts of the Americas[26]—also helped birth what can justifiably be described as a Canadian dimension of the Caribbean Radical Tradition and what Cedric J. Robinson has described as the Black Radical Tradition that is rooted in the history of black resistance and "an accretion, over generations, of collective intelligence gathered from struggle."[27] In Robinson's view, this tradition manifested itself in the early twentieth century in the work of James, George Padmore, W. E. B. Du Bois, Richard Wright, and Oliver Cox, a list to which we must add Claudia Jones, Elma Francois, Kathleen Cleaver, and Angela Davis, among others.[28] Since the publication of Robinson's classic book, the analysis of this tradition has been expanded in ways that seriously consider the role of gender, the arts, and sexuality within this tradition,[29] all of which is important in terms of appreciating the legacy and significance of the congress today.

James' connection to the CCC also signified the passing of a torch of sorts from the older to the younger generation of Caribbean radicals. And while the CCC had essentially disbanded after its third conference in 1967, this by no means meant an end to the Caribbean group's collective work.[30] By then several members of its core, including the three H's (Hill, Harvey, and Hector), had returned to the Caribbean while Cools was sojourning in England (Roberts remained in Montreal), but the CCC's work continued through the work of Caribbean Nation (CN), which published a one-off issue of *Caribbean International: The Dynamics of Liberation Opinion*,[31] a revolutionary journal established by former CCC-CLRJSC members and the publication of which coincided with the convening of the 1968 Congress of Black Writers. In some respects, the CN journal represented a Caribbeanized rendition of *International African Opinion*, the pan-African journal edited by James in the 1930s in London for the International African Service Bureau (IASB), led by fellow Trinidadian George Padmore and involving Amy Ashwood Garvey and Ras Makonnen of Jamaica and Guayana respectively, and future African heads of state Kwame Nkrumah of Ghana and Jomo Kenyatta of Kenya. In other words, not only did the CCC-CLRJSC and now CN work closely with James, but its members situated themselves within the political tradition of James and his fellow pan-Africanists in the 1930s.

Despite the fact that it was not a CCC event, its core members considered the congress to be the climax of the "consciousness-raising" activities[32] that the group had organized between 1965 and 1967, and Franklyn Harvey appears to have influenced the meeting's direction from Trinidad through his correspondence with Rosie Douglas.[33] As the subtitle of the congress and *Caribbean International Opinion* suggests—"The Dynamics of Black Liberation" and "The Dynamics of Liberation" respectively—the journal might perhaps be described as a Marxist-oriented complement to the growing sense of black nationalism and Black Power that the congress represented. The choice of titles could hardly have been coincidental and as the term "dynamic" implies, both the editors of the journal and the organizers of the congress imagined freedom as a process, riddled with tensions and contradictions out of which liberation took form, and in this sense, the term "dialectic" could have made a suitable substitute. In terms of the scope of the journal's content, in addition to the submissions by three former CCC-CLRJSC members—Alfie Roberts on sugar and the Caribbean revolution, Franklyn Harvey on the May 1968 revolts in France, and Tim Hector on the plight of

CARIBBEAN
INTERNATIONAL
OPINION

DYNAMICS OF LIBERATION

october 1968

Caribbean International Opinion (cover).
Alfie Roberts Collection

the Vietnamese in both North and South Vietnam—it also contains two contributions by C. L. R. James, the first on political economy and the second entitled "State Capitalism and the French Revolutionary Tradition." Other contributors included two future Caribbean prime ministers: Arnim Eustace of St. Vincent and the Grenadines (listed as a member of the congress co-ordinating committee) who wrote about the economy of the Caribbean; Rosie Douglas who examined racism in Canada; S. (Stanley) Chiwaro of Zimbabwe (also a member of the congress co-ordinating committee) who discussed neo-colonialism in Africa; M. A. Farray on "The Historical Development of Capitalism and Its Effects on the New and Afro-Asian Worlds," M. Barrow on "Art and Bourgeois Reality," and Feleon on Haiti under François Duvalier.

The departure of several prominent members of the group to the Caribbean or England signaled the arrival of a new political sensibility among black and Caribbean women and men in Montreal and across Canada. A political shift began to take place among both Canadian-born blacks and Caribbean immigrants who increasingly drew inspiration from the Black Power movement, as they had before from the Civil Rights movement in the United States. Many in the growing Caribbean community began to turn their attention away from the region and toward the domestic needs of people of African descent in their adopted home. Between October 4 and 6, 1968, another outgrowth of the CCC, the Conference Committee, MTL (Caribbean and Other Black Organizations), otherwise known as the Canadian Conference Committee, organized a conference at Sir George Williams University focusing on "Problems of Involvement in the Canadian Society with Reference to the Black Peoples" under the leadership of, among others, Clarence Bayne, a Sir George Williams University economics professor from Trinidad, and the social worker and educator Dorothy Wills, originally from Dominica.[34] Guests included prominent African-Canadians, such as Dr. Howard McCurdy of Windsor University, US-native Daniel Hill, director of the Human Rights Commission of Ontario (also father to acclaimed author of *The Book of Negroes*, Lawrence Hill), and the African-Canadian Richard Lord, who was then vice president of the Quebec Liberal Party. The conference consisted of workshops related to employment, housing, political, cultural, and social alienation, Black Power and economics in Canada, and poetry and drama.[35]

As the Jamaican sociologist Dennis Forsythe wrote, this conference was more "pragmatically rather than ideologically oriented—a fact deduced from its various resolutions and composition of its panelists, but since pragmatism is also part of the dialectics of change, we should give the conference due credit, if not for its achievements, then at least for its designs."[36] Several resolutions were passed during the meeting, including the call for the educated and professional blacks to play a more direct role in education and employability of members of the black community, and a demand for a Royal Commission to investigate the issue of black civil rights in Canada.[37] Most significantly, a resolution was passed that called for a national black organization capable of meeting the growing and changing needs of blacks across Canada. Within a year this group founded the National Black Coalition of Canada (NBCC).[38]

But if the Canadian-focused conference was primarily pragmatic and local, the Congress of Black Writers was its opposite. Organized in Montreal the week after the Canadian-focused event at Sir George, the congress was ideologically driven by the spirit and force of radical Black Power politics, black nationalism, and black internationalism in ways that, judging from the extensive state security files on the event and those who organized and participated in it, clearly raised the alarm within the state security apparatus.[39] Raymond Watts envisioned the congress as part of the tradition that spawned the First and Second Congresses of Negro Writers and Artists (1956 and 1959 in Paris and Rome respectively) that brought together many of the leading African, African-American, and Caribbean intellectuals of the time, including Frantz Fanon, Aimé Césaire, Richard Wright, George Lamming, and Léopold Sédar Senghor.[40] In the end, the event was convened by a wider group of black students at McGill University and a co-ordinating committee that included students from Sir George Williams University and members of the wider black community that had been shifting in the direction of Black Power,[41] a shift that was captured in Canada by Austin Clarke's remarks about Martin Luther King Jr. Clarke's scathing critique of King's non-violent approach and what he described as moralistic attempts to appeal to the conscience of whites[42] was characteristic of a new phase in black struggle, the tenor and tone of which was reflected in the atmosphere of the congress, despite the fact that it was dedicated to the memories of both King and Malcolm X.

In his seminal study of the black diaspora, internationalism, and transnational politics, *In Search of the Black Fantastic: Politics and Popular Culture in the Post-Civil War Era*, Richard Iton suggests that the experience of the diaspora affords "the capacity to imagine and operate simultaneously within, against, and outside the nation-state," the possibility of challenging racialized exclusion and domination from within the nation state while transcending its boundaries and limitations.[43] Prevailing notions of diaspora are not as flexible as the term might imply, and despite the political possibilities that its porosity suggests, the word diaspora is often deployed in ways that imply stasis. But by 1968, Canadian, US, British, and Caribbean intelligence agencies were fully aware and mortally afraid of the transgressive, disruptive, and transnational political possibilities that Iton refers to.[44] In response, and as part of a process that I have referred to as biosexuality, or biosexual politics—a primeval fear of blacks that is rooted in slavery and the recurring need to control black bodies (and minds), a phenomenon intimately connected to a fear of black rebellion and self-activity and rooted in a primal fear of the biological and political spread of blackness through black-white solidarity and sexual encounters[45]—the state resorted to extraordinary security measures. Canadian state security was particularly concerned that Canada would somehow be "blackened" and radicalized by the growing presence and political persistence of blacks in Canada who were connected to blacks in the US, the Caribbean, and the UK; and that Canada, and particularly Montreal, was becoming a centre of international black radical activity.[46]

Black politics in the 1960s represented a struggle of people of African descent to realize their full humanity within the constraints of anti-black racism and economic imperialism. It was a public exorcism, the unleashing of centuries of pent up anger, anxiety, and frustration, and it attempted to abandon the demons that slavery and colonization had invested in their minds and bodies. Georgio Agamben has argued that, under the present crisis-ridden system of global capitalism, human life is increasingly reduced to naked or bare life in which states exert increasing control over human bodies.[47] But while the Italian philosopher has documented this growing phenomenon in Europe, he is seemingly oblivious to the fact that Césaire, Fanon, Angela Davis, Achille Mbembe, Saidiyya Hartman, and many others have documented this phenomenon in their work, and that blacks have been intimately familiar with this regime under slavery, colonialism, and institutional and systemic forms of anti-black racism. Reduced to mere bodies under slavery at a critical moment in the history of pre-capitalist and capitalist production, black slave labour was crucial, that is to say, to both constitutive and constituent parts of global capitalism. But slavery also resulted in the negation of

congress of black writers
congrès des écrivains noirs

towards
the second
emancipation
the dynamics
of black liberation

❖

vers la seconde
émancipation
dynamique
de la libération
noire

october 11th-14th, 1968
students union and leacock building
mcgill university
montreal, canada

souvenir
program

Congress of Black Writers Souvenir Program. Alfie Roberts Collection

blacks as intellectual beings and creators of culture. It should come as no surprise that black art forms are also frequently reduced to an essential essence and physicality that precludes appreciation of the work and dedication, intellectual or otherwise, that its production involves. The congress attempted to counter this phenomenon by validating black humanity on its own terms, and by rejecting master-slave dynamics in favour of self-recognition and self-affirmation. To the extent that these efforts were successful, they ushered in an era of heightened political consciousness in which blacks, through various processes, asserted their right to exist as human beings and to become, that is to say, to live a life of freedom. In response to this assertion of humanity came the calculated inanity of state security forces that took quasi-legal steps to eliminate its expression,[48] a potent reminder of the challenges involved in organizing for social change today.

The Event

The congress was dedicated to the memory of Dr. Martin Luther King Jr. and Malcolm X, whose images, along with Frantz Fanon, Patrice Lumumba, and other black political figures, adorned the walls of the student union ballroom that is today named after the Montreal actor and McGill alumnus of Star Trek fame, William Shatner. King was murdered several months before the congress convened and in the wake of his death, black neighbourhoods across the US erupted in rebellious fury as their frustrations boiled over into the streets. The palpable spirit of Black Power was symbolized in the militant rhetoric and actions of the Black Panther Party (BPP) and the shift of the Student Nonviolent Coordinating Committee (SNCC) toward the BPP, but also in a cultural revival in which blacks donned Afro hairstyles and, in some cases, African dress. The symbolic importance of dress and style was not lost on educator Yvonne Greer, who recalls seeing lawyer Richard Small dressed in African garb as he delivered his presentation at the congress on race in Britain. This taught her that blacks did not have to "become white," conform to a stereotype of an educated person, or ignore less privileged members of the community in order to be intellectuals or professionals.[49] Greer was not alone in her observations: Canadian state security also took note, with more than a hint of alarm, that "the dress of 75% of the negros [sic] present was of African type, possibly worn to indicate they were revolutionaries."[50]

The shift in consciousness was also explicit in the gathering's statement of purpose, signed by the McGill graduate students and co-chairs Elder Thébaud of Haiti, a future New York psychiatrist,[51] and Rosie Douglas, future prime minister of Dominica. The statement declared that "modern white oppression . . . has always sought to justify its oppressive control over the other races by resorting to arrogant claims of inherent superiority, and attempting to denigrate the cultural and historical achievements of the oppressed peoples."[52] The organizers also acknowledged that black struggles took place on the cultural, spiritual, as well as political and economic fronts, and that:

> In the face of this total colonial stranglehold, it is clear that the task of self-liberation involves much more than freedom from economic and social oppression. Genuine freedom can only come from the total liberation of the minds and spirits of our people from the false and distorted image of themselves which centuries of cultural enslavement by the white man have imposed on us all. The struggle for liberation of black people is accordingly not only an economic or political question, but also a cultural rallying cry, a call to re-examine the foundations of the white man's one-sided world, and to restore to ourselves an image of the achievements of our people, hitherto suppressed and abandoned among the rubble of history's abuses.
>
> It is in this context that this Congress of Black Writers hopes to make its contribution. Here for the first time in Canada, an attempt will be made to recall, in a series of popular lectures by black scholars, artists and politicians, a history which we have been taught to forget: the history of the black man's own response (in thought and in action) to the conditions of his existence in the New World; in short, the history of the black liberation struggle, from its origins in slavery to the present day. For the sake of to-morrow's victories, it is imperative that we take another look at the events of yesterday . . . in the Congress, black people will begin to rediscover themselves as the active creators, rather than the passive sufferers, of history's events; the subjects,

rather than objects, of history. It is only when we have rediscovered this lost perspective on ourselves that we can truly begin to speak of emancipation; it is only when we have returned to our authentic past that we can truly begin to dream about the future.[53]

In other words, history and memory were central to the conception of the congress and the organizers argued that memories of the past could be recast in the present to help shift the prevailing dynamics of power that devalued black humanity. In this sense, and notwithstanding the somewhat flawed absolutist conception of an "authentic" history, the organizers also understood the congress and the use of history as a significant step toward not simply authenticating the past, but ultimately confronting the economic and cultural underpinnings of white economic and political dominance and the presumption of cultural superiority that undergirded it in what they referred to as the "second emancipation": that is to say, the struggle for freedom in the post-slavery, post-colonial era.

Congress participants and attendees included the Trinidadian-American Stokely Carmichael, as well as Americans James Forman, Alvin Poussaint, Ted Joans, and Harry Edwards; C. L. R. James and Darcus Howe of Trinidad, both of whom were based in England; Richard B. Moore of Barbados, based in the US; Richard Small and Robert A. Hill of Jamaica; Walter Rodney of Guyana; and Canada's Burnley "Rocky" Jones. American poet LeRoi Jones was unable to attend because of a gun charge in New Jersey. BPP leader Eldridge Cleaver and the Haitian writer René Depestre were also absent. The government of California under Ronald Reagan annulled Cleaver's parole, effectively preventing him from traveling,[54] and, according to congress co-ordinating committee member Adeline Magloire Chancy, Depestre, who was then living in exile in Cuba, he did not respond to the invitation.[55] All three are nonetheless listed on the conference program, a reminder that documents alone can never tell the entire story.

News of an incident on the opening day of the congress helped to set the tone for the four-day gathering. The custodians of the St. Croix cemetery in Windsor, Nova Scotia, had recently refused to allow a young black girl to be buried there, based on a company by-law that permitted the prohibition of the burial of blacks and Indigenous peoples.[56] This incident drove home the fact that racial exclusion was not simply alive, but thriving in Canada, just as hundreds of people attended the congress to discuss the history and struggles of black people and the contemporary meaning of Black Power in the face of widespread anti-black racism in the West, and the impact of colonialism, neocolonialism, and imperialism in the Third World. Rocky Jones had been a

Congress co-chairs Elder Thébaud and Rosie Douglas at press conference. Courtesy of Elder Thébaud

member of the Friends of SNCC in Toronto before returning to Nova Scotia in 1966 where he co-founded Kawacha House in Halifax, a black community and political organization that worked on a range of issues affecting blacks. By 1968 he was well known for his work among blacks in Halifax who largely lived in *de facto* segregated and poor communities. Referring to the cemetery incident in his opening speech (only a fragment of the speech has survived), Jones described Canada as "Raceville," and discussed Halifax's black ghettoes and the existence of poor schools and teachers and the high dropout rate in black neighbourhoods. He argued that it would be an act of genocide for blacks to engage in gun violence against whites. Instead, he chose to focus on the need for blacks to be better organized politically and more attuned to what was happening with blacks internationally, in Kingston, Jamaica, or in Montreal and New York, as examples. Jones also called for a black media organization as a counter to the "white man's press," one that would serve to remind blacks that they were part of a global revolution. For Jones, it was also important to work with Indigenous and French-Canadian allies who were fighting against their English-Canadian oppressor, but, ultimately, people of African descent needed to consolidate power so that the "capitalist complex," as he described it, would see blacks as a force to be reckoned with, a force that was going to "change the history of mankind . . . now. [*Applause*]"

Elder Thébaud and unknown panelists. Courtesy of Elder Thébaud

In a follow-up interview with Radio McGill journalist George Lewinski, Jones renewed his call for African-Canadians, French-Canadians, and Indigenous peoples to work together, not necessarily because they liked one another, but in order to "fight a common struggle." Jones also expressed his opposition to the idea that blacks should build their own universities, instead arguing that existing universities could meet their needs while blacks learned their history in freedom schools or in their kitchens. Echoing Malcolm X, and later Stokely Carmichael and Charles Hamilton's analysis in their popular book *Black Power*, he also argued that whites must work in their own communities in order to confront racism and politicize other whites in "Raceville" rather than telling black people how to change their condition.

Darcus Howe, Carmichael's childhood friend in Trinidad and C. L. R. James' nephew, was one of the lesser-known figures to participate in the congress. According to his biographers Robin Bunce and Paul Field, it was after his participation in the congress that Howe—who would later become one of the most important popular left political figures in Britain's post-Second World War period—"made radical politics his vocation."[57] Howe was not a scheduled conference speaker, but he did find himself on the conference podium, and as Bukka Rennie recollected, he spoke about the "mash up" of the short-lived West Indies Federation (1958–1962) and, with a touch of humour, according to Rennie, the "number of institutions . . . born in Trinidad that outlasted the Federation. He was talking about Renegades Steel Band. [*Laughter*]"[58] But as James informed the audience following Howe's remarks, his nephew was "not a comedian," as his comments were intended to highlight the importance of learning from popular creativity and knowledge.[59]

As Howe himself recalled, the congress offered "some of the most brilliant speakers at that conference: Walter Rodney, Bobby Hill"—Hill "used to bounce on two feet like Fidel Castro! Tim Hector . . . I was terrified, I thought 'I'm among the big guns now.' C. L. R. mastered it. Carmichael graciously would accept that."[60] His allusion to Robert (Bobby) Hill and Walter Rodney is of particular interest here. Hill's presentation was not one of the most anticipated of the congress, but its resounding appeal was evident in the ample applause he received after he addressed his audience. His talk might be described as a phenomenology of Black Power, or what he referred to as the "metaphysical principle of black liberation and black resistance." From the Haitian Revolution to the phenomenon of Marcus Garvey and the emergence of the Black Power movement, Hill counterposed what he called moments of silence with the conscious actions of blacks to shatter that silence and assert their humanity. In this sense, the title of his talk, according to the congress program, "The Fathers of the Modern Revolt: Garvey, etc.," left much to be desired, and it could have perhaps been more appropriately titled "Beyond the Mournful Silence," the title of his 1966 presentation in Detroit before members of the Facing Reality group.[61]

Following the congress, Hill also delivered a lecture to a McGill sociology class on "Frantz Fanon and the Problems of Nationalism in Past [*sic*] Colonial Society," during which he discussed black nationalism as a product of white oppression and the failure of white humanism.[62] Hill linked the global chaos of the moment to the history of slavery and recalled how slaves developed a "national" consciousness once they were free to roam from one plantation to the next. A white system had created chaos all over the world and blacks, he argued, now needed to recreate society from the bottom up using nationalism and unity as the basis for black liberation and creating a new world. And, according to the *McGill Daily* report on his lecture, Hill also argued that violence could not be ruled out as an option in terms of blacks achieving their goals.[63]

Rosie Douglas had anticipated the importance of Hill's contribution to the congress in a *McGill Daily* interview when he described his relationship with Rastafarians in Jamaica, his central role in organizing the various events of the Caribbean Conference Committee dating back to 1965, and as someone who was now doing important work in Jamaica on the Garvey movement. In the same interview, Douglas also mentioned a young historian who had travelled from Jamaica with Hill, someone whom he described as just "as committed as Bobby" and whose presence, along with Hill's, would be vital to the congress. Douglas was referring to Walter Rodney whom he felt, along with Hill, might be the surprise of the entire event. He also prophesied that the public would be hearing much more in the months to come from the two young scholars.[64]

In the lead up to the congress, Hill and Rodney had collaborated in the "grounding" sessions in Jamaica that have since become famous as a result of Rodney's 1969 book, *The Groundings with My Brothers*.[65] While Rodney is perhaps best known today as the author of *How Europe Underdeveloped Africa*, it was in *Groundings* that he made three important statements in Montreal in October 1968: "The Groundings with My Brothers," which was delivered following his expulsion from Jamaica by the government of the country; "Statement of the Jamaica Situation" (co-authored with Robert Hill); and "African History in the Service of Black Liberation," both of which were delivered at the Congress of Black Writers.

"Statement of the Jamaica Situation" exposed the myth of the harmonious "Out of Many, One People" multi-racial Jamaican society and championed the "epochal march forward of the Black Humanity." The mood and movement of Jamaica's black sufferers was typified in the spirit and example of Rastafari, which rejected the trappings and symbols of official Jamaican "Babylonian" society;[66] and in the government's desperate attempts to maintain the facade of plurality in the face of oppression and abject poverty, inequality, and the suppression of information that was exemplified in its prohibition of Stokely Carmichael, James Forman, and H. Rap Brown from entering the country, and the banning of literature by Carmichael, Malcolm X, and Elijah Muhammad.[67] State repression was used against the restless black poor majority, including savage attacks by black police officers who, Rodney duly noted, were as brutal as white officers in the US, in order to maintain the dominant order.[68] But Rasta, and black consciousness, fired by Garveyism, Ethiopianism, and then US Black Power, meant an interest in "things African" and black, a phenomenon that challenged the epistemological order of things.[69] Even police brutality and violent state repression pointed the way forward for "black youths" who were increasingly "becoming aware of the possibilities of unleashing armed struggle in their own interests."[70]

"The Groundings with My Brothers" speech was a logical extension of the "Statement." It was a mistake, Rodney argued, for the government to believe that by banning him it would somehow halt or stall the movement of Jamaica's black masses against racialized class oppression.[71] He invoked a

Rocky Jones and Walter Rodney. Courtesy of Rocky Jones

poem that Ted Joans recited at the congress, "Integrated Nigger," or what Joans calls "The Nice Colored Man" (see below), as way of challenging the myth of the multiracial integrated Jamaican society, and he once again recalled Rastafari as an example of black Jamaica's rejection of the society that had derided, despised, and dismissed Rasta. As Afro-Jamaicans looked toward the African continent,[72] he called upon black academics and intellectuals to attack the "distortion of white imperialism, white cultural imperialism" as he had attempted to do in discussing African history at the congress;[73] and to move beyond the myth of Jamaica as a multiracial society and to attach themselves to the struggles of the black majority.[74] This is what Rodney had done during the groundings or reasoning sessions in Jamaica, sharing the experience that he had gained through traveling, his social and political analysis, and his knowledge of history with Jamaica's dispossessed sufferers in some of the most economically deprived neighbourhoods in the country. These groundings contributed to the emergence of a black political consciousness in the country and highlighted the importance of blacks speaking to each other without white interference, a point that he himself had highlighted during the congress.[75]

Lastly, Rodney reiterated his respect for Rastafarians and their philosophy and recalled how they had taught him, among other things, humility during his ongoing exchanges with them in Jamaica.[76] He also emphasized that it was the class of sufferers, Jamaica's dispossessed, whose potential was expressed in their own artistic creativity, that held the key to the country's future.[77] Given the events that surrounded Rodney's expulsion from Jamaica in the aftermath of the congress—events that were of profound importance for the emergence of a new wave of left politics in the Caribbean—it is hard to say which of his Montreal statements was most significant, and it perhaps makes sense to understand them as part of an extended and interconnected discourse. This said, it was in "African History in the Service of Black Liberation" (the version below is the actual presentation and is not identical to the version published in *Groundings*) that Rodney demonstrated the erudite command of history for which he would become renowned. The presentation also gave his audience a glimpse of his capacity to bring history to life by linking the past with the present. In the presentation, Rodney avoided what we might describe as the "great kings and queens syndrome," which measured a society's worth based on the existence and power of its royalty, the size of its army, its political structure, literature, etc. Rodney rejected this conception of civilization in favour of more human concepts that reflected the humane ways in which people related to one another in a given society—the practice of hospitality, the principle of gerontocracy, and law in Africa. Having presented his notion of African history to a primarily North American and Caribbean audience, Rodney suggested that beyond its cathartic value, African history was more relevant to the social development of Africa and that the history of blacks in the "New World" would better serve as a tool for developing a "revolutionary strategy" for the Americas.[78]

But equally as important as his presentations in Montreal, the Congress of Black Writers ushered Rodney onto the world stage as an historian of Africa and an important emerging political voice. In England, Rodney had been a precocious young scholar from Guyana who was quietly making academic waves with his writing on African history. Like many Caribbean and pan-African figures before him, he also delivered public talks at Hyde Park, and he was among a number of young West Indians who participated in a study circle in the London home of C. L. R. and Selma James. But it was in Montreal that he came into contact with some of the key figures of the Black Power movement in the United States, and the combination of his stature among Jamaica's dispossessed, his presence at the congress, and the international attention that this and his expulsion from Jamaica received catapulted him onto the world stage, marking the beginning of a trajectory that would eventually lead him back, via Cuba and Tanzania, to Guyana, his first and final resting place, where he was callously killed in 1980.

Rodney's expulsion from Jamaica warrants particular attention here. In Jamaica, he engaged in a dialogue among equals, according to Hill, who is now a prominent historian of black popular movements and Caribbean and pan-African history. From Rodney's own admission, he learned more from Jamaica's sufferers than they did from him,[79] all of which helped lay the groundwork for a popular movement. It is not, then, surprising that protest against his expulsion unleashed the pent-up anger and resentment of the country's dispossessed and disenchanted. As Hill suggests, Caribbean history can be divided into the pre-October 1968 Rodney-inspired protests and the period after them[80] in which the political group Abeng was spawned in Jamaica, and various other left groups and movements across the anglophone Caribbean that would culminate and then decline with the Grenada Revolution.[81]

By 1967, C. L. R. James was a kind of elder statesman who embodied the Caribbean, black, and pan-African and socialist tradition that had come to define subsequent generations. He had left the Caribbean for London in the 1930s where he worked alongside his boyhood Trinidadian friend, the legendary pan-Africanist George Padmore, and with a number of Africans, including Kwame Nkrumah and Jomo Kenyatta. As a prominent socialist in Europe, he collaborated with Leon Trotsky when the former leader of the Russian Revolution was exiled in Mexico; and in the 1940s and 1950s, while living underground in the US, he made important contributions to Marxist theory as a member of the Johnson-Forest Tendency, an organization that he co-founded with the theorist Raya Dunayevskaya and the philosopher Grace Lee. James was the author of one of the anglophone Caribbean's first major novels, *Minty Alley* (1936), books on Marxism, international socialism, and pan-Africanism, including *World Revolution: 1917–1936, The Rise and Fall of the Communist International* (1937), his classic study of the Haitian Revolution, *The Black Jacobins: Toussaint L'Ouverture and the San Domingo Revolution* (1938), and what would eventually be published as *Notes on Dialectics* (1948). He also wrote a marvelous book on cricket, *Beyond a Boundary* (1963), which has been described as one of the best books ever written about sport in general. All of this is to say that James was a man of great political and intellectual stature who, as the consummate polymath, had made profound political and intellectual contributions in multiple areas, and his exemplary body of work meant that his presence at the congress was highly anticipated.

James delivered three presentations at the congress: one on Negritude, which he presented in French in the place of René Depestre, and two on slavery, including one on the Haitian Revolution, the only presentation that has survived in full, and which is published in this book. There is however a clip of James's Negritude presentation in which he shifts between English and French as he describes Aimé Césaire's contribution to African consciousness:

> And this is what I said and which I want to repeat and I would like the discussion to end there. He first gave *le coup de clairon* (the trumpet's call) *du mouvement vers l'Afrique et la civilisation africaine* (towards Africa and the African civilizations). *Parce qu'il était impossible* (because it was impossible) *de chercher une vie vraiment humaine* (to seek a life truly human) *dans la civilisation européenne du 19e siècle* (it was impossible to find a truly human life in the European civilization of the nineteenth century, still more in the twentieth). This is what Césaire was putting

forward and it is astonishing to me that he could see that so clearly as early as 1938. If there was anything that we should see more clearly than ever today, it was the conception that he was concerned with putting forward the fundamental contact with nature of the imaginative views that we have of the African people against the blue steel rigidities and the complete domination of machinery and things of the kind that Western civilization represented then and which it represents still more today. I want to say that that is what I refer to and that is what I think, after the discussion, is the fundamental issue of this poem and its conception of things African and dealing with the black people. Thank you, Mr. Chairman. [*Applause*][82]

In his sweeping presentation on "The Haitian Revolution and the History of Slave Revolt," James situated the slave revolution within the context of the American, French, and Cuban revolutions. He argued that there was a symbiotic relationship between the French Revolution and its Haitian counterpart, with each revolution feeding into the revolutionary fervor of the other, and that the Haitian Revolution was the precursor to its Cuban heir. In "The History and Economics of Slavery in the New World,"[83] James' description of Cuba as "the finest advance made in modern history since the decline of the Russian Revolution" was enthusiastically received. He also referenced the French anthropologist Claude Lévi-Strauss, who argued that slaves brought a civilization of their own to the Americas and that this civilization helped to sustain them. If these remarks received an enthusiastic response from the audience, his view that Ancient Greece represented the high point of civilization was met with disapproval by some in the audience, and the irony that slavery, albeit of a different kind, was practised in Ancient Greece was not lost on a *McGill Daily* journalist who was present during James' talk.[84]

James' presentation also focused on the centrality of slavery in the making of modern capitalism: slave labour produced the cotton that fed the industrial revolution, without which there would have been no proletariat to confront capitalism's bourgeoisie.[85] The argument was perhaps somewhat redundant in so far as if there was no capitalism, there would be need to overthrow its bourgeoisie, but the point served to highlight the constitutive relationship between slavery and capitalism, a point that was consistent with his argument that the "sugar factories" on the plantations of the North Plain of Haiti were the jewel of colonial trade.[86] James initially made this point in *The Black Jacobins* where he described the concentrated presence of large numbers of slaves labouring and being socialized in these proto-capitalist sugar factories. In

Rocky Jones, C. L. R. James, and Stokely Carmichael, with a copy of *Caribbean International Opinion* in his hand. Courtesy of Rocky Jones

this sense, this system was the most "advanced" economic system and enslaved Africans were, for James, closer to the modern proletariat than their counterparts anywhere in the world[87]—a point that Cedric Robinson described as "rhetorically powerful."[88] The social and economic significance of this point has yet to be fully appreciated. African slaves and their descendants were the "conscripts of modernity," to borrow a term from the Jamaican anthropologist and theorist David Scott, who were socialized in the production process in a manner that, as Marx argued in relation to the proletariat, would lead to the overthrow of the system that dominated them. But James' point was that the systematic and systemic practice of disciplining, regulating, and controlling African bodies under the regime of slavery in the Americas was a unique manifestation, a new point of departure, and a crucial and component part of the emergence of capitalism that predated or, at the very least, coincided with the proletarianization of Europe.

Radio McGill journalist George Lewinski recalled in his broadcast shortly after the congress how James related black liberation struggles to the liberation struggles in Vietnam and Latin America, and that he de-emphasized racism in favour of highlighting imperialism as the real enemy. Comparing him to the German American philosopher Herbert Marcuse, Lewinski's James was an academic first and a revolutionary second, who would begin his lectures by outlining his main argument and method, and whose presentations were "always precise and meticulous" with "ironic asides and humorous anecdotes." James was "not a firebrand like Stokely Carmichael," but an intellectual who preferred facts to emotionalism and "frequently during the congress he chided black leaders" who ignored "historical realities in their speeches." This perhaps is what set James at variance with younger black leaders and writers who, according to Lewinski, "took offence at some of his comments. James' lectures are indicative of this variance, directed as he said to anyone, black or white, who would see the destruction of capitalism, while many of the younger speakers were clearly directing their speeches to a primarily black audience." While the young journalist (he was a student) captured much of what made James an important intellectual, his bifurcation of James into an intellectual on the one hand and revolutionary on the other overlooked the contribution that his revolutionary politics contributed to the form and substance of his ideas. James' political convictions sustained his thinking throughout most of his adult life, and it was his understanding of revolutionary history and politics that facilitated the quiet ease with which he spoke about the prospects for freedom and the dynamics of liberation.

Lewinski's program also included an extended clip of James' talk on "The History and Economics of Slavery in the New World," the rest of which has not survived. Among other things, James attempted to clarify the meaning of Black Power in light of post-colonialism in the Congo and Haiti. As historian Sean Mills has demonstrated in *A Place in the Sun: Haitians and the Remaking of Quebec*, by the 1960s, Montreal's growing Haitian population was having a significant impact on the cultural and political life of the city and in the province of Quebec in general.[89] A number of Haitians were already familiar with James as a result of the French translation of *The Black Jacobins*, a book that congress co-chair Elder Thébaud described as the "best book that has been written on the Haitian Revolution: It has been used in Haiti, in schools, in universities, and none seriously studying the history of Haiti can ignore it."[90] And many Haitians were in attendance when he spoke at the congress, including Adeline Magloire Chancy,[91] who was a central figure in Montreal's growing Haitian community and part of the Haitian-exile left that was committed to the transformation of Duvalier's Haiti. It was in her capacity as a member of the Congress of Black Writers' organizing committee that she met James:

> I spent some hours with C. L. R. James . . . typing and translating parts of his incomplete paper, in his hotel room. What [a] great honor for me to work with this famous historian (I had read *The Black Jacobins*) and revolutionary thinker! I took the occasion to inform C. L. R. of the actual situation in Haiti and the courageous resistance struggle in various sectors of the population. While in exile, it was our aim to prove that Haitian people did not accept the dictatorship of Duvalier and, at the same time, to call for solidarity.[92]

Despite her precarious immigration status (she had arrived as an exile and was not a legal Canadian resident), Chancy assumed somewhat of a public role, and not only in relation to the Haitian community. For example, Chancy was among those (Rosie Douglas was another) who organized a protest that ended at Montreal's Square Victoria in response to the shock and sense of revulsion that she felt following the assassination of Martin Luther King Jr. on April 4, 1968, the same day as her birthday.[93] She would later collaborate closely with other members of the anglophone black community, including Alfie Roberts.

As Chancy recalls, James' presence at the congress "*était une événement,*" that is to say, was a major event, perhaps the highlight for Haitians who were present. Chancy and Elder Thébaud used their ability to speak English to discuss the political situation in Haiti and to forge links with other anti-imperialist individuals and groups outside of the Haitian community.[94] No doubt the following remarks by James on Haiti, informed as they were by his conversations with Chancy and perhaps other Haitians in Montreal, would have had a particular resonance for Haitians in the audience:

> I know very well that Black Power can be today a very oppressive power, so that the slogan Black Power is a general slogan against colonialism, neocolonialism, and against what Frantz Fanon was so clear about— native local governments that are merely continuators of the period of imperialist government that has been overthrown. We must be quite clear about that. Stokely used to say, for him, Tshombe[95] was not a black man [*applause*] because Tshombe served the interests of imperialism. And we are very clear about that —I from personal experience.
>
> That Doc Duvalier[96] is black, that does not matter at all. I myself am waiting, and a lot of other people are waiting, for the day when the Haitian people are going to overthrow him. That is certain to come. [*Applause*] Maybe not as quickly as some of you Haitians might like, but you must understand and take it for certain, he cannot continue indefinitely. Many of them have tried and he is certain to go. The population everywhere is aware of that and I am waiting every day at any day. . . . The other day I saw in the paper that he said he was going away, he was ill, and he wanted to go to the United States for medical attention, and some of his friends told him "no, you don't go to the United States for medical attention. All the medical attention you need we will give you here." [*Laughter*] So he's still there, but he had reached a stage where he wanted to get out. I read that in the French paper *Le Monde*, which tells less lies than the other bourgeois papers. [*Laughter and applause*] So that a few month ago, Duvalier thought it was best to go and seek medical advice abroad. We don't know when he will need to [go] abroad for medical advice again, but we can hope for the best.[97]

James mentioned the experience of Haiti and the Congo as a warning against facile notions of Black Power that embraced conservative and repressive black figures, or analyses that paint all blacks as saints and all whites as devils. His years of experience in political life had taught him otherwise, and during the question and answer period following his presentation on slavery and revolt, James also made the following remarks about his position on Haiti, Duvalier, and the Cuban Revolution:

> I have been invited to Haiti. I was invited by the head of the military mission when they had read my book, *Les Jacobins noir*, translated into French.[98] And I was able to tell them, very politely (I'm a polite person), that I am afraid that I couldn't possibly come there under any circumstances. I would have to go and say, "Well, I'm very happy to be here and I think you are doing well enough," or something. I would have to do it. I preferred not to go. That is why I have not been able to go to Haiti. [*Applause*]
>
> Secondly, I hope my friend there knows that the real support of Duvalier is the United States government. [*Applause*] Duvalier's government is the worst and most corrupt government in Latin America. There is no doubt about it. [*Applause*] But he is able to continue because, although he is rude to the United States and he robs tourist who go there, etc., nevertheless, the United States continues to support him, and not to support anybody who wants to overthrow him. And the reason is very simple: they prefer a thousand Duvaliers to another revolution that might produce another Fidel Castro. [*Applause*] They can stand Duvalier, any number of Duvaliers. They have some at home, too [*laughter*], but a revolt, they don't want to have. And we must be aware of this.
>
> I have no doubt whatever that the American State department and the rest of them are quite aware of what took place in the San Domingo Revolution. They are more than ever aware of what took place in the Cuban Revolution, and they are aware—they ran to the Dominican Republic quick in order to prevent [revolution] because any revolution that takes place in the Caribbean is going to do what the other two have done, it's going to make a clean sweep. [*Applause*]

Stokely

For many, Stokely Carmichael's speech was the highlight of the congress. At the time, the Trinidadian-born African-American was at the height of his popularity, one of the most recognizable faces on the planet, and perceived by many as the heir apparent to Malcolm X. He had also been designated

"Prime Minister" of the Black Panther Party—all of this at a time when the US Black Power movement served as an inspiration for liberation movements and struggles all over the world. Carmichael's reputation as a brilliant, captivating speaker who could enthrall audiences was legion, and his congress speech did not disappoint. The congress was also one of several important international platforms from which he delivered speeches in 1967 and 1968, and by situating his Montreal speech within the context and continuum of other speeches that he delivered in the same period, we are better situated to appreciate the importance of his Montreal speech.[99]

Convened in London's Roundhouse, July 15–30, 1967, the Congress on the Dialectics of Liberation was organized by four radical psychiatrists, including David Cooper of the Institute of Phenomenological Studies. Speakers also included the philosopher Herbert Marcuse, poet Allen Ginsberg, *Monthly Review* co-founding editor and Marxist economist Paul Sweezy, and the Scottish psychiatrist R. D. Laing. But it was Carmichael's presence that captured the headlines of the British press and he was enthusiastically welcomed by members of the black community in the neighbourhoods of Brixton, Hackney, and Notting Hill.[100] His main talk (he also participated in other events, including a panel with Ginsberg) began with some critical remarks on the incessant focus on the individual in politics, arguing that, for black Americans and the people of the Third World, it was the system of international white supremacy that was at the root of the problem and that needed to be destroyed, not individual figures. To support his point, he quoted Frantz Fanon's criticism of Sigmund Freud's insistence on the pre-eminence of the individual factor in psychoanalysis: the problem "is a question of socio-diagnostics. The Negro problem," according to Fanon, "does not resolve itself into the problem of Negroes living among white men, but rather Negroes exploited, enslaved, despised by the colonialist, capitalist society that is only accidentally white."[101]

Carmichael then made a distinction between what he described as individual racism and institutional racism. Individual racism refers to overt acts of racism or racial aggression. This might include the bombing of a black church in which children are killed in Birmingham, Alabama. The second type, more subtle and difficult to identify, but equally destructive, included the many black babies that died every year in Alabama due to poverty, malnourishment, inadequate health care, etc. These conditions persisted because the state has no interest in tackling institutional racism, because those who most benefit from capitalism have a vested interest in ensuring that the poverty and alienation upon which capitalism is based is not tampered with.[102]

Carmichael also discussed the subconscious racism that is sustained by narratives of history that place Europeans and their descendants at the centre of humanity and civilization with all of the attendant assumptions of superiority that have rendered blacks inferior in their eyes. Acknowledging that blacks have internalized these external definitions of themselves and, drawing on Frederick Douglass and Albert Camus, he argued that only when slaves stop obeying their masters, or the oppressed refuse to be defined by definitions imposed upon them by their oppressor—only then would the creative process of liberation begin.[103] This, he argued, was precisely what blacks and people of the Third World were fighting for—to define themselves and to retain the integrity of their cultural identities against the onslaught of American and European cultural imperialism.[104] Turning to economic imperialism, he then argued that black communities in the US were actually colonies in so far as the economic and political capital of those neighbourhoods was controlled by whites who did not live there and were not socially or politically invested in them. The struggle, then, was two-pronged: organizing to confront capital in communities in urban centres where blacks were strategically placed while the people of the Third World waged their struggle against imperialism outside of the US.[105]

For Carmichael, capitalism was intricately connected to racism and he criticized the labour movement for its unwillingness to confront race and for settling for higher wages at the expense of worker control, particularly when higher wages and improved working conditions came at the expense of the people of the Third World who do the work that workers in the West refuse to do, and under conditions that the same workers refuse to work.[106] In essence, Carmichael tied the fate of African-Americans with that of the Third World, and, given the logic of his argument, along with the tension and tumult of the time, it is not surprising that, while drawing on the Third World liberation struggles in South Africa and Rhodesia (Zimbabwe), among other places, and in light of the violence inflicted by American imperialism in Vietnam, Carmichael embraced violent struggle. The violence of imperialism was both psychological and physical and blacks reserved the right to defend themselves by responding in kind: "We are fighting a political warfare. Politics is war without violence. War is politics with violence. The white West will make the decision on how they want the political war to be fought. We are not any longer going to bow our heads to any white man. If he touches one black man in the U.S., he is going to go to war with every black man in the U.S."[107] This said, and having assessed that, given the size of the population, blacks could not take on the US state by force, he envisioned blacks becoming "a disruptive force in the flow of services, goods, and capital" and that, as blacks "aim for the eye of the octopus, we are hoping that our brothers are disrupting externally to sever the tentacles of the US."[108]

Carmichael not only stressed that African Americans were fighting to salvage their humanity, but that "we are fighting to save the world."[109] In other words, blacks and the people of the Third World were the vanguard of a global struggle to save humanity from itself and, turning conventional Marxism on its head, he argued that the people of the Third World—including the Third World in the US (African-Americans)—were *the* global proletariat at the forefront of confronting capital. This phase of struggle, he argued, was both physical and ideological: "And the fight must be waged from the Third World. There will be new speakers. They will be Che, they will be Mao, they will be Fanon." They were, for him, emblematic of the new voices of liberation, and to emphasize this point he added, speaking to what must have been a predominantly white audience of left intellectuals and activists: "You can have Rousseau, you can have Marx, you can even have the great libertarian John Stuart Mill."[110]

This last comment no doubt raised the eyebrows of C. L. R. who, although his speech does not appear in the published proceedings of the conference, was present according to Carmichael. In fact, it was James and his measured critique of some of the assumptions of Black Power, not Carmichael, who captured the attention of a young Tariq Ali who thought Carmichael overstated the case about the prospects for black revolution.[111] Perhaps Ali was perturbed by Carmichael's heightened sense of black nationalism and perhaps Ali found displeasure in Carmichael's dismissal of the trio of Rousseau, Marx, and Mill. But to Carmichael's credit, he was attempting to transform the paradigm, to shift the "geography of reason," so to speak, from western Europe and North America to the Third World. He was not simply attempting to substitute one body of ideas or set of thinkers for another, but to make a larger argument related to what and who counts as universal and, the particular, the centre and the periphery, and the so-called "civilized" and "backward." Carmichael was painfully aware that much of the struggle for freedom both in the US and in the Third World was intricately tied to discarding the legacy of cultural imperialism, or what Sylvia Wynter, referring to the Caribbean context, has aptly described as European "epistemological imperialism."[112] In other words, Carmichael understood that without waging a struggle against both the economic and racial assumptions inherent in global capitalism, African-Americans and the people of the Third World would continue to be victimized by the same praxis of cultural and political alienation as their predecessors.

Carmichael's incendiary OLAS (Organization of Latin American Solidarity) speech was delivered in Havana as black rebellions ignited American cities.[113] He arrived in Cuba as blacks erupted in the July uprising, during which forty-one people were killed,[114] and given his stature as a spokesperson whose words gave credence to the pent up anger and frustrations of African-Americans, was treated like a head of state in Cuba and he was chaperoned about Havana by Fidel Castro himself.[115] The speech captured the temperament of the times and, in addition to the international attention it received, was widely circulated and discussed throughout North America and in cities as far apart as Montreal, where it was published in pamphlet form by Caribbean Nation, the outgrowth of the CCC-CLRJSC, and Los Angeles. Carmichael called for an end to plundering of the wealth of the world for the privilege of the few, and for a world in which "civilizations can retain their cultural sovereignty instead of being forced to submit to foreign rulers who impose their own corrupt cultures on those civilizations they dominate."[116] This would have no doubt appealed to his audience, given that the bulk of the Havana conference's delegates hailed from countries that had direct experience with colonialism and imperialism.

Despite the fact that Black Power had reached a fever pitch by 1967, it was viewed with suspicion by many socialists who traditionally spurned forms of nationalism. Aware of this skepticism, Carmichael's presentation was replete with references to the struggle of the people of Vietnam as well as quotes from Che Guevara, and he pointedly stated that the Black Power movement viewed "Cuba as a shining example of hope in our hemisphere."[117] He also exhorted his audience to look beyond the words "Black Power" that, for him, was "more than a slogan; it is a way of looking at our problems and the beginnings of a solution to them," but the inevitable coalescence around race "is not the totality."[118] This last point recalls Fanon's polemic against Jean-Paul Sartre in *Black Skin, White Masks*, where Fanon argued that Sartre failed to understand and appreciate blackness in its universality—that the so-called universal is not race-free, as Toni Morrison has reminded us[119]—instead viewing it as a necessary step toward the universal struggle of humanity. Fanon took issue with Sartre's view and remarked that "the Negro suffers in his body quite differently from the white man" and that although "Sartre's speculations on the existence of *the Other* may be correct, their application to a black consciousness proves fallacious. That is because the white man is not only *the Other* but also the master, whether real or imaginary."[120] For Fanon, black consciousness was not a minor term, but an integral part of the human struggle for freedom. Interestingly, it is Carmichael in this instance who reduces black consciousness to a precursor status, describing Black Power as "only the necessary beginning"[121] or step in the process of universal emancipation, and he does so precisely at a time when the Black Power movement in the United States was extending the boundaries of emancipation for

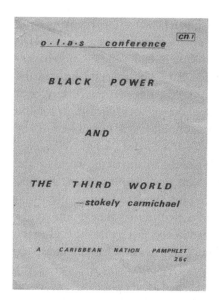

o·l·a·s   conference   [cn.1]

BLACK   POWER

AND

THE   THIRD   WORLD

—stokely carmichael

A   CARIBBEAN   NATION   PAMPHLET
25¢

Caribbean Nation's publication of Stokely Carmichael's OLAS speech. Alfie Roberts Collection

all oppressed Americans and people around the world.

Carmichael also argued that the white American working class had a lot of work to do before it would be fit to march alongside America's black vanguard. As we know from his Dialectics conference speech, for him, the genuine proletariat was to be found among the toilers of the Third World and not the privileged white workers of the First World who had lost their militancy and revolutionary zeal, a point that he repeated in the Havana speech.[122] In America, the Black Power movement represented "the real revolutionary proletariat ready to fight by any means necessary for the liberation of our people."[123] Echoing Malcolm X, he once again argued that African-Americans represented a colony within the United States[124] that was aligned with, if not a part of, the Third World. What was then required was "a two-pronged attack" against the twin evils of racism and economic exploitation that would cut across racial lines.[125] But at this stage, despite the exploitation that white workers' experienced, they see their "own interest lying with the power structure," a reality that vitiated genuine racial solidarity.[126] If and when, however, "the white workers realize their true condition, there will then exist the possibilities for alliances between ourselves and them," although Carmichael was neither waiting for this happen nor despairing if it didn't materialize.[127] In other words, black self-activity was not predicated or dependent upon demonstrations of white solidarity with people of African descent.

He concluded his speech on a note that echoed Fanon's appeal to the Third World to abandon Europe with all of its barbarism "and try to set afoot a new man."[128] For his part, Carmichael declared: "It is a question of the Third World starting a new history of Man, a history which will have regard to the sometimes prodigious theses which Europe has put forward, but" without forgetting Europe's crimes "committed in the hearts of man . . . the pathological tearing apart of his functions and the crumbling away of his unity."[129] Such was Carmichael's analysis in 1967 and the two speeches, tailored to the particular audiences that he was addressing, complemented one another. While his bedazzling elocution kept his audiences enthralled, not everyone was enamored and awed with his oratory. At the time, SNCC was transitioning toward a more overtly militant approach that advocated armed resistance when necessary. The transition process was far from seamless and, according to James Forman, then head of SNCC's International Bureau, Carmichael's speech in Cuba, and several other international speeches that he delivered during this period, were not sanctioned by the SNCC.[130] For Forman, Carmichael's incessant reckless rhetoric brought unnecessary attention and repression upon SNCC field organizers and the general black population.[131] Forman and other SNCC members were also unimpressed with the level of sophistication and clarity of his speeches related to race and class, or what was described as his excessive emphasis on race.[132] And while, for Forman, this deficiency was corrected during the OLAS speech, he also took issue with Carmichael's suggestion that blacks in the US had been content to coexist with capitalism prior to the emergence of the Black Power movement. For Forman, this point essentially negated the history of black resistance beginning with slavery.[133]

Over a year had passed before Carmichael took to the podium in Montreal in 1968. If by this time his analysis was more elaborate and complex, it was perhaps in part due to his communication with C. L. R. James, who, like Forman, had been critical of Carmichael's earlier speeches. In a 1967 presentation on "Black Power," James described a letter that he wrote to Carmichael after hearing him speak at Montreal's Sir George Williams University in March of the same year.[134] In the letter, James suggested "that there were certain doubtful points in his speech which he should bear in mind" and "that there were grave weaknesses in the whole Negro struggle in the United States," including a lack of a "sound historical and theoretical basis" in terms of where the struggle had emerged from and where it was heading.[135] Within that same year James identified a marked improvement in the depth and scope of Carmichael's presentations, and he hinted that his letter had something to do with the change.[136] But there were certainly other developments that would have impacted Carmichael. In 1968 Martin Luther King Jr. was assassinated, followed by the assassination of Robert Kennedy. Given his previous collaboration with King, and given that, for some, Kennedy represented the US's last liberal hope for the fulfillment of genuine democracy—and having borne witness to how America eats its own—Carmichael's congress speech captured the tenor and tone of the terror of the time and, in this sense, the speech represented a veritable call to arms.

Carmichael was the final speaker, and the anticipation of his speech rose to a fever pitch when Walter Rodney set the stage for his entrance:

Exposure to this black question is a tremendous thing for both black people and white people. I know some brothers who argue that if you go to a black man who doesn't know himself you have to go slow at first. Don't press him too much or else it might be traumatic, it might destroy him. Well, we've had a lot already for the morning.

Referring to Michael X, Edwards, and Forman's speeches (poet Ted Joans also performed his poems just prior to Harry Edwards' speech) Rodney humorously warned, "We've had three speakers and we've had Fanon thrown in too. So that's a lot of exposure. I don't think the conference committee can hold themselves responsible for any traumas that are produced, [*laughs from crowd*] but you'll have to cope with brother Stokely coming up next. [*Applause*]" And when Carmichael finally spoke, "near pandemonium broke out."[137] This is how former SNCC member Ekwueme Michael Thelwell described himself: on his feet and in near tears along with young students "shouting with intensity of feeling every bit the equal of theirs. Not my usual style." He later discovered that C. L. R. James had a similar reaction upon hearing Carmichael speak in public.[138]

Thelwell's recollection was characteristic of how many reacted as Carmichael elocuted. For Adeline Magloire Chancy, Carmichael's speech, alongside those of Harry Edwards and James Forman, were unforgettable in so far as they highlighted the idea that blacks in the US represented an internal colony and that the solution to changing their condition was to engage in a global, anti-imperialist, and revolutionary struggle against capitalism in the US, while valorizing the lives, experiences, and identities of blacks who have been dehumanized by white supremacy, but without reducing the struggle to a black-white conflict.[139]

But some in attendance had a more critical view of his speech and the audience's general reaction to it. For LeRoi Butcher, who would play an active role in the Sir George Williams University protests in the immediate aftermath of the congress, many of the congress participants were caught up in the signs and symbols of blackness—beads, dashikis, etc.—"without having to define the enemy as the oppressors of the masses." And while he gave a nod to Carmichael's allusions to Cuba, China, and the Arab world, Butcher dismissed the speech for what he described as its anti-white sentiment and for suggesting that "white people were no good and should be blamed for all of our problems."[140] Butcher's harsh criticism was perhaps a bit too categorical, and as Carmichael himself confessed much later, he often deployed different performance styles, depending on his audience: a "standard-English speech for the merely affluent and curious" in which he presented reasoned and

Stokely Carmichael's closing address, with Michael X and Ted Joans. Courtesy of McGill Archives

thought-provoking arguments;[141] the "harder, more analytic, and ideological argument for more serious political and intellectual forums," and the "down-home, nitty-gritty idiom," a style heavily influenced by "Harlem street-corner nationalists and the Southern black preachers" that was reserved for "the brothers and sisters on the block."[142] But as a former philosophy student at Howard University, Carmichael's congress speech might, at least in part, be understood as a dialectical reasoning on colonization that combined all three of his categories of presentation.

He began his speech by acknowledging the challenges involved in being the last presenter in so far as much of what he wanted to say had already been discussed. He nonetheless set out to bring together and deepen some of the ideas of the previous speakers and clarify a number of terms related to revolutionary struggle, the first of which was the distinction between oppression and colonization that, he noted, was crucial to developing an ideology for black liberation. While exploitation referred to economic oppression, colonization involved both the economic and racial domination of people of African descent whose natural resources in Africa were pilfered by imperial powers. And while he exempted French Canadians from this dynamic of exploitation, he reminded the audience that France too was a principle exploiter on the African continent.

During what he described as colonialism's first phase, the "entertainment" phase, the colonized/oppressed find their voice and verbally express their contempt for whites, akin to what he describes as a warm-up session before a boxing match. But this "feel good session" is insufficient, and the second phase involves a shift from entertainment to the development of strategies to concretely change the situation. This is the most dangerous level for the oppressor, who does everything possible to subvert this effort, including co-optation, the deployment of agent provocateurs, and, if necessary, armed force. Then, elaborating on the impact of colonization, he referred to black self-hate and the adoption of the values of the oppressor and, invoking Fanon, he argued that self-loathing is expressed in the form of internecine violence. For Carmichael, the counterweight to oppression and self-hate involved an undying love of the self while challenging negative emotions toward the oppressor.

Carmichael then turned to the question of land and argued that African peoples needed to develop a global ideology to confront pan-African dispossession that was itself the result of racism, capitalism, and imperialism. Richard Gott has argued that, in Havana, Carmichael had denounced socialism and communism as irrelevant for African-Americans because they were incompatible with black struggles in the United States, where the scourge of racism took precedence over class.[143] For Max Elbaum, this shift occurred in 1968 when Carmichael dismissed communism as a "white ideology," arguing instead that black folks needed not a left or right ideology, but a black one.[144] By the time he arrived in Montreal in October, Carmichael was arguing that the struggle against racism, capitalism, and imperialism involved a fight for political alternatives, but he had also developed a critical analysis of socialism and communism that questioned the ideological and racial position of the Soviet Union, although he embraced Fidel Castro and Che Guevara. He

Leon Jacobs and a pensive Stokely Carmichael. Courtesy of Rocky Jones

argued that blacks needed to avoid being trapped within foreign ideologies and, to this end, he recalled the experience of the Trinidadian communist George Padmore, who had left the Comintern and broken with the Soviet Union because the Russians compromised with the colonial powers of Britain and France. His point was that it was important for blacks to recognize that the Soviet brand of socialism did not operate in the best interests of Africans.[145]

Carmichael was ultimately calling for revolution, or what he described as "the total destruction of the old system—total destruction—the re-emplacement of a new system which speaks for the masses of the people of a given country." Revolution was about taking power, and so to "talk about revolution before you take power is to be, at best, politically naïve, at worst, stupid. [*Applause and laughter*]" To make his point, he invoked the example of Fidel Castro, who had fought in the Sierra Maestra during the armed struggle phase of the Cuban Revolution but, having seized power, "Fidel walked into Havana with guns in his hand, Che on his side and said, 'this day I claim this country for the masses of Cuban people.' Then the revolution began . . . then the revolution began. [*Applause*]" Here we arrive at what was, for many in attendance, the most contentious part of Carmichael's speech—the question of violence. The only way to take power, he argued, is through revolutionary violence:

Now for me it is clear, there are only three ways you get things [*laughter*]: you ask, you beg, or you take. [*Applause*] You work for it, you beg for it, or you take it. No, you don't steal it, you take it. You only steal it when you don't have power. If you have power, you take. [*Applause*] I don't think that white Canadians would say that they stole Canada from the Indians. [*Laughter*] They said they took it—and they did. [*Applause and laughter*]

Well then it's clear that we can't work for these lands, we can't beg for 'em, so we must take them. Then it's clear that we must take them through revolutionary violence.

But while his call to arms captured the attention of his audience, he failed to frame the specific form the revolution would take or to identify the specific context he was referring to. Did armed struggle involve the seizure of land and the state apparatus, or simply land? What mechanisms or processes and what strategies or tactics would be employed in the revolutionary struggle? Who would lead the struggle and what form and structure would this leadership assume? And, of course, the penultimate question: was armed struggle a genuinely viable alternative in terms of seizing power within the US context, assuming that this was the specific context to which he was referring? And while Carmichael's notion of revolution was limited to two phases, armed struggle and seizing state power, as the post-independence period in Africa had already begun to show, statist notions of liberation that ignored popular forms of democratic participation and social organization were destined to reproduce many of the inequalities of colonialism—but this was not accounted for in his analysis.[146]

Even the distinction that he made between begging, stealing, and the ultimate goal of taking power offered very little in terms of thinking through how power is assumed. Whites, he argued, took power from Indigenous people in Canada because they had the power to do so, and they did it with what he later sarcastically referred to as a "pioneering spirit." But how would people of African descent, or specifically African-Americans take power? In the place of a concrete analysis or program, Carmichael offered the following:

White western society has legitimatized everything for us. We have never been able to legitimatize. They legitimatized religion; they legitimatized wars; they legitimatized education; they legitimatized beauty; they legitimatized everything. We must now seek to legitimatize for ourselves. We must say to people in the United States it is more honorable to kill honky cops than to kill Vietnamese. They have done nothing to us. [*Applause*] We have to seek to legitimatize because they will not let us legitimatize. If I were in power and you were arming against me, I wouldn't let you arm against me. Destroy you. Have to if I'm going to stay in power and we have to recognize that. That's our struggle. The struggle is that much harder, the victory is going to be that much sweeter. [*Sporadic applause*]

White racists were armed in the US and the state used its apparatus, including the police, to suppress black aspirations. Carmichael's non-violent days as a SNCC organizer were now behind him and a growing number of African-Americans believed that non-violent struggle had run its course.

This was not only the spirit and assumption with which the Black Panther Party operated, but it was very much in the tradition of Robert F. Williams, the former NAACP leader who advocated and practised armed self-defense. "Tom Paine, Washington, Jefferson, and Patrick Henry were all honorable men," wrote Williams, "who are supposed to represent the true spirit of America. These noble men advocated violence as a vehicle of liberation. They are not considered wild-eyed, bloodthirsty fanatics by a long shot."[147]

Perhaps more than any other individual, Williams' defiant stance in the late 1950s and early 1960s embodied the spirit of what later emerged in the form of Black Power in the US. It was the example of Williams, perhaps even more so than Malcolm X or the writing of Frantz Fanon, that inspired Carmichael's advocacy of violence. Carmichael's call to arms, then, had a history and a tradition behind it, tied to organizing against racial oppression in the perilous South. As he later wrote, "Myself, I had no problem with Bro Williams's position then and I have no problem with it now. We come from a long line of patient people," but that patience, he argued, was finite, and among his "peers in the movement, as for a great many in the African nation, Brother Williams had simply been stating forthrightly what we all were feeling. We may not have adopted his position on self-defense then, but within the ranks of the young movement was a great deal of sympathy for it."[148]

Long before King's assassination, and given the brutal force used against participants in the Civil Rights movement, sixties African-American politics were often framed in terms of non-violence and violence in which King was often counterposed to Malcolm X. As we have seen, in Canada author Austin Clarke repudiated King's non-violent approach in favour of a more radical posture in the context of what he described as a state of moral apostasy,[149] but in the heat of that tempestuous time, King's critics perhaps misread the "radical King," as Cornel West has described him, who was, according to Coretta Scott King, a socialist. He was a voice of moral outrage against American imperialism and the war against the people of Vietnam.[150] Sometimes context is everything, and as Charles Johnson has written in *Being and Race: Black Writing Since 1970*, by 1968 the US had experienced almost a full decade of political assassinations as well as the unpopular war in Vietnam and protests against it. Not only was there a new level of militancy that was connected to these events, but "the dominant themes in black arts and letters were paranoia and genocide. The 'evidence' for a black American holocaust seemed irrefutable" as historical analysis of the black experience in the US "drove home the sense that black history was, and might always be, a slaughter-house—a form of being characterized by stasis, denial, humiliation, dehumanization, and 'relative being.'"[151]

The Black Panther Party now defended the right to use arms to protect black neighbourhoods from the police. Rebellions gripped US cities as blacks lashed out in the urban ghettoes, to which so many had been confined, against systemic racial oppression that limited their life possibilities. In this context, and even after accounting for the performative nature of his presentation in which he masterfully manipulated the emotions of his audience, Carmichael's remarks on the use of violence reflected the political temper of the time, and he was clearly not alone in his analysis of violence. During an exchange following Alvin Poussaint's presentation on "The Psychology of Subjection: Race Relations in the United States of America," Walter Rodney challenged Poussaint to explicitly state his position on violence as a means of catharsis. But Poussaint was clearly uncomfortable with the question and ultimately suggested, to the disappointment of some in the audience, that violence was not his field.[152]

Echoing Fanon once again, Carmichael reminded his audience that colonialism was the purveyor of violence, and that this violence assumed various forms:

> We do not see that poverty is violence; we do not see that race is violence; we do not see that cultural degradation is violence. We have allowed white society to define violence as only the man with the gun. How stupid. It is violent for white society to rape Africa of copper, gold, aluminum, everything. It is violent . . . it is violent . . . it is violent. [*Long applause*] It is violent to have little black children get up and feel that they are ugly. It is violent . . . it is violent. [*Applause*]

His appreciation of the myriad ways in which social and psychological violence attacked the black psyche must have been well-appreciated by the black women and men in the audience, and particularly those who had grown up in North American cities where blacks were in the minority in relation to the dominant white majority. While it is true that much of his speech focused on revolutionary violence, his closing remarks echoed James Forman—as did much of his presentation—when he returned to the issue of political ideology:

> Fanon is correct. There is lacking an ideology for the Africans, but the Chinese didn't have their ideology in a blueprint of revolution. They struggled, they fought, the contradictions arose, they resolved. If they didn't resolve the contradictions, the contradictions resolved them. It was not until they conquered that they began to develop a real revolu-

tionary ideology. [*Applause*] The same then is true of Cuba and the same must be true for us. We must work, struggle, develop that ideology but we must be conscious of what we're against—racism, capitalism, and imperialism. That is our fight.

The necessity of a clear ideology was Carmichael's ultimate point, but as he argued, ideology is forged in the process of struggle. If this was the case, what organizing principles would be required to wage a struggle out of which this ideology would emerge and lend shape and direction to the ongoing struggle? What set of ideas would serve as the point of departure for organizing for revolutionary change? These questions were not lost on C. L. R. James as he listened to Carmichael's speech. James had great admiration for Carmichael, and the feeling was mutual. As a young man growing up in Harlem, James' name was frequently mentioned among the soapbox speakers and orators, and his *The Black Jacobins* had been a powerful influence on the young Carmichael. Moreover, the fact that James, along with George Padmore, was from Carmichael's native Trinidad only added to the sense of affinity between them[153] and Carmichael discovered in the elder James someone who was willing to share his vast political experience and theoretical insights; someone to whom—as Walter Rodney would remark in relation to his own political development[154]—he could turn as an example of an elder who had stayed the revolutionary course well into his senior years. Unlike in Rodney's case, James did not have to write an obituary for Carmichael and, given the number of black revolutionary figures who had been callously killed in the US and abroad, James cautioned Carmichael to take steps to prevent a similar fate,[155] a point that Carmichael no doubt took to heart.

In an interview conducted by Michael Smith of the *McGill Reporter* following Carmichael's speech,[156] James was happy to report that Carmichael now "speaks with a scope and depth and range of political understanding that astonishes me," something James recognized as a testimony to Carmichael's abilities, but also "to the speed with which the modern world is moving politically."[157] He described Carmichael as "one of the most remarkable personalities in contemporary politics."[158] And, having read Carmichael's OLAS speech and noting the ways that he linked the struggles of African-Americans to that of the people of the Third World and to a critique of capitalism; and having heard him speak at Sir George Williams University and at the Dialectics conference the previous year; putting this all together, James was now of the opinion that Carmichael was one of the strongest voices representing socialism in the United States.[159]

This said, James had a few criticisms for his protégé as he commented on the distinction that Carmichael made between exploitation and colonization at the congress: "The distinction that he makes *can* be a valid distinction" but, while Carmichael was entitled to emphasize race within the colonial experience, at its core colonialism for James was a form of economic exploitation. James chose to interpret culture very differently from Carmichael, for whom it was largely structured along racial lines. As an example, James dismissed the idea that the cultures of French president Charles de Gaulle or Spain's Franco were identical to the cultures and values of the French and Spanish population as a whole.[160] In other words, culture was inherently defined by, or at least intricately tied to, class. James' view was very much aligned with Amilcar Cabral's, who would later have a profound influence on Carmichael. Cabral spoke of the context of Guinea-Bissau in terms of horizontal and vertical cultures within the same society, with the horizontal referring to more communally structured groups, whereas the vertically organized groups had more delineated roles and responsibilities that were structured along hierarchical lines.[161] While James lacked Cabral's complex and intricate understanding of West African societies, both his and Cabral's analysis of culture was more nuanced than Carmichael's somewhat essentialist understanding of the continent's culture at this stage.

James also questioned Carmichael's call to arms and the use of armed struggle in the US context:

> If a man talks about picking up a gun and going into the streets, I am not going to oppose him, because that is the revolution, and we may come to that. But I don't think that in 1968 in the United States it is correct to talk about the revolutionary struggle in terms of picking up a gun and going into the streets. I don't quite see that people in Harlem should pick up guns and go into the streets. There *are* times when you have to use violence and many of the American Negroes have been using violence under certain circumstances. I don't oppose anybody doing that. That means he is on the correct side. But there is a lot more to the social revolution than merely picking up a gun and going into the streets.

When asked to elaborate, James argued that ultimately "social revolution means that the great mass of the population have come to the conclusion that the life they are living cannot continue and they want to change it." This is what happened, according to James, in Britain in the seventeenth century during Cromwell's revolution, as it did during the American Revolution of 1776, and during the revolutionary process in Hungary in 1956 before it was crushed by the Stalinist regime and Russian tanks.[162] The same was also true of Cuba, which was attempting to forge socialism under very difficult circumstances. As James buoyantly remarked: "I should say a socialist revolution in the United States—nobody will be in any doubt as to what it really is. That will be something that will write itself across the sky. No, there's no problem."

It's a Man's World

As the anxiety that congress organizing committee member Josie Wallen experienced when she discovered that Carmichael (aka Kwame Toure) had contracted cancer in the 1990s reflects,[163] his speech and his presence in Montreal in general left an indelible imprint on the minds of everyone who heard him speak. But it was the range of black political figures, among other factors, that made the congress particularly rich. Despite the absence of speakers from the African continent, Latin America, and the non-anglophone Caribbean, this was a black international event that tenuously bridged generations and political perspectives.

If the Congress of Black Writers represented the passing of the torch from one generation of pan-African and black radical figures—such as James and his Barbadian and American counterpart Richard B. Moore (formerly of the African Blood Brotherhood and the US Communist Party)[164]—to another generation that included Stokely Carmichael and Walter Rodney,[165] the intergenerational transition was far from seamless. A combination of intra-generational political dynamics, differences, and divergent ideas on how to address anti-black racism led to a number of tense moments, even conflicts. I have chosen to highlight these differences and omissions here, not in the interest of airing dirty laundry, as one critic has suggested,[166] but in appreciation of the reality that tensions are an integral and necessary part of building a sense of cohesion in movements. It is only by highlighting and working through such contradictions—devoid of romantic representations of history or of how people engage one another in social movements—that we can gain some perspective from past struggles that inform our understanding of the exigencies of liberation in our time, and perhaps avoid some of the pitfalls that have trapped previous generations who harboured the same freedom dreams. I have discussed some of these tensions, contradictions, and differences in *Fear of a Black Nation: Race, Sex, and Security in Sixties Montreal*,[167] and elsewhere I have argued that the political moment of the 1960s "represents a goldmine for our understanding of many of today's pressing issues,

Raymond Watts, Stokely Carmichael, Miriam Makeba, and Rosie Douglas. Courtesy of Rocky Jones

including gender, race, class, security, sexuality, and political solidarity. It represents a moment of enlightenment on the road, I hope, toward a more expansive vision of freedom for our time," but only if we are willing to pose and attempt to respond to difficult questions and grapple with the challenges that movements present.[168]

Without a doubt, the most glaring weakness of the congress was the total absence of women speakers, despite the fact that women had played a crucial role in organizing the event. Even the celebrated singer and South African exile Miriam Makeba did not speak or sing but was simply present in the shadow of her husband, Stokely Carmichael. (A photograph taken the weekend of the congress captures the symbolism of Makeba's silence. A diminutive Makeba looks upwards with her gaze fixed on a tall Carmichael.) According to Michael O. West, at least one woman was able to mount the congress speaker podium where she "advocated a natural African look." Citing state security files, according to West, the speaker was Dorothy Jean Hughes, aka Dorothy Jean Hughes Farrow or Sister Koko, and she too attended the congress in the company of Stokely Carmichael, apparently serving as his secretary.[169]

Stokely Carmichael, Joan Jones, and Walter Rodney. Courtesy of Rocky Jones

Trinidadian Barbara A. Jones was a brilliant plant geneticist, one of the very few black academics and scientists that were employed by McGill University at the time. She was also an accomplished poet. Writer Ramabai Espinet has described the influence of Jones' 1967 book of verse, *Among the Potatoes*, in the following way: "It was the first time I had read erotic poetry on the subject of a black woman's sexuality. It was an inspiring read because its liberatory intent leapt off the page."[170] Reading her poetry, it is a wonder why she herself was not invited to participate in the four-day congress. Perhaps the sensuous love poetry was off-putting in that heightened moment of Black Power:

> dream after dream
> my eyelids flutter
> hues of my love concubine
> to make erotic weaves
> from lovers yarn[171]

But Jones' poems were also political. "Viet Nam" describes the Cold War carnage, the "blooming blood" and "charred bodies" in the war,[172] and "To Martin Luther King" pays homage to King as "the great magician" who called for black freedom:

> the gross rough red necks
> rolled in and said
> never nigger never
> and two white eyes
> lit up with fight
> in the plight
> and fight for
> freedom[173]

In "Le Roi Jones," the speaker calls upon the American poet, the "skin brother," to

> vivisect
> the whole
> amputate
> cancerous bitterness
> and leave
> prophetic morsels
> for
> immortality[174]

In "Mixed Emotions," Jones wrote:

> let now the black man free
> let now the white man flee

from those he f—ed and sucked
and kept beneath his feet[175]

In the poem "The Bridges," the speaker describes the chasm separating blacks from whites, "the schizophrenic unity of the real/unreal reality wedded to it," and then observes:

how often on the bridge ive looked
to see who died to fill the gap
between the real and unreal too
between the bodies one and two
between east and west unwon
between old and young anon
between bodies black and white
between the living and the dead[176]

These are haunting words when we consider that Jones died under mysterious circumstances, allegedly committing suicide. Espinent was gripped by what she described as "the unspeakable loneliness experienced by the poetic persona of the text. She was locked in isolation. Why? Was it because she was saying the unsayable?"[177] It is difficult to discern the circumstances that led to her death, but depression appears to have been the factor that pushed her over the precipice. Perhaps her emotions and state of mind are captured in the following lines in the poem "Life":

oh barren nothingness of life
why do we prolong
the endless strife[178]

or in the poem "Depression," in which she writes:

and through the abyss of her mind it came
depression
the silent bastard of past hates and worst of all
repressions[179]

It is thanks to Barbara Jones that we have a summary assessment of the congress. In her November 1968 article, "A Black Woman Speaks Out," Jones provided a summary of the congress in which she remarked:

The Congress of Black Writers . . . featured the opinions of black men from Africa, the Americas, Asia, and Europe, and put the question of black liberation in a world context. They feel that the racist, capitalist and imperialist white Western world which emasculated and humiliated the black man can only be a comfortable place for black men after a complete social and violent revolution takes place. In the public lectures, but more importantly in the all-black caucuses, there were efforts to define the problem of the black man and construct a world-wide strategy for his liberation. This unifying ideology, it is felt, must precede the arms struggle and final violent revolution."[180]

Jones' emphasis, as a black woman, on the fact that only black male voices were represented at the congress and her emphatic use of the pronouns *they* and *his* perhaps implies a distance between black men and women, almost as if she were referring to a separate species. Even if she was not consciously making a statement about gender, in hindsight, the title of the article speaks to the palpable silence on the subject as we consider how gendered dynamics unfolded from the vantage point of the present.

Another Jones, Joan Jones, deserves a special mention here, as she has received very little attention. Joan Jones was originally from Oakville, Ontario, had roots in Montreal, but made her mark in Nova Scotia as an activist and community organizer. But despite her seminal role, she has lived in the shadow of her former husband, Rocky Jones, and this is true despite the fact that she played a central role in his coming into political consciousness. From Rocky Jones' own account, "It was Joan who got me reading" and "challenged me and made me articulate what was in my head" while feeding his interest in "politics and Black consciousness." Moreover, her interests were not restricted to Canada and the US, but to international politics, as she read figures like W. E. B. Du Bois, Frantz Fanon, C. L. R. James, Ralph Ellison, James Baldwin, and Malcolm X, among others.[181] In other words, Joan Jones was a political animal in her own right, and although she was not a speaker at the congress, she was not simply present, but was clearly a presence, as is obvious in several congress photos (see pages 44 and 55). She would no doubt have many stories to tell about her life and experience as a black woman in the movement, and perhaps, one day, it is hoped, someone will write her biography, or better yet, she will share her own story.

While black politics of the time was considered "a boy's game," according to Norman Cook, Brenda Dash also played a prominent public leadership role that was, for him, comparable to that of black male figures. This view was shared by Canadian state security, which kept tabs on her activity,[182] and as Cook recalls, Dash was a Black Panther-like leader, a black Canadian woman with a following among other Canadian-born black women and a powerful influence over male leaders. Much more remains to be written about her. [183]

Anne Cools arrived in Canada from Barbados in her early teens. She finished her secondary school studies in Montreal and went on to become a core member of the CCC-CLRJSC, the only woman prominently featured in that position. Cools was an avid reader of philosophy, politics, and history and an important contributor to the group's wide-ranging political discussions, and it was as a member of the group that she traveled to Cuba, armed with the mission of having C. L. R. James' classic study of the Haitian Revolution, *The Black Jacobins*, translated into Spanish. Cools was also actively involved in the Sir George Williams University protest, for which she served a prison sentence. Like many women who experienced the constraints of participating in groups that were dominated by men, she became an active feminist who collaborated with Selma James on the International Wages for Housework Campaign.[184] As Patricia Hill Collins has written, "Social science research typically focuses on public, official, visible political activity even though unofficial, private, and seemingly invisible spheres of social life and organization may be equally important."[185] In relation to the CCC, this issue is further complicated because women who were involved in the group have generally downplayed the significance of their role as organizers. In the case of Cools, she was actively involved in the group's political-intellectual work but, like many women who found themselves in this position,[186] she went on to become an active member in the women's movement. In her short essay "Womanhood," Cools argued that black women have carried "all the burdensome, backbreaking and stultifying labour of both black and white society" on their backs, and that through their work and actions, they paved "the way towards economic independence for the women of the world," but that it was now time that "society in general, and black men in particular, take a careful look at black women." Cautious not to limit the problem to individual female-male relations, Cools concluded with a call for the destruction of the economic and political system that limited the life chances of women and men: "Black women, the slaves of the slaves, can have no peace, no rest until they have evolved new social structures within which men can be Men, women can be Women, and their children, free-thinking total creative human beings."[187]

Cools was writing in 1971 and our appreciation of the gender spectrum was not what it is today, but despite the awkward gender divide, she ultimately called for a new society in which human beings can live up to their creative potential. She was not a prolific writer and so she has left no considerable

Anne Cools and Selma James, ca. 1971. Courtesy of Carolyn Fick

paper trail of her work within the CCC-CLRJSC, but her role as an important figure in the local and international women's movement, and her collaboration with Selma James, Marlene Dixon, Quebec's Pauline Julien, and other prominent feminists, has been all but excluded from narratives about the women's movement. Her absence from the dominant feminist narrative has deprived us of much-needed insight into the inner workings of gender in black and Caribbean political groupings and in social movements and left politics in general, and into how gender dynamics within these groupings inform our understanding of the dynamics of liberation.

Anne Cools was living in England as the congress unfolded, and the absence of black women's voices—and the fact that the bulk of the speakers characteristically directed their comments to the "brothers" in the audience—reflects the prevalence of male dominance that, as former SNCC organizer and Black Panther Kathleen Cleaver has reminded us, is embedded within the wider society.[188] Referring to academia, Njoki Nathani Wane has argued that despite advancements, "Black women and other marginalized groups have been accused of being incapable of producing the type of interpretive, objective analytical thought that is labeled theory in the West," effectively excluding women, and in this case particularly black women, from consideration as legitimate intellectual beings.[189] But while intellectual invisibility has been part of a broader complex of issues, as Audre Lorde reminded us, these issues are also complicated by sexuality, which for her meant finding herself marginalized among blacks with whom she was politically active. In "Learning from the Sixties," Lorde refers to what she describes as the horizontally expressed anger between blacks in ways that mirrored what she describes as the "impotence" that blacks at times felt at their powerlessness to vertically attack the "corruption of power and true sources of control" over their lives.[190] In response to anti-black racism and oppression, blacks often sought unanimity that ultimately resulted in attempts to downplay or entirely negate gender and sexuality differences. "As a Black lesbian mother in an inter-racial marriage," Lorde writes, "there was usually some part of me guaranteed to offend everybody's comfortable prejudices of who I should be." Ultimately, she concluded: "If I didn't define myself for myself, I would be crunched into other people's fantasies for me and eaten alive. My poetry, my life, my work, my energies for struggle," she adds, "were not acceptable unless I pretended to match somebody else's norm. I learned that not only couldn't I succeed at that game, but the energy needed for that masquerade would be lost to my work. And there were babies to raise, students to teach."[191]

As Carole Boyce Davies argues in her seminal study of the life and work of Trinidadian-American-British feminist and communist Claudia Jones, to be a black woman on the left is to be even further alienated and diminished as a human being. But as the case of Claudia Jones highlights, to be a black woman in this position is also to be positioned politically to the left of Karl Marx in so far as, in the case of Jones, her writing grappled with the simultaneity of gender, race, and class, as opposed to class alone or even race and class.[192] When we consider the Congress of Black Writers in this spirit, the silence around gender dynamics represented an even more significant lack, not only because the "black woman's burden" was ignored, but also because of what Adrienne Catherine Wing refers to as "the strength and love and transcendence" was also missing.[193] In this sense, the congress was reminiscent of its precursor, the 1956 Congresses of Negro Writers and Artists in Paris, where women were equally invisible, leading the novelist Richard Wright to remark that, "When and if we hold another conference . . . I hope there shall be an effective utilization of Negro womanhood in the world to help us mobilize and pool our forces" and that in "our struggle for freedom, against great odds, we cannot afford to ignore one half our manpower, that is, the force of women and their active collaboration. Blacks will not be free until their women are free."[194] Unfortunately, the congress organizers were either unaware of Wright's admonishment or simply failed to take it seriously. Perhaps belatedly conscious of this absence, a resolution was passed at the end of the congress to emphasize the role of black women in black struggles.[195]

All in the Family?

If gender and the role of women in black struggle received scant attention during the congress, race dynamics in relation to the presence of whites was palpable and, for some blacks, it was a source of great consternation. This was a black congress that was not only organized on a university campus, but on one of the historically "whitest" university campuses in Canada , as the work of Rosalind Hampton illustrates,[196] and named after a former slave owner. This irony appears to have escaped the congress organizers who were perhaps unaware of the history of the university's namesake and benefactor, James McGill. His *duppy* (ghost) haunted the university's hallowed halls during the congress and the presence of whites and the rejection of their presence by some blacks almost disrupted the entire congress.

In a 1969 essay on the "militant Black writer," Stephen E. Henderson declared:

> Black writers do not write for white people. They write for black people and they write about their blackness, and out of their blackness, rejecting anyone and anything that stands in the way of self-knowledge and self-celebration. They know that to assert blackness in America is to be "militant," to be dangerous, to be subversive, to be revolutionary, and they know this in a way that even the Harlem Renaissance did not.[197]

This was the kind of sentiment that animated many of the conference discussions. From the outset, the belief that whites should not be allowed to participate in the congress sparked considerable debate and generated strong criticism,[198] and what has been described as the unsettling presence of Maoists during the congress probably did not help. According to Bukka Rennie, who was part of the congress' organizing committee and who later played a role in the Sir George Williams protest, the Maoists were eventually asked to leave because they were disrupting the proceedings and circulating papers describing James as a Marxist revisionist.[199]

The black-white split during the congress also created divisions between blacks who were opposed to excluding whites and blacks in favour of it. Barbara Jones described the split in the following way: "At one point it appeared that the inhibiting presence of white observers, sympathizers, the CIA, RCMP, and the press might cause a rupture in the participating groups, but such a fracture was averted."[200] In light of what we now know about state security's surveillance of participants in the congress and its infiltration of black groups, Barbara Jones' reference to the RCMP and the CIA could not be more ominous. Not only did the congress elicit anxiety within Canadian state security, but former CCC member Jean Depradine suggests that in the aftermath of the Sir George Williams protest, ordinary police and many white Canadians began to fear the presence of blacks.[201] But it is Jones' next remark that most concerns us. The rupture she refers to was partially averted by black-only meetings. As she writes, "the most important issues of the congress were debated in all-black caucuses because it was felt that black people, having always feared white oppression, are not prepared to share the strategy for action with the white man."[202] Jones added that separation does not negate the possibility of whites showing solidarity with blacks, but is rather a realistic approach to addressing the needs of blacks while being conscious of the danger of what Harry Edwards referred to as having a "black cobra in the house"—there were black agents who infiltrated the movement and provided intelligence—as opposed to a "white wolf outside the door."[203]

This debate was typical of the moment. Many blacks saw themselves as part of the vanguard of the revolution that was sweeping the globe and were dismissive of the perspectives of "white experts." It was this reasoning that contributed to the occupation of the 1969 joint African Studies Association (ASA)/Canadian African Studies Association conference in Montreal's Queen Elizabeth Hotel by many of the same individuals who had been involved in the Congress of Black Writers and the Sir George Williams protest.[204] Blacks openly called upon black writers to write for and speak to blacks as part of their duty as writers and to keep "family discussions" within the "home" while promoting self-knowledge and self-celebration.[205] Shorn of the tension and antagonism during the congress, it was perhaps an early version of philosopher Anna Stubblefield's notion of family, in *Ethics Along the Color Line*, that some black participants had in mind. It was eventually decided that restricting whites from a public meeting was untenable, but that smaller black caucuses would be reserved for black delegates and participants.[206] Given that the conference was a public event, it was inevitable that tensions among blacks, and between blacks and whites, as a result of what was perceived as anti-white sentiment, would emerge. For example, during his presentation "African History in the Service of Black Liberation," Walter Rodney made it clear that he was speaking to "fellow blacks," to the brothers in the audience. However, unlike some participants who called for the removal of whites from the meeting, Rodney stated that whites were "perfectly entitled to listen" but he was not setting out to prove to whites that blacks were human beings by demonstrating that they had built civilizations. "Those whites who want to join the black revolution will certainly do so for reasons which are far more profound than their . . . acquaintance with African history."[207] Richard B. Moore also discussed African history during his presentation, but whereas Rodney attempted to discredit the idea that some societies were more civilized than others, Moore focused on ancient African civilizations in order to challenge the stereotype of the primitive and backward African. During the question and answer period Rodney, whose presentation had preceded Moore's, challenged what he perceived as Moore's attempt to appease whites by reminding the audience that Canadian and American companies dominated and exploited the Caribbean, including the mining of bauxite in his native Guyana and in Jamaica that was manufactured into aluminum in Arvida, a city in the Saguenay region of Quebec, a short distance from Montreal. In this sense, Rodney argued, based on the standard of living that this industry afforded Canadians, "Every white Canadian who lives off of the profits of that company is my oppressor, objectively. [*Applause*] Now, what happens is this: A white is going to look at me and see me as I see myself. I am going to define it. This is crucial and we can only define this among ourselves, first and foremost, because there is too much intervention . . . [and we] are too aware that the [white] man is present." In connecting Alcan to the Caribbean, Rodney injected a race-class analysis that concretely linked the privileges that white Canadians enjoyed to the economic underdevelopment of the Caribbean prompted by foreign investment, in this case from Canada. He also rejected the notion that blacks had to demonstrate their equality with whites or perform their humanity before a white audience. Instead, in disagreement with Moore, who had emphasized the importance of white allies, Rodney insisted that blacks must define themselves for themselves, and that there are times when they need to do this among themselves in order to avoid outside interference. While he believed that blacks needed to arrive at the point where they did not feel the need to have to plea for white acknowledgement or feel threatened by their physical presence, he believed that there remained a need "to resort to the elementary device of retiring to caucus and say, 'Well look, let us examine things now.' You see, we have to define the position. It is no use talking about a white friend or a white ally. To ally with what? To aid what? We must define what is to be done. When we define it, we can see if there is an ally."

Perhaps the most outspoken exponent of excluding whites was poet Ted Joans, who at the time was living in Timbuktu, Mali. During what he called a spontaneous non-academic "Afro-astonishment," he told the audience: "We want to turn you on to some truth, as brother Michael X has suggested, since this is a black writers conference or congress." He also chose to let his "black poems" speak for themselves, but just before doing so he added:

And unfortunately, some of the brothers here in Montreal, the black brothers, have an attitude about what you think poetry is. Man, I don't write like that. I don't even have any of them kind of books on my shelf. I happened to go through one of them white universities in America unbrainwashed so see I don't need Shakespeare and I don't think he needed me. The only time I was ever even interested in him—when he had that black cat standing over choking that neck. I forgot that cat's name, but anyway, that's the only interest I had in Shakespeare. [*Applause*] And I don't need that alcoholic, Dylan Thomas, I don't need him either. See, I don't buy their books and I don't need their books. I can learn, I learn everything about them, but after that you must get rid of it. See like Bird, Charlie Parker, Lester Young, Coleman Hawkins, Ornette Coleman, you see, black jazz musicians they take those European-made instruments and they do other things with them. [*Sporadic applause*] The Brothers are getting themselves together, you get yourself together, and we're not going to have no questions and answers, and if we did, there's certain people we are not going to talk to at all. We're not going to talk to them because the brother stood up here earlier this morning and said I don't even see you [referring to Walter Rodney].

There were clearly divergent views on what represented genuine poetry, and although there's no evidence of this, it is likely that many of the Joans' interlocutors were from the Caribbean and still very much wedded to the English canon that Joans was familiar with, but rejected in favour of an aesthetic rooted in jazz. Having made his point, he proceeded to read the poem "The Truth":

If you should see
A man walking down a crowded street
Talking aloud to himself
Don't run in the opposite direction
But run toward him
For he is a poet
You have nothing to fear from the poet,
But the truth

Joans then recounted an experience at the Africa Centre in London where, after reading one of his "black poems about black situations," he was told that he would never be permitted to read there again. Next came "Hallelujah, I Love Jazz So," otherwise known as "Jazz is My Religion," a poem that brings to mind "Jazzoetry" and "Bird's Word" by The Last Poets. In Joans' poem,

Ted Joans, Walter Rodney, Rocky Jones, and Joan Jones. Courtesy of Rocky Jones

jazz becomes the narrator's religion and its African-American musicians its hallowed priests—"Reverend Dizzie Gilespie," "Ministers Miles and Monk," "Reverend Horace Silver," "Brother Basie and Brother Bird," "Sister Ella," and "His Holiness Pope John Coltrane"—all of whom "preach a sermon that always swings. [*Applause*]" Jazz is then tied to the tradition and cultural heritage of the blues, "is black and blue" in hue and, by necessity it excludes European-American musicians such as Dave Brubek and those he describes as "a few other phony mothers" who "never have a sermon for me to swing. [*Sporadic applause*]" For Joans, jazz is an essence tied to being, and one is born into it; it is part of the dyed in the wool African-American experience and "a weapon to battle black blues."

Joans followed up with what he called "a violent poem" and warned the audience, "hold on to your seat." "The .38" is about a man who brutally beats his wife. The speaker describes the blows that are administered on the woman's body as she screams and pleas, ultimately for her life, before her enraged husband kills her with a .38 special revolver. The murder is punctuated by an eerie silence before the murderer enters the apartment of the speaker and kills him, too. It is notable that in introducing the poem, Joans said that it is about a situation that could have happened to him, the point seemingly being that, for Joans, the climax of the poem occurs when the poem's speaker is shot, and not the woman.

"My Ace of Spades" was dedicated to and about Malcolm X and his commitment to truth. Joans had met Malcolm in Paris and, in his words, Malcolm "turned me on," and he described Malcolm as "one of the greatest black men that ever walked the face of the earth." Joans then read "The Nice Colored Man," which he sarcastically dedicated—again reflecting some of the tensions that had surfaced between himself and some of the blacks he encountered—as the "nice coloured men working behind the lines" or the "nice coloured people pulling these strings" in Montreal. The affective rhythmic repetition of the word "nigger" brought some members of the audience to their feet and they laughed, cheered, and clapped as the poet described the range of "niggers," from the passive or "nice nigger" to the "clever nigger" and more "militant" or "brave nigger" that reflect the poet's ideal types. As he recited the poem's climactic lines, many in the crowd were aroused in a fervor:

> Eeny, Meeny, Miny, Moe,
> Catch a Whitey by the throat,
> If he hollers nigger,
> Cut it.[208]

Having closed with these lines, he repeatedly shouted the words "Black Power," but there was clearly some commotion and tension following his reading, and after some caucusing, Joans took to the microphone and informed the audience that the session was about to come to an abrupt end:

> I said this was a little Afro-American or black-astonishment that we ran in on the nice colored people, so now we have a note here saying that we have to stop this at once . . . because they have another program scheduled. If some of the black students—I'm not talking about the negro students—if some of the black students here could find another room or something downstairs, we'll continue and we'll have Brother Bob Hamilton and Brother Michael X speak to you and I'll read some more black poems. But we'll have to go downstairs, we'll have to get out of the hall, we have to do it.

On the last day of the conference, Joans once again read his poetry, this time just before Harry Edwards, James Forman, and Stokely Carmichael took to the stage. Rodney introduced "Brother Ted Joans" as a jazz poet who is "back in his own roots" in Timbuktu "right in the heart of the old tradition of Mali" where the poet resided at the time. Joans dedicated his readings, to the applause of the audience, to Langston Hughes and Richard Wright, "two great black writers." He then dedicated a poem "Why Try" to his sister, mother, and lover—a poem that describes brown beauty in the form of a brown woman's brown thoughts, a brown woman's body, brown eyes as she listens to brown sounds of brown music. A white woman encounters the brown woman, after which she feels compelled to throw away her suntan lotion and pose the rhetorical question, "why try?" to which the audience erupted in raucous laughter and applause.

In "Africa," dedicated to "two warriors in Newark," LeRoi Jones and Brother Abu Ansar, Joans displayed clever wordplay to describe the aspirations of "A-free-con-tinent." The poet also dedicated an unnamed poem about black athletes to Harry Edwards, "the tallest brother on the stage"

(Edwards stands at 6 feet, 8 inches tall). Joans then read a poem that immortalized the executed Congolese politician Patrice Lumumba, once again to resounding applause.

"Two Words" described black poets who have embraced the black aesthetic and rejected Shakespeare and Thomas in favour of Black Power. He also read "The Truth" once again, describing it as the only poem that he has memorized; and "The Nice Colored Man," which he claimed he had not intended to read, but "was inspired by some of the fellows yesterday." His announcement of the poem sparked loud applause and when he finished reading it there was, predictably, resounding, extended applause, cheering, and laughter, prompting Rodney to simply remark to the audience: "Comments on the last speaker would be superfluous," before introducing Harry Edwards.

While other delegates were more tempered in their attitudes toward whites than Joans, several of them also insisted that they would not discuss strategies for black liberation in front of whites. The London-based Jamaican lawyer Richard Small of the Campaign Against Racial Discrimination (CARD) fit into this category. In his insightful and detailed presentation on race relations in Britain he discussed the history of slavery and the overall contribution of people of African descent to the economic development of Britain. He also discussed the growing xenophobia and racism against people of African and Asian descent and the general climate of fear to which blacks were subjected, fostered by British politicians such as Enoch Powell and Cyril Osborne. Having said this, Small then made it clear that the public congress was not a suitable place to discuss strategies and solutions to the problems that confronted blacks in Britain. Following his presentation, and much to the dismay of the audience, the Trinidadian economist Lloyd Best criticized what he described as the "absolutely scandalous" intellectual level of the congress. The co-founder of the New World group also accused the speakers of dividing the world into "cowboys and Indians," resulting in a response from the audience that was less than flattering: "I do not believe Mr. Best should come here and wash our dirty linen in public. [*Applause*] Speak to the people involved and let them right the conference. We have a whole day to go. I don't want to hear Mr. Best and I'm sure many people feel the same way."

Did Best fail to realize that the congress was neither a writers' conference *per se*, nor an academic gathering where formal papers are delivered? Most of the invited guests were attached to various movements, and their speeches and the general spirit of the congress were very much in keeping with the surge in global black consciousness of the era. As was his inimical way, Best went against the grain and, as he recalled years later, he was the only one who directly spoke to what he described as the anti-white hostility during the congress:

> I got up and I said that I didn't think this dignified the Congress; it [was] not the kind of thing we wanted, and I disassociated myself from it, and they booed me. And some people called me an Uncle Tom. But I was quite happy to say what I said. I also thought [they] should not have been saying the things about white people that they were saying because Kari Levitt was there, a lot of our white friends were there who were completely part of the movement, and fully lived it [and they] quite insensitively attacked them without thinking. And I said that I didn't think we should proceed in that way and as usual I made my position very clear.

For Best, speaking up was a matter of principle:

> C. L. R. James didn't like what I said. He said I should not have said it then. I don't understand what that means. I think it is opportunistic not to say it when that's when you have to say it. I don't belong to any orthodoxy. You can't railroad me with any position that [does] not discriminate properly. And I said so, I made my position clear. A lot of people who felt the way I did said I should have done it afterward and outside. I didn't feel that way. And they stayed quiet, including C. L. R. He stayed very quiet . . . His wife was also white and she was there. And these people were just talking about honkies without any kind of discrimination, and no kind of restraint and so on. He sat down there and took it, I couldn't.[209]

Despite the implicit and explicit critiques of facile attacks against whites and the calls for a systemic critique of racial capitalism, there is little doubt that the tenor of the conference left little sympathy for Best's stance. Raymond Watts recalled Best's "arrogance" at refusing to be brief or for failing to pose a question following Richard Small's presentation on race in Britain.[210] The tone of Watt's comments hint that the crowd's response to Best was somewhat justified.[211] But perhaps if Watts had been in agreement with Best's remarks, his recollection of the event would have been different. Best was also heckled by some members of the audience, a moment that his friend and colleague Rosalind Boyd recalls as being a humiliating experience for him,[212] but Best was unperturbed and does not appear to have been unduly affected by the hecklers in the room. The melee threatened to descend into

Harry Edwards' presentation with Michael X and Stokely Carmichael. Courtesy of Rocky Jones

pandemonium and this was only averted due to the patience, skill, and stature of the Guyanese writer and polymath Jan Carew who was chairing the session. But given that most people whom I interviewed recalled Best's intervention with disfavour or indifference, it is worth mentioning that Best remembered the congress some thirty-five years later as "one of the great times" of his life, adding: "I have never heard such beautiful and powerful oratory as I heard on that occasion, particularly from Stokely. Of course, it was a who's who in the real sense. Everybody from the Black Power movement or the radical movement in North America was there."[213]

Best was not alone. Norman Cook, then an African-Canadian McGill student with roots going back several generations in Canada and with family ties even further back in the southern US, believed that the anti-white sentiment was immature, offended potential allies, and polarized the black community. Best's criticisms were at least partially vindicated by Rocky Jones who, as we have seen, discussed the need for black people to build coalitions with Natives and French Quebecers since African-descended people were only a small minority in Canada. Harry Edwards too, speaking on the final day of the congress, cautioned those present not to get caught up in attacking individual whites as opposed to "the system" itself. For Edwards, who helped spearhead the Black Power protest at the 1968 Mexico Olympics, but who did not travel to Mexico out of fear, according to Michael O. West, that he might "disappear" like his Mexican ally, the student leader Hector Jaramillo,[214] it was crucial "to understand that we are not dealing with an individual psychopathic, inhumane beast such as Hitler," but with a "worldwide system which turns out Hitlers in the same sense that it turns out Chevrolets, Jaguars, hydrogen bombs, and rifles. [215] [*Applause*]" Edwards added that "we have to recognize that as long as there are more than three of us in a room and all of our faces are black, the white man is there somewhere because his eyes and his ears and his mind and his mentality is there. We have to recognize this."

Edwards' sobering speech was followed by James Forman's Fanonian analysis of class and nationalism in the Third World.[216] As historian Fanon

Che Wilkins has remarked, Forman's presentation mirrored his well-received November 1967 speech, "Liberation Will Come from a Black Thing," which was at least in part a critique of Carmichael's brand of Black Power nationalism and what Forman interpreted as his evasions of class.[217] But, in retrospect, it is obvious that Carmichael's analysis owed a debt to Forman who, much more succinctly and with much less fanfare and theatre than his younger counterpart, captured the spirit and essence of the dynamics of colonialism, imperialism, race, and class under capitalism. Forman began with a minute of silence in tribute to the fallen heroes and martyrs, including Frantz Fanon, Martin Luther King Jr., and Malcolm X, whose images, along with Patrice Lumumba's, adorned the walls of the meeting room. The former civil rights leader and executive secretary of the Student Nonviolent Coordinating Committee, who had, up until a few months before the congress, been associated with the Black Panther Party, then proceeded to deliver a tightly organized analysis of Fanon's ideas on colonialism and post-colonialism. Fanon "fought and died for revolutionary socialism throughout the Third World, especially in Africa," according to Forman, "with the same aspirations as Che Guevara did in Latin America," preaching "against narrowness and pitfalls of a purely nationalist revolution that won a flag, a new style of dress, and underneath the dregs of humanity remained the same."[218]

Forman's presentation was no doubt an implicit warning to leaders of the Black Power movement in the United States as he sought to clarify the distinction between colonialism and exploitation by providing an American example. Once again invoking Fanon, he urged his audience to come to terms with the fact that "all colonized people are victims of racism and exploitation, [*sporadic applause*] but that all exploited people are not colonized." In the United States, for example, "we see whites who are oppressed and who are exploited, many of them, but they do not suffer directly from the racism which is inflicted upon blacks by whites. They are not a colonized people, but a part of the exploiting group of people. They, in fact, form a part of the colonizing race."[219] Forman concluded by unequivocally declaring that racism cannot be eliminated without the control of state power.

Racial and intra-racial tension played itself out in other ways that exposed differing perceptions of the black-white divide. Among those present was the Trinidadian-born Michael X (born Michael de Freitas), the British Black Power figure whose presence Best described as "a disservice to the Congress because he made a speech for five minutes only in four-letter words." Watts, Rennie, Cook, and Hill all alluded to Michael X's disruptive presence at the congress. In an attempt to instill a sense of intellectual rigor in the congress, Robert Hill remarked during his presentation on Marcus Garvey and Black

James Forman's address with Ted Joans, Stokely Carmichael, and Harry Edwards. Courtesy of McGill Archives

Power that "If you haven't read what Garvey said today, I don't know that you can be a brother at all. I don't know because we have been fooling around, a lot of intellectual bullshit going on [*applause*] and men believing that they are making a serious contribution to black liberation and black resistance." Hill implored the audience to ground themselves "in the communities of black people wherever you are, live with them, think with them, organise them and they will point the word forward."[220]

While for some, C. L. R. James' presence was one of the highlights of the congress, as Hill recollects, James' white American colleagues encountered "a kind of very sharp-edged reaction from the black participants. . . . James would go between his hotel and the congress sessions, from the congress sessions back to his bed in the hotel and his American colleagues who were all white would travel with him and would help him in and out of cars, getting him into the auditorium, etc. So here were these white people surrounding James and blacks looking on wondering, what's going on."[221] According to a *McGill Daily* report, some blacks chose to walk out at the beginning of James' talk to protest the presence of whites at the congress.[222]

Raymond Watts recalls bitter disagreement between Richard B. Moore and James, the two elder statesmen of the meeting, over James' presumed indifference to the malicious abuse embedded in the history of the word Negro.[223] He also remembers Carmichael's insistence on a "black solution" to black problems without the assistance of Marx, Lenin, and Trotsky,[224] as does Bukka Rennie, who recalls that James later wrote a letter to Carmichael impressing upon him the importance of grounding his ideas in history.[225] Here we stumble upon an interesting dilemma of memory. Rennie is perhaps unconsciously referring to Carmichael's March 1967 Montreal presentation at Sir George and not his October 1968 congress speech at McGill, a conflation that would have occurred with the passage of time, serving as a reminder of why we should perhaps think of memory as what I have described as a kind of patched quilt that evokes the spirit of the past as opposed to recreating the past as it actually occurred.[226]

Another issue emerged among blacks during the congress that highlighted some of the challenges involved in building a political movement. Several participants—Robert Hill, Raymond Watts, and Leroi Butcher recalled tension between James Forman, Stokely Carmichael, and members of the Black Panther Party (BPP). Forman was alleged to have been forced at gunpoint to accept a merger between his SNCC and the BPP during a meeting in Puerto Rico.[227] The story was released in *The New York Times* on October 7, four days before the Congress of Black Writers began, and the issue was no doubt on Forman's mind as he participated in the Montreal conference alongside Carmichael and other members of the BPP who were in attendance. But Forman insisted that the rumor was false and part of the FBI's plan to disrupt and destroy both organizations.[228] In any event, the proposed merger was called off, although years later Carmichael stated that he eventually quit the BPP over the alleged incident.[229] This said, during his congress speech, Carmichael made several references to Forman's presentation. At one point he remarked: "There is exploitation and there is colonization. Forman explained that. I want to go into it more deeply because I think when one talks about exploitation, the question of race is not present." In light of the conflict between the SNCC and the BPP, and given that Carmichael was still a prominent member of the BPP, and that Forman and Carmichael had fallen out over what Forman described as Carmichael's lack of discipline and individualism when he was involved in

SNCC,[230] the idea of pursuing the question of exploitation and colonization "more deeply" might be interpreted as a playful but not entirely innocent jab at his erstwhile associate. At another point during his presentation, Carmichael attempted to recall a passage from Fanon's *The Wretched of the Earth*, and then asked Forman to find the passage for him—Forman was considered an expert on Fanon and had plans to write a book about him[231]—almost as if he were speaking to an assistant ("Can you get it for me, brother Forman?") and then laughed in his characteristically charismatic and mischievous way.

The Long Aftermath

Elsewhere, I have discussed the immediate aftermath of the congress and how it contributed to a renewed spirit among blacks in Montreal and helped to spark the Sir George Williams protest, which in turn played no small part, along with Walter Rodney's expulsion from Jamaica, in catalyzing a new left politics throughout the Anglo Caribbean.[232] This is how I understood the significance of the event in 2007:

> The activities of the Caribbean Conference Committee, the Congress of Black Writers, and the Sir George Williams Affair were part of the dialectical development for Montreal's black community. Symbolically, the events were like a knot in the brain, a proverbial signpost in the collective consciousness of Montreal and Canada's black population that pointed toward new horizons. The entire society was infected and after the Sir George Williams Affair, new groups and organizations were created and older ones were resuscitated in order to serve Montreal's expanding black population. As a follow-up to the Canadian Conference Committee's inaugural meeting, and on the heels of the events at Sir George Williams, the National Black Coalition of Canada was founded. Local organizations emerged, including the Côte-des-Neiges Black Community Association, the Black Coalition of Quebec, the Notre-Dame-de-Grâce Black Community Association, the Lasalle Black Community Association, the Quebec Black Board of Educators, the Black Study Centre, Black Theatre Workshop, Black Is Television, the Black Action Party, as well as black community newspapers such as *Uhuru* (July 1969 to November 1970) and *The Black Voice* (May 1972 to October 1974). These groups and institutions made critical contributions to the social development and quality of life of black Montrealers and Canadians at a crucial stage in the community's evolution. And in

so doing, they also made critical contributions to the social fabric of the wider society and, to that extent, helped to make both Montreal and Canada more humane and livable places while, at the same time, profoundly influencing political developments in the Caribbean.[233]

More than ten years have passed since I wrote those words, begging the questions: in light of the present political predicament, what can we make of congress in terms of its long aftermath, and how do the issues that were raised then reverberate, resonate, and echo into the present? And how might it inform our understanding of politics today?—a question that, ultimately, takes us beyond the romance of the event and into dynamics of liberation in our time.

The Congress of Black Writers was part of a political moment in which some issues took precedence over others that were equally present in their absence—present in absentia—as a result of what Michel Rolph-Trouillot has referred to as the "dialectics of mentions and silences."[234] In this sense, it is not enough to simply dismiss the exclusion of gender and sexuality as a reflection of that time. Rather, it is important to appreciate that it is precisely the reaction to this absence at the congress, in the wider Afro-diasporic world and the world in general, that, through the concrete actions of the *engagé*—and especially women—these issues have been and continue to be placed on the political agenda today. This reality is evident today in the genesis of Black Lives Matter (BLM), a movement that was sparked by the actions of three women —Alicia Garza, Patrisse Cullors, and Opal Tometi—in the aftermath of the acquittal of Trayvon Martin's killer, George Zimmerman, and one in which women have played and continue to play a central role. In other words, and in keeping with the unruly nature of the dialectic, in the long aftermath of a gathering that was so invested in black manhood and, to a lesser extent, class, the silence on gender and sexuality, among other issues, has, in the *longue durée*, given voice to these issues. Today these same issues occupy a more prominent, growing, but by no means yet central, place in black political discourse. To the extent that some priority has been afforded them, it is partly because they had not been prioritized before and therefore needed to be. Put yet another way, today's movements, including BLM, rest dialectically on the shoulders of the historical movement that the congress embodied, with all its glaring absences.

But 1968 is not 2018. It was inconceivable to most fifty years ago that the US would boast of a black president, but that moment has come and gone and we now live in a post-racial society, but not in the sense that has been hitherto discussed. Canada, too, had a black and female official head of state in Michaëlle Jean, a Haitian-born former journalist whose tenure as Governor General (the Queen of England's official representative in Canada) coincided with Obama's. The moment is post-racial in so far as, having had a black president in the US, we can disabuse ourselves of the idea that racial exploitation, inequality, and repression will dissolve simply by virtue of having a black figure in the White House. Oppression exists in multiple places and has many faces, and this reality encourages us to, more than ever, appreciate the dynamics of race and class alongside global imperial designs, how class is an important ingredient in the practice of racial and gender oppression, and how racial exclusion reinforces class oppression and inequality. Clearly, this is not to dismiss race, but more to appreciate how it is a coeval of class, as people in the Third World are fully aware. This is the point that C. L. R. James made on multiple occasions during the congress, as did James Forman, Harry Edwards, and, in his own inimitable way, Stokely Carmichael. Rodney, too, made the same argument in both his congress statement on the situation in Jamaica and his Montreal speech following his expulsion from Jamaica.

The myth of American exceptionalism and the American Dream suggests that anyone can achieve economic success in the US by dint of their hard labour, by sheer power of their will. The Canadian equivalent is the equally prevalent myth of Canadian innocence that depicts the country as a haven for those who have historically sought refuge and fortune—including the history of Harriet Tubman's underground railroad—while conveniently negating the colonization of Indigenous peoples, the enslavement of people of African origin, and the history of indentured labour *in Canada*. While the history and legacy of cultural genocide of Indigenous peoples in Canada has gained some traction in recent years—though it has not by any means fully pierced the consciousness of the majority of Canadians—the roots of contemporary anti-black racism in Canada and its everyday manifestation remain clouded in denial, despite the publication of books such as Afua Cooper's study of slavery in Canada, *The Hanging of Angelique: The Untold Story of Canadian Slavery and the Burning of Old Montreal*, and Barrington Walker's *Race on Trial: Black Defendants in Ontario's Criminal Courts, 1858–1958*. Both books critically examine crucial moments that situate Canada within the context of racial oppression and exclusion in the complex of territories that make up the Americas. Despite the many books on Canadian anti-black racism or the "black experience in Canada" have been published to even try to produce an exhaustive list here, but the point is that, despite overwhelming textual and experiential evidence to contradict them, the idea of American exceptionalism that is manifested in the American dream and the myth of Canadian innocence persists, shielding legacies and continuities of enslavement, colonialism, and imperialism that have affected, and continue to adversely impact, black lives in North America, and, in very particular ways, as the work of geographer Katherine McKittrick reminds us, the lives and narratives of black women.[235] These and similar myths and obfuscations combine within the wider web of colonial and post-colonial history to obscure the persistence of power dynamics. They negate the life and death issues, problems that cannot be resolved by resorting to facile theories that, while rooted in histories of suffering and woe, neglect the plight of society's dispossessed, that is to say the people down below. As the miners in Marikana, South Africa, know all too well, the fight for genuine and meaningful social change is hard graft. There is no easy road to freedom, and naked power in the black skin can be just as deadly and unfriendly as power in the white skin, irrespective of who possesses the ultimate reins of power.[236]

Martin and Malcolm

The Congress of Black Writers was dedicated to two prominent fallen black figures whose narratives in many ways defined black politics, not only in the US, but also in Canada and the UK, and in many other parts of the globe. It is then fitting to end on a note inspired by the legacies of Martin and Malcolm. But first a word on socialism.

Socialism is a simple word that has assumed multiple meanings in varied contexts over time. It comes with a great deal of baggage from the past, tied to failed states and disastrous attempts to exercise a new sense of freedom that was not defined by markets and capitalism. From Grenada to Belarus, socialist experiments failed to deliver the utopia that the idea has come to represent. The reasons for this are varied, yet, if we define socialism as a social, political, and economic system that provides, but is not limited to meeting, the basic material needs of the population; as a set of ideas, beliefs, and values tied to the collective will of a society in which the majority of the population plays the defining role in determining its fate, while striking the delicate balance between collective rights and the freedom of individuals to develop and realize their creative potential as human beings; as a way to create in ways that nourish the human spirit while not being subsumed to the collective will; and to be able to do so without fear of discrimination, recrimination, or reprisal based on gender, sex, race, sexuality, or any other form of exclusion that denies human beings their humanity; to the extent that this is socialism, then socialism is a universal ideal that cannot simply be reduced to a set

Malcolm X Congress of Black Writers button. Courtesy of Adeline Chancy

of ideas and practices that evolved within the context of Europe, or be limited to a Western conception of the world tied to pseudo-social and pseudo-scientific notions of progress and development.

Socialism is a human phenomenon and people of African descent have played an important role in critically engaging and redefining it: C. L. R. James, Claudia Jones, Angela Davis, Aimé Césaire, Elma Francois, Frantz Fanon, Julius Nyerere, Amilcar Cabral, Walter Rodney, and perhaps most surprisingly, the founder and leader of the Universal Negro Improvement Association, Marcus Mosiah Garvey. Garvey once declared that "the whole world will take on the social democratic system of government now existing in Russia. It is only a question of time"[237] and he praised the two most important leaders of the Russian Revolution while encouraging his followers "to do for Africa what Lenin and Trotsky had done for Russia in overcoming Czarist despotism."[238] He was particularly fond of Lenin, who had called for communist support for the struggles of African-Americans,[239] and in his reflections on Lenin following his death in 1924, he declared that "Russia promised great hope not only to Negroes but to the weaker peoples of the world."[240] As a mass organization dedicated to the transformation and uplifting of people of African descent internationally, Garvey argued that the UNIA "could not but favor the existence of a social democratic government in Russia or in any other part of the world, because we are of the class that rules in Russia and naturally our sympathy should be with the people who feel with us, who suffer with us."[241] And when the conflict between Trotsky and Stalin developed in Russia, Garvey expressed his concern about the split and also reminded his followers of his great admiration for Lenin, whom he described as "a savior of his people or a savior of his country. Lenin to us has pointed the way where the majority of the people will rule, and Lenin has pointed the way for a better system of government through which humanity will, I hope, have peace and perfect peace."[242]

I signal Garvey here because, as Robert Hill argued during his congress presentation, it was Garvey, more than any other figure in the US, who paved the way for what would later be known as Black Power. Garvey is often derided and dismissed as a black nationalist and, by extension, anti-socialist figure, but his sympathy for the Russian Revolution, and the rationale behind it, suggests that his legacy is much more complicated and deserves more attention in this area. W. E. B. Du Bois, Garvey's occasional nemesis, was a communist for much of his adult life and was intrigued with the Russian Revolution from its inception. He traveled to the Soviet Union and other parts of Eastern Europe several times, beginning in 1926,[243] and as the Reverend Martin Luther King Jr. once remarked, "It's time to cease muting the fact that Dr. Du Bois was a genius and chose to be a communist" because "irrational, obsessive anti-communism has led us into too many quagmires to be retained as if it were a mode of scientific thinking."[244]

This brings us to King himself, whom Coretta King described as the first black socialist she ever met.[245] Martin Luther King realized that capitalism exacts a heavy toll on society: global warfare and the callous taking of life, environmental devastation, and the decimation of the human spirit. He had read *The Communist Manifesto* and *Das Kapital*, but as a minister of the church, he could not accept a dialectic—dialectical materialism—that ignored the spirit that was so fundamental to G. W. F. Hegel, a fair analysis from a reverend.[246] But socialist as he may have been, for King, "communism forgets that life is individual" while capitalism "forgets that life is social. And the kingdom of brotherhood is found neither in the thesis of communism nor the antithesis of capitalism, but in a higher synthesis. It is found in questioning the whole society, it means ultimately coming to see that the problem of racism, the problem of economic exploitation, and the problems of war are all tied together. These are the triple evils that are interrelated."[247] For him, in the months and weeks before he was assassinated, race, class, and war were intricately connected, as opposed to fragmented parts of a whole.

In the spirit of Afro-diasporic communities across the Americas, King invoked the revolutionary traditions embedded in biblical parables and lore that he then translated into contemporary analogy. While orthodox socialists or Marxists might be quick to dismiss King's ecclesiastical critique of communism, his analysis represents a criticism of the depletion of spiritualism, that metaphysical sense that we are all part of and connected by something greater than our material existence. We only have to read accounts of some aspects of life in Soviet-era Russia to appreciate the significance of King's critique.[248]

King's critique of both capitalism and communism leads us beyond a conception of society in which humans are treated as fragmented beings to be exploited and executed for the benefit of capital. This was Cornel West's "radical King," whose analysis of the Vietnam War led him to challenge the American military-industrial complex, which was willing to spend billions abroad on war while millions were mired in poverty at home, including African-Americans who fought for "freedom" in Vietnam while they lived a life of un-freedom in America.[249] But while King began to publicly denounce capitalism and the American war machine in Vietnam in 1967, Malcolm's resolute critique of the war in Vietnam, which he also tied to the US war machine in Africa and the war against African-Americans at home, began in the early 1960s. For him, like King, there was no contradiction between his political-economic analysis and his faith or, put another way, in the spirit of liberation theology, their spiritual beings did not conflict with their appreciation of the dynamics of liberation from economic and racial exploitation.

Malcolm described the US as a "neoimperialist power" in Africa[250] and frequently referred to the nefarious role of "Uncle Sam" in Cuba, the Congo, Cambodia, Vietnam, and South America. He died an internationalist who, through his travels in Africa, Saudi Arabia, and Europe, shifted his analysis of race in the US, but by no means diminished its significance, situating it in relation to other forms of oppression across the globe. Malcolm was particularly incensed with the murder of Patrice Lumumba[251] and what he described as the "criminal" role of the US and the "American power structure" in the Congo in terms of supporting the recruitment and training of mercenaries who destabilized and eventually helped to overthrow Lumumba.[252] He was shifting to an increasingly more radical, that is to say revolutionary, position, a direction that was more than evident in his March 19, 1964 interview published in the socialist journal *Monthly Review*. The interview, conducted by the poet and jazz critic A. B. Spellman, is revealing in terms of Malcolm's rapid radical and revolutionary internationalist shift in outlook only a few months after parting with the Nation of Islam, although the thrust of his views would suggest that he had already been thinking through these "new" convictions before his rupture with the Nation. In the interview, Malcolm called for a black revolution, as opposed to a revolt, that would radically change the system in America. Despite his call for a sweeping, systematic, and structural change, Malcolm was clear that there could be no working-class, inter-racial solidarity as long as the white working-class racism persisted, and that black self-organization and "black solidarity" was of paramount importance for the black revolutionary struggle.[253]

In the last two years of his life, Malcolm also delivered a number of speeches on the Socialist Workers Party (SWP) platform and did interviews with socialists. This was the same organization in which C. L. R. James had played an active role in the 1930s and 1940s, and for which he had helped to formulate the autonomy, self-organization, and self-determination of the "Negro" that was outlined as early as 1939 during his historic meeting with

Leon Trotsky in Coyocan, Mexico, and later published as *Leon Trotsky On Black Nationalism and Self-Determination* (for some reason the title does not include James' name) with Malcolm's image gracing the cover.[254] For many years the SWP had not only promoted black nationalism but, taking its cue from James and Trotsky, has described the black movement as the vanguard of the imminent socialist revolution in the US.[255] Malcolm was increasingly shifting toward an analysis of class that complemented his analysis of racial oppression, a position that was enthusiastically supported by the SWP as well as Grace and James Boggs, both independent Marxists who had been James' collaborators; and he was also looking not only to African countries, such as Ghana and Tanzania as examples, and the class and racial oppression of neo-colonialism in the Congo, but also paying close attention to developments in China, Vietnam, and Cuba as examples of socialism and anti-imperialism at work,[256] framed by a Jamesian conception of self-organization, or what has been described by Manning Marable in his biography of Malcolm as "James's belief that the oppressed possessed the power to transform their own existence."[257] It would not be a stretch to suggest that Malcolm had read James and Trotsky's position on the self-determination as well as James' *The Black Jacobins*. If so, it would also be safe to say that, along with his Garvey connections (recall that both his parents were staunch Garveyites and very active UNIA organizers), James, via Malcolm, would have played an important role in formulating the central position of Black Power that Stokely Carmichael and the Black Panther Party later developed. He veered toward an internationalist position and began to consistently connect the plight of African-Americans with the dispossessed, damned, and condemned of the earth—in Vietnam, Congo, and Cuba, among other places—and consistently critiqued the US war machine,[258] but he also described capitalism as a "vulture" that sucked "the blood of the helpless."[259] Malcolm's analysis echoed that of Karl Marx who described capital as "dead labour, that vampire-like, only lives by sucking living labour, and lives the more, the more labour it sucks."[260] As Malcolm argued, as "the nations of the world free themselves, then capitalism has less victims, less to suck, and it becomes weaker and weaker. It's only a matter of time," he optimistically professed, "before it will collapse completely."[261] He used similar language in another speech, describing various independent countries of Asia as "socialistic" and suggesting that various African countries have also turned to socialistic methods to solve their problems.[262]

During a speech at the Militant Labor Forum of New York, Malcolm, fresh from his travels in Africa, discussed the growing power of China as a communist state, invoked the spirit of the Cuban Revolution, and alluded to various revolutionary struggles in Africa. When he was asked to describe his economic platform, he delved even further into what I am suggesting was a shift in the direction toward socialism: "As was stated earlier, all of the countries that are emerging today from under the shackles of colonialism are turning towards socialism. I don't think it's an accident." He went on:

> Most of the countries that were colonial powers were capitalist countries and the last bulwark of capitalism today is America and it's impossible for a white person today to believe in capitalism and not believe in racism. You can't have capitalism and not believe in racism. You can't have capitalism without racism. And if you find a person without racism and you happen to get that person into conversation and they have a philosophy that makes you sure they don't have this racism in their outlook, usually they're socialists or their political philosophy is socialism.[263]

To suggest, as Malcolm did, that white socialists were essentially, by definition, not racists was, for someone of his acute intelligence, somewhat surprising, particularly when we consider how racism has been the single-most significant contributing factor in what Richard Iton referred to as the "solidarity blues."[264] And yet, what this quote does suggest is that arguably the most influential African-American figure of the post-Second World War period was contemplating a conception of socialism that seriously accounted for anti-black racial oppression. At the very least, these words leave little doubt that Malcolm X was an anti-imperialist whose revolutionary vision was shifting toward a socialist position as he connected the plight of African-Americans to the oppression, exploitation, and liberation of the damned and condemned of the earth. Malcolm had become an internationalist who was now connecting the plight of US blacks with the conditions of the people of Africa, Asia, and Latin America. This shift is further evident in Malcolm's relationship with the Tanzanian revolutionary Abdul Rahman Muhammad Babu, who would later be associated with Walter Rodney, and whom Malcolm invited to speak during an Organization of Afro-American Unity (OAAU) event in New York in 1964. At the same event, a solidarity message from Che Guevara, whom Malcolm appears to have met in private in New York, was read to the audience.[265]

Both Malcolm X and Martin Luther King Jr. had arrived at a point where they believed that freedom from racial oppression was incompatible with capitalism; that capitalism was antithetical to humanism in so far as it reduced the toilers of the world to fragments of themselves for the benefit of the few while eroding the spirit of all who were caught in its web. We have no way of knowing what directions King and Malcolm would have taken in their respective lives if they had lived longer, but it is perhaps fair to speculate that their critiques of modern capitalism would have been more, and not less, resolute—perhaps adding an acute analysis of gender dynamics, sexuality, environmental devastation, and the prison-industrial complex. As Keeanga-Yamahtta Taylor suggests, the Black Lives Matter movement—and here I include the BLM in Canada and the UK—has a great deal in common with the radical Black Power movement of the 1960s and 1970s in terms of its systemic analysis of racism in relation to capitalism, but one of the big differences being that in BLM, gender, sexuality, and ableism, among other forms of discrimination, have assumed a much more prominent role.[266]

We will never know, but what is clear is that their critique of the coevals of race and economic class exploitation, alongside the military-industrial complex, was unequivocal, and gestured toward a socialist vision—this is small "s" socialism, a vision of social justice in the broadest sense of the word; that is non-patriarchal, embraces members of LGBTQ community; and that is anti-racist, anti-colonial, and anti-imperialist; and in which the accumulation of capital and conspicuous consumption that has brought such dread to the planet is called into question and confronted.

Socialism is the word I have chosen to use here, but if there is another word that more adequately captures these ideals, then so be it. While I am invoking a term that is laden with preconceived meaning, the strength of the socialist ideal, as I have defined it, and not as ideology, posits an egalitarian vision of the world with the potential to work across identity lines and toward a common egalitarian good. Of course, the issue of solidarity is an important consideration here. Malcolm, and later Carmichael, argued that blacks do not need whites to join their movements, but to work within white communities to address racial oppression. But where do movements and struggles for social justice converge? Do they connect? Or, put another way, where is the space for human solidarity and organizing for economic and political justice across identity lines, but without negating particular experiences, a practice that has served as a major obstacle to human solidarity? The very meaning of solidarity is defined by differences brought together in order to work toward a specific goal or set of objectives. As the pervasiveness of racism and paternalism persists, blacks and other racialized groups remain skeptical of movements that purport to be universal and humanist, including socialist groupings, but nonetheless proceed to tell racially marginalized groups that identity does not matter; that identity is fractious, when, in so many ways, their socioeconomic lives have been defined by the very identities that institutional power, largely in the hands of people of European descent, continues to ignore or treat as incidental. As Toni Morrison and Afro pessimists have argued, the American conception of freedom is intricately tied to the metaphysics of the racialized Other, the permanently bounded and unfree who serve as the measure of freedom for American society as a whole:[267]

> Expensively kept, economically unsound, a spurious and useless political asset in election campaigns, racism is as healthy today as it was during the Enlightenment. It seems that it has a utility far beyond economy, beyond the sequestering of classes from one another, and has assumed a metaphorical life so completely embedded in daily discourse that it is perhaps more necessary and more on display than ever before.[268]

Freedom, as Morrison suggests, "can be relished more deeply in a cheek-by-jowl existence with the bound and unfree, the economically oppressed, the marginalized, the silenced."[269]

Black labour—which was once a major source for the production of surplus value and was both constituent and constitutive of the rise of capitalism—is now superfluous in the post-slavery, post-colonial, and increasingly post-industrial age, resulting in the wholesale incarceration of a now economically redundant surplus black population. Black bodies and minds continue to be policed—and here again it is important to note that we are also talking about both Canada and the UK, among other places, where, proportionately speaking, the same problems that plague the US persist.[270] In these contexts retreats into pessimism, futurism, or fictitious kingdoms in which royalty rules, however benignly, over its subjects; or reductionist conceptions of identity that falsely separate blacks from the global realities of modern crisis-ridden capitalism, and how the crisis impacts blacks and other oppressed peoples across the globe, are counterproductive. In other words, the tendency to think of identity as a fixed and immutable essence is problematic in so far as it fails to consider the dynamic of being and becoming that essentially defines what it means to be a healthy human living an "authentic" life; an existence that takes it for granted that freedom does not imply abandoning one's self in a sea of universality. As Keeanga-Yamahtta Taylor succinctly puts it, the African-American struggle for liberation (and here I take America to mean the Americas) is a crucial part of and intricately connected to the struggle to end social, economic, and political exploitation and the overall "project of human liberation and social transformation."[271]

In the 1960s, many blacks concluded that overcoming the systematic racial exclusion involved negating what Fanon described as a worm-eaten and rotting system that was responsible for producing it. Blacks assumed a place at the forefront of the struggle to transform the United States, the Caribbean,

Canada—the Americas in general—as well as the UK, and the world. And despite its small size, the black population in Montreal played an active role in this global struggle. The Congress of Black Writers was one, albeit important, manifestation of this phenomenon that, by promoting the need for revolutionary change and the abolition of anti-black racism, highlighted the important role that blacks can play and were playing in "moving against the system," to use Harry Edwards' words. This is the lasting legacy of the Congress of Black Writers, a legacy that is part of our appreciation of the dynamics of liberation. Fifty years have passed since that historic event, and while the geopolitical landscape has changed considerably, the fundamental antagonisms and contradictions of our time have not. With all its challenges, the congress attempted to chart a course into the future and to imagine and create a new, more egalitarian world. Malcolm X's ideas were foundational to the radical wave of Black Power. As early as 1964 Bobby Seale ordered a subscription to OAAU's paper *Backlash*,[272] and many within the Black Power movement, including Stokely Carmichael, echoed Malcolm's ideas as they moved further to the left. Chicago Black Panther leader Fred Hampton died with a copy of *Malcolm X Speaks* at his bedside, the book that contains some of Malcolm's most concise and clearest anti-imperialist and socialistic remarks. Black Power was the prevailing ideology among Afro-diasporic people in North America, the UK, and, to a certain extent—in light of Rastafari and on the heels of the protests that ensued after Walter Rodney's expulsion from Jamaica post-congress—the Caribbean. But what body of ideas can we draw on or turn to today to not simply interpret the world that we live in but to dramatically change it for the better?

Martin, and especially Malcolm, were shifting in a direction that was anti-capitalist and pro-socialist in their last years. In Malcolm's case, his shift in the direction of socialism can be understood as an extension of his incessant critiques of the black bourgeoisie that had turned its back on the black majority, as well as his early embrace of the Cuban Revolution.[273] The fact that early FBI interest in Malcolm X within the Nation of Islam was primarily predicated on the impression that he might be a communist[274] suggests that there is something threatening about the idea of challenging the international economic underpinnings of society. However, as James Boggs, the Detroit-based, African-American theorist, wrote in the aftermath of Malcolm's murder, change requires movement, and movement requires building organizations, and organizations demand organization—they have to be organized—but with a clear analysis, idea, and vision of what we are organizing and fighting for, and how these aspirations might be realized—tactic and strategies. This cannot rely on spontaneous eruptions of protest and rebellion as catalysts for change.[275] As Boggs was also quick to point out, such a movement cannot rely and is not contingent on feigned manifestations of solidarity that patronize black folks as opposed to recognizing that blacks have historically played, and continue to play, a crucial role in liberation aspirations and served as inspirations for global movements for social transformation.[276] This is not black hubris, but an historical fact that takes on added meaning within the current global context, and especially, given the growing and alarming rates of black incarceration, for black lives. As Boggs reminded us in 1969, the issues involved are a matter of life and death:

> The rapid development of automation and cybernation to reduce the need for human toil and to create opportunities for human development; the distribution of goods according to need; the overthrow of the existing educational system with its built-in racism Western biases; a new revolutionary constitution which will establish a new law and order between nations and within this nation on the basis of the right to self-determination by those who have been systematically damned to underdevelopment—these are only some of the issues to which Black Power naturally and urgently addresses itself. Thus the perspective of Black Power is a new society much closer to the classless society projected by Marx than anything that the old Marxists have even dared to envision.[277]

Boggs went on to state that "the Black Revolution is not anti-socialist or anti-communist, but is very much anti the Socialist and Communist Parties," which have historically pushed for black solidarity with a white working class that was just as virulently racist as its bourgeoisie and hostile to the precepts of an egalitarian society.[278] In other words, Boggs was calling for a socialism that would be divested of its old ideological baggage and biases, as well as of the practice of anti-black racism that impeded and continues to impede genuine solidarity, and he refused to subsume the needs of the black working class to this confused conception of socialism. Socialism, as I have described it, is a set of ideas and values associated with a more just, egalitarian, and anti-oppressive society. It is the antithesis to the rabid capitalist exploitation, crude consumerism, cultural and economic imperialism, racial oppression, and environmental destruction that characterizes our current moment, and it is tied to what Stefan Harney and Fred Moten have characterized as speciation. Speciation is characterized by flawed notions of progress and improvement that translate into the "general reduction of the earth to productivity and submission of earth to techniques of domination that isolate and enforce particular increases in and acceleration of productivity"[279] at the expense of our individual and collective capacity to be human in the best sense of that word. In this context, the renewal or reinvention of the socialist or socialistic ideal, to use Malcolm's word, and in the sense that I have described it, holds a key to unlocking the human potential and creativity that is necessary for building a new society, and people of African descent have an important role to play, as they have in the past, in defining how the movement toward such a society might unfold in the coming years.

JAMES FORMAN

James Forman est né à Chicago en 1928. Il a passé cinq ou six ans dans une ferme du Mississipi. En 1957 il est diplomé de l'Université Roosevelt, puis a fait un an de recherches au Département des Etudes Africaines à l'Université de Boston. De 1961 à 1966 il occupe le poste de Secrétaire exécutif du SNCC. En 1967 il participe à un Séminaire international sur l'arpatheid organisé par les Nations Unies. A ce séminaire il présente une communication qui définit la position du SNCC sur l'Apartheid, le racisme et le colonialisme. En janvier 1968 il publie une plaquette: HIGH TIDE OF BLACK RESISTANCE. Actuellement James Forman dirige le Bureau International du SNCC.

ROCKY JONES

Rocky was born in Truro, Nova Scotia, fourth in a family of ten. He has spoken extensively in Canada on the necessity of our brothers and sisters organizing to fight racism in Canada, to identify with the struggle in the United States, and with the struggle in the third world. In the face of heavy criticism and opposition form the white controlled religious institutions in Nova Scotia, he has continued to fight to keep alive the flames of change and the hope of liberation.

COMMITEE

CONGRESS OF BLACK WRITERS COMMITTEE

R. Douglas – Dominica
E. Thébaud – Haiti — Co-chairmen
B. Baldon – Trinidad & Tobago – Publicity
R. Watts – Trinidad & Tobago – Secretary (Mtl)
W. Look-Lai – Trinidad & Tobago – Secretary (N.Y.)
M. Alfred, Miss – Barbados – Financial Secretary
P. Filsaimé – Haiti – Coordination
J. Pierre-Louis, Miss – Haiti — Public relations
J. Wallen, Miss – Canada
C. Nurse, Miss Barbados
E. Thornhill, Miss – Barbados — Registration
J. McColla, Miss – Jamaica
E. Howell, – Barbados – Graphics
S. Chiwaro – Zimbabwe
J. Depradine, Miss – Grenada
R. Martin – Canada
K. Kumi – Ghana
B. Walker, Mrs – U.S.A.
K. Prempe – Ghana
B. Joseph, Miss – Grenada
K. Kimi – Ghana
K. Ajisi – Ghana
R. San-Vincente, – Venezuela
R. John – St. Vincent
J. Johnson, Mrs – Jamaica
D. Collins – Canada
V. Daniels, Miss – St. Vincent
M. Evans, Miss – Grenada
K. Charles, Trinidad & Tobago
J. Wyatt – U.S.A.

CONGRESS OF BLACK WRITERS
CONGRÈS DES ECRIVAINS NOIRS

Towards the Second Emancipation
The Dynamics of Black Liberation

Vers la Seconde Emancipation
Dynamique de la Libération Noire

Students Union and Leacock Building
McGill University
Montreal, Canada.

October 11th - 14th, 1968

REGISTER NOW – $4.00

Congress program. Alfie Roberts Collection

Chapter 1

THE PSYCHOLOGY OF SUBJECTION

Race Relations in the United States of America

ALVIN POUSSAINT

B EFORE I go on to the body of what I want to talk about, I want
to give you a framework, a little bit for thinking about what I'm
going to say. I'm a psychiatrist, which means that I was trained,
basically, in Freudian-type psychoanalytical methods with some variations
on a theme, which is basically a European, Western, white science. You have
to remember that Freud got most of his theories from analyzing upper-class
white women in Europe and that, from this, he developed a whole type of
psychoanalytic theory. So, there's some question of how relevant this type of
thinking might be to black people, and particularly for people who are from
different cultures—the Asian people, the African people—and whether we
can really see them in a type of Western, Freudian framework.

The other thing about psychiatrists is that they tend to see psychopathology. We're trained as medical doctors and we're trained to look for problems,
disease, and illness. So we tend to be negative or lean toward picking up disease without taking a look at the strengths of people, what their assets are,
what their abilities for a good adaptation are. And this is very true in terms of
the black man. When sociologists or psychiatrists study the black man in the
United States, they're looking for problems, for a hotbed of pathology that

social scientists rush in to study; and not just white social scientists, but also black social scientists. And this goes on so much that you would think that black people were completely mad, or completely diseased in some way. We have to remember, too, that psychiatrists, by the very nature of their operation, tend to support the status quo because they're usually dealing with individual sickness. They take out an individual and they define him as sick.

Now frankly, it doesn't matter to them too much that the society may be sick because they don't know how to deal with the society. So, they take the patient and they try to help him adjust or adapt to that society. Scientists frequently will tell you that they're letting people be themselves. But often this can't be so. The very nature of the operation frequently gets them to help you to feel better, and sometimes to feel better you have to come into more harmony with the system. So that if you define black people's problems in terms of psychopathology or individual psychopathology, you're letting the system off easy, you're making the victim of the problem somehow responsible for the illness in the larger society.

Let me give you an example of how this works. Suppose you have a family and you have a child in it, say a college student. And the college student develops a problem. And his family sends him to a psychiatrist and defines that student as sick. Now, suppose the psychiatrist learns through the patient that really a lot of his illness is because, say, the family—mother and father—are oppressive. Then what is the psychiatrist's duty in that case? By accepting the patient as sick in the first place, he may be supporting the oppressive system if he doesn't also address himself to that. So that some psychiatrists now take in the whole family because they want to deal with the oppression or the problems in the family unit or that little society.

Now, how do you deal with the problems and sickness in the larger society? You have to remember too that frequently psychiatry, although based on some scientific principles, is basically a value system. That is, instead of defining things as good or bad, we have developed other types of words to describe these phenomena. So, we call things sick, unhealthy, neurotic when actually what we may be saying is that thing, you know, this is good and that's bad—a morality sometimes similar to religion. And that's why you can find so many different types of "scientific" approaches among psychiatrists themselves and physicians, because they basically act on what their values are, frequently, and not out of an objective, scientific approach.

When I was working in Mississippi I had some contact with the University of Mississippi's psychiatry department. And these were psychiatrists trained to be "objective and scientific," and we have to put all of that in quotes. When it came time for them to integrate their unit—not integrate it, I shouldn't say that. The unit was all white. They didn't bother to set up a segregated in-patient service for black people, they kept all of it for white people. But the federal government was putting pressure on them, because of the new laws, to integrate the unit. Psychiatrists sat down and had meeting after meeting in conference to talk about this and each time came up with the feeling—objective, scientific conclusions—that it would be detrimental to the mental health of both white and black patients if they integrated their unit. So they were using their science to directly support the status quo.

Now, they finally did integrate—that is, they allowed a few Negro patients on the ward (I don't know any of them)—when the federal government threatened to withhold about three million dollars' worth of federal research money for the unit. And after they had this little experiment with some patients on the ward, the chairman of the department told me in private that all of the things that they thought were going to happen, that would happen, most of them didn't happen. It was all in their minds. And because they were products of the system, even as psychiatrists, they were unable to cope or deal with, essentially, what was a social-political problem. And you wonder about psychiatrists being in this whole area. Again, they're writing about black people, and even if you talk to these psychiatrists in Mississippi, any psychiatrists, they could tell you all the problems about blacks. And there's much more a danger in this, I think, than people realize, because most of it is very, very unscientific to begin with.

There are books and articles coming out defining the psychology of the black man that we really have to take with a grain of salt and be very, very careful about. See, white society in America very seldom writes about white psychopathology; they don't do that because they don't see their problems in terms of psychopathology because they are the society. Yet they seem almost titillated, over and over again—you can write book upon book upon book about the messed up mind of black people and it sells. And whom does it sell to? To the white population. And they read over and over again about the black man's anger, the black man's sexual hang-ups in relationship to racism, but they never talk in detail about the racism.

Now you have people writing about black psychopathology who start off by saying, "Well, all of this is secondary to racism, white racism," but that's all they say about it. Then they spend the rest of the time talking about the sickness that black people have as a reaction to racism. In some of this you get the feeling that the white society, even some black people writing about this problem, seem to think that somehow black people are putty, their minds are putty in the hands of white racism; that they don't see it or understand and know how to deal with it—or haven't known, it supports, how to deal with it—or that black people are somehow robots reacting to white racism and doing all the things that they're supposed to do and adapting to this. Because the effect of writing about all this black illness really reassures the white man and confuses, I think, black men about the nature of the problem. Somehow you think that, well, if you tell them about the problem, if you tell them how messed up we are because of racism, you're gonna win friends and they're gonna be sympathetic and that you're gonna change attitudes—it doesn't work that way.

We have probably thousands of books talking about the sad predicament of the black man. It doesn't change white attitudes. In fact, it might do exactly the opposite. Because if you define someone as sick, even though you say, well, it's due to racism—you know you can say, well, someone's got that disease that's making his skin fall off, and so on, and it's due to cancer, that doesn't mean you're going to want to deal with or be around that person with that illness, or who you see as having that illness. Or you might even cause further division among black people themselves because some start thinking they're "healthier" than others. And it also provides a type of thinking that gets away from the fundamental problems, because if you see things as individual psychopathology, then you think, well, that's the way you treat it, you know, let's support mental health. Then you set up community psychiatry programs. You start getting psychotherapy and other programs for poor people, black people, and you let the system that's producing the problem and turning out defective individuals go untouched. So that again, even in community psychiatry programs, you might be supporting all the factors that produce the problem in the first place.

Psychiatrists, I guess, have to determine what they want to do. And we're basically clinicians, supposed to make people feel better, and some want to do that, and that's fine. But I don't think that we should kid ourselves about what we really are doing. In a book I recently read, speaking about black pathology, blacks were defined as having paranoia—and I think this will clinch the whole thing for you about how the status quo and everything works together— blacks were defined as having a paranoia, a cultural paranoia produced by the culture. Now, paranoia, in psychiatric terms, means that you're delusional and you're psychotic, that what you perceive is not in reality. Blacks don't have that. Blacks have an appropriate suspicion about the motives and intentions of white men based on concrete experience. That is not sick behaviour. In fact, if you wanted to even think in such terms about cultural paranoia then you would have to define the white man in America as having this problem because he has acted in a paranoid, out of reality fashion to the supposed threats of black people in the country—what they're going to do to them:

what they're going to do to them economically, what they're going to do to them sexually. That's mostly a matter of their fantasies.

But we get stuck with your labels. I think there's even some joy on the part of some people in somehow exposing themselves or having a catharsis about, you know, their hang-ups, say, as black men or black women. And that's a curious thing too—that blacks are able to do that. And what does that mean, particularly when a lot of it is not scientific? So that you'll get people writing, say, about the black man's hang-ups on white women and they'll generalize this to all black men. And that, scientifically and statistically, is not true.

Now, you can come up with a whole lot of theories about it, that this is the way it's supposed to be because of, well, the racism. But is it? Or are the people writing about it, do they have a special type of experience and a special type of concern? Were people and blacks in the Civil Rights Movement a special type of black that was looking for a special type of thing? That's not the major point I wanted to make there. But you know the black writers will do this over and over again. Do you know of any white writer anywhere in the United States, including the South, who's ever talked, say, about their hang-ups on black women? They don't write about that. It's almost as if they know better than to write about that, that they wouldn't be that foolish to expose themselves. So, we know that, particularly in the South and in the North, white men are continually cruising, looking for black prostitutes. The black woman has been continually sexually exploited and we know that the white man has all sorts of hang-ups about that, but they don't write about it. And if someone knows of a book or even a good novel where this is taken up—and don't say *The One Hundred Dollar Misunderstanding*,[1] because that's a non-sense book.

But I raise this again, to have you think about why you have these types of differences? Is it, somehow, that coming out with a lot of these things on the part of the black writer, actually an acceptance of the stereotypes, the racist stereotypes, they really have come to believe themselves inwardly, and then sort of have a catharsis of confession and truth? Or are they, too, really just victims, even though it may be done under the guise of attacking the system or attacking racism?

Now that I said those things, I just want to talk in a general way, and it has to be a general way, [about] some things I feel are important about the psychology of blacks. And I feel they're important because they're things that we can have a program around, a planned program. I'm not denying that there are overall effects of racism on people, both white and black, but it may not be as clear-cut or as defined as some people would like to have it. And blacks have things that are unique to their experience—slavery, segregation—but

I think the most profound effect, if you want to call it that, is that the black man has been sort of forced into a very submissive role. And you don't have to be a mental giant or a psychiatrist to figure that out.

Blacks have been made to be docile and accepting of a very oppressive system and you had to be docile in the face of that system for survival. If you wanted to live, you frequently had to make the choice between being assertive and aggressive or being acquiescent and docile to the system. And since most human beings usually choose to live, blacks frequently tended to go in this direction. That doesn't mean, though, that there wasn't rebellion, because there was rebellion. And that doesn't mean that in many different ways blacks fought back on very simple things, and all you have to do is talk to, you know, a Negro maid and she'll tell you the many ways they had of letting anger back out at the oppressors without being murdered.

Now, it's also a fact that the whole oppressive system in America was particularly directed toward the black man, to keep him emasculated and to keep him castrated. And that's not too subtle either. Their courts do it, the schools do it, all the racial etiquette does it. I'll just remind you that, you know, even now the "courts of justice" in the United States inflict severe penalties on black folks for aggressive behaviour, particularly black men, and there's very much of a double standard that operates. But right now, some people seem to be clouded in their thinking about it or don't see it, and it's still very obvious. I just want to mention a few of them to really remind you that it still very much exists.

Rap Brown was caught with a gun on an airplane and they sentenced him to five years in jail for that violation. At the same time they give gun lessons, target shooting lessons, to white housewives in suburbs in how to shoot. And that's legitimate behaviour. They sentence LeRoi Jones to two to three years in jail for carrying a gun—he didn't shoot anybody—during the Newark riots. At the same time, white vigilante groups with rifles and all sorts of things are not touched, not even arrested, and probably very frequently encouraged. Mr. Hatchett, a fellow who was just dismissed by New York University because he called Nixon, Humphrey, and Albert Shanker of the United Federation of Teachers racist bastards—and that, you know, is impolite [*laughter*]—and they kicked him out. Now we have a man running for president of the United States [who] legally calls niggers "niggers." [*Laughter*]

We have a man, governor of Georgia, who used guns publicly to violate the law and threaten to kill Negroes, and he is governor of Georgia. Now, you know what would happen if LeRoi Jones or Rap Brown ever tried to run for governor of anything in the United States. Do you think they would let him on a ballot? Whose crimes—and it goes without saying—we know whose crimes are greatest, and those are the crimes of the racist. This double standard in order to keep blacks submissive also operates in relationship to violence and there's a campaign going on now in the United States to scapegoat the black community and make them responsible for the violence in the society. And I want you to know that we haven't produced one assassin in the black community. Most of the violence in the United States, when you weigh it all up, beyond a doubt, has been committed by whites against blacks—beyond a doubt. It was the whites who killed the Indians and it was the whites who did all the lynching. It was a white policeman who shot down all the people during the riots. Yet, this is the way it operates and probably will continue to operate, because both black and white people in the United States have been attuned and conditioned to accept this double standard in some intuitive way. So that black people say, "Well, Rap Brown violated the law. Now he should be sent to jail for five years."

[*The recording is interrupted and then resumes with Poussaint responding to questions from the audience.*]

I think there is a relationship to all of this. I think it has to do with groups that are potentially a threat to the established system in some fundamental way. You noticed that now, say, with the peace students and peace groups in the United States, the more they begin to confront the system and to challenge it in fundamental ways—or maybe not so fundamental, just around the war—the system then begins to treat them more and more like niggers. A lot of things become legitimized; that the police can then move in with force and beat them. They begin to call them all sorts of names, make them sick and strange—not normal people. And all your presidential candidates, as you know, are doing this now. I think it's the same thing with communism. They see a fundamental threat to the whole system in communism and they get very paranoid about that and begin to treat them with oppression, etcetera. That goes for most groups that challenge in that way, because it becomes a question of very important and crucial power relations that people are not going to give up easily.

QUESTION: Yes, with regards to psychiatry in relation to man. Now, this is very controversial . . .

POUSSAINT: In relation to what?

QUESTION: To man. Psychiatry in relation to man, that is the black man, the white man, etcetera. This is my idea of the whole situation: Psychiatry was originated in a cold and calculating world. I think the psychiatrists themselves have failed the situation. For instance, man was endowed with a special, well, inborn qualities.

MODERATOR: Questions please, questions.

QUESTION: Would you wait a minute, please. [*More murmurs from the crowd*] Are you here to say what a man should regard as a question? However, the entire idea is this: That black man, the psychiatrist defines this man as a man who is living in a dream world wondering. But then, who really has the measure of defining who is really in a dream world?

For instance, men like Shakespeare, Keats, Shelley, all these people, they live in a world of themselves and what I want to say is that the psychiatrists, they leave inner conflict in the present generation, that is among students, etcetera, because they want to project an idea to the world that, when they go for counseling, the psychiatrists say, "Well, you are nutty." The hippies, if we look at these people, they have something also to offer. I think you can say a little more on this then I will. Well, I'll leave two with you here, with regard to religion. Now, "blessed be the meek" is as true as it is written and if the black man feels that he is wrong in following this trend, he will be just embarking upon an idea perpetuated by the white man. He is right. The whole idea is this: The evolution of life caters for another race to rise and if, I feel, the white man doesn't reconcile, he would be enslaved.

MODERATOR: I have been asked to announce that only questions will be accepted and that Dr. Poussaint will have to leave at eleven o'clock.

QUESTION: Sir, I wanted to ask you, when you talked about the confrontation, the conflict between black Americans and white Americans, you were talking, in a way, to different groups—one exploiting the other, one hurting the other. But to me, I come from Greece and Americans there never used psychology to explain their relation to our country. And I wonder, since black Americans are Americans also in the sense that they live there and they definitely participate in the society and the economy and everything, is there a way in which, without getting themselves completely identified with something other than America, is there a way in which they can struggle to change America? And what do you think can be done by the American whites? Do they have to feel identified, and with what, in order to be able to change America or will they never change America? If blacks get to be equal with whites in America, will that mean that we are going to have black CIA and black troops in Greece and in other places? [*Applause and laughter*]

POUSSAINT: That's an interesting idea, huh. How many of you for black troops in Greece? [*Laughter*] You know, that's a large order of question that I can't really answer simply. You know, I think that people have all different feelings. I still think that, basically, it seems a thrust of most groups, even many on the militant side, is in some way to get into the system, but in a new way. That is to get into it in a real way, the way the system operates, that is, with power relationships among people. They want to get in in this real way and not in a way in which they are subjected.

Now, as to what blacks would do, say, if they took over America, and the whole question of capitalism and racism and all that, is a big question. In some ways, the capitalist system is very intimately connected and intimately tied up with racism and supports it, and the whole question of whether you would have to fundamentally change a whole apparatus in order to eliminate the racism is a question that, you know, is unresolved. I know it's possible, know that if things are a little bit different it would be black people subjugating the whites. I would like that a little bit better, in a sense, if that turned out as an equalizer.

What I'm saying is that I'm not giving blacks any hold on all sorts of special types of morality, necessarily, that other human beings don't have. You know it could be partly a whole bunch of types of circumstances that puts groups in different types of relationships. It's possible if you have black nations, you know, black nations may fight each other and fight white nations, exploit. Who knows what's going to happen in this world. So, the question you really asked [about] is a lot of fundamental things, about what kind of society we want to live in as people, whether black, white, or black in power, white in power, or what have you.

WALTER RODNEY: I've come a long way to gain some insights from this brother and from other black brothers who either have skills, or a least brothers and sisters who have an experience to share and, in order to do this, I have to make a short statement on which you'll comment. I'm very sorry about the last ruling. The statement relates to the question about violence as a therapeutic. Now, my understanding of that statement on two levels: firstly, for myself I find it very applicable. I mean I am sick, you see. This society has made me sick. I don't think an ordinary human being ought to have the type of preoccupations that I have about destroying things and destroying people. That's an illness. Now, I want some therapy and I think violence is part of that, an essential part of that. [*Applause*] That's the first thing.

The second thing is that our people have a very unbalanced conception of force and violence, as I see it. It's not that we don't contemplate this; we see it every day. But we don't see it as something inherent in us. It is something that people always do to us and, again, that unbalance. For the whole mass of black peoples over the world, it seems to me that violence is a therapy. I mean, I wouldn't go on. One could quote the sort of examples that Fanon did in the Algerian War, the sort of thing that Che Guevara writes about, about the peasant in the guerrilla war; how he has to see the state system—the police, these brutal pigs—actually the violence being applied to them before something begins to happen to him up there.

Now, I would like this brother to use his insights to go into the question a little bit more. In other words, I felt he glossed over the term "violence as therapeutics." So, my question is to ask him to say some more. [*Applause*]

POUSSAINT: Now, all I can say, let's say we have theories about all of this. One is that violence is therapeutic and has to happen. And then we get in a problem about defining what's therapeutic: what is therapeutic and what is it supposed to do to you if you're violent? What happens that is therapeutic? A release? A catharsis? Does this make you a new being? What does it do to you? Because it's conceivable you could be violent and ain't nothing gonna happen about improving your state of mind.

See, violence is an assertive type of action that changes your relationship to someone. You know that? In other words, if you're violent, you are initiating that act, that's an assertive, positive act that the other person has to respond to. So, you change your relationship, say, to the white man if that's what you're trying to do. On the other hand, there are many other ways, too, of changing that relationship, of confronting, and of being assertive, that it seems to me could be just as therapeutic.

I'll get out of this whole thing by saying we really don't know— see, Fanon had a theory and we really don't know if he's correct or not, whether the violence or anything else is indeed therapeutic. How do you find that out, see, except to have a feeling or say, "Well, I felt good doing that." Well, see, I don't know if that's enough to accept this as sort of a principle that's not fallible or that is one that somehow you should operate on in a revolutionary way. I don't know if that's even, if that's the only way of bringing about revolution. But that's not my field.

SOMEONE FROM THE AUDIENCE: But that has to be your field.

MODERATOR: I would like to ask that no more questioners come up to ask questions, number one, and, number two, that we have no more comments from the audience.

SOMEONE FROM THE AUDIENCE: No man!

QUESTION: Well, being a white American, I can only view the problem from Western, white orientation. And the first question that occurs to me is, how does the situation affect me? And I'm scared, not of my black brothers or my white brothers, but of myself and what I'm not doing and what

I am doing. And so, I come to you, Doctor, as more or less a patient [*applause and laughter*], to suggest therapeutic treatment for me [*laughter*] as a sick white American.

POUSSAINT: I should have some people in the back suggest the therapy [*laughter*] that they would like to prescribe. Again, I think, you know, in part, a lot of the answer to that—you know that's a question a lot of white folks ask, but after you tell them what to do they don't act on it anyway. But, fundamentally, I think it's to deal with the racism in the society, the white racism, in the ways that you have to deal with it, that it's not nice and that you have to take risks and things may happen to you from confronting the system, just like it has always acted on black people. I'll just generally say that.

And the woman's remark when I said that wasn't my field (revolution), I want to explain what I mean by that. And it's a relationship that I've held with the movement. Frequently I feel, particularly as a psychiatrist—not that I don't have my feelings and opinions—but that politics and some other types of social action sometimes is better left to a people who have more experience with that type of thing. In some cases, I wouldn't presume, say, or try to make policy when I'm working this out, say, with SNCC [Student Nonviolent Coordinating Committee] about what their political action should be—that this is what they're working in and where they have developed or develop expertise. I wouldn't, sometimes, presume, say, to try to determine the direction of where something. . . . Those are things that happen in another type of way and I, in fact, don't think, probably, psychiatry should infringe on it.

QUESTION: I want to ask you, Dr. Poussaint, some questions about black American psychopathology. So far this morning, all you've said about black American psychopathology is that studies of black American psychopathology reflect the prejudicial interests of the white community in seeing images of black sickness as sickness by which white America can define the blacks as inferior. I want to ask about the black community as interpreted by a black psychiatrist, not as interpreted by prejudicial white interests. What are the sources of mental health within the black American community, given the very great complexities of that community? We have everything from Uncle Toms to radical militants defining personality on ideological spectra. We have everything from unemployed sharecroppers to a Supreme Court Justice defining personality on a vocational hierarchy. Do you define personality in terms of the particular historical situation blacks are in and, therefore, finding the sources of personality in black responses to situations created by white society? Or do you define personality in terms of universals that occur in all individuals, regardless of race, and are expressed in varying degrees because of the socialization the individuals are given?

POUSSAINT: Big people have very big questions. [*Laughter*] Let me answer, I think, what I think the most important part of it was and that is what are other ways of looking at, say, the black community or "black psycho-pathology" or how does a black psychiatrist view it? I already said at the beginning of this session that I was trained in America with a certain type of perspective and knowing that things affect you in all sorts of ways and, unconsciously, I know that there's a certain bias to the way that psychiatrists see things—perhaps including myself. First of all, we know some things about the black community, that they have a very great capacity to deal with and adapt to stress; to move on with it under very, very dire circumstances; to, in a substantial way, support each other, and to grow. Because otherwise we wouldn't have survived.

And no one knows too much about what these things are, frankly, because problems aren't approached in this way. There are a lot of other types of sub-cultural things in the black community, from music to dance to forms of communicating with each other that are quite unique and have special value. And this is something, I think, for some group, not only psychiatrists but black people in general, to come together and find out what things are very important and vital to the black community that are not, say, the stigmata of oppression, but things that grew from black people, not only as part of their American experience, but also as part of their African experience. Because, remember, even slavery was operating continually on a matrix and that matrix was an African heritage.

And don't let people say that there's no connection between the black man slave with Africa because that's absolutely not true—it can't be true—and that there's linkages here also. So, let's say that there's too much talking about the negative things or what are supposedly "negative" things about black people and not enough research and looking into all of the many, many strengths that black people have as a people.

QUESTION: We have heard many talk about violence or whether violence is the solution for black people. The question I want to ask is can we find another way, other than violence, to have a solution to our problems, to our hang-ups? Now, to me, it seems that it has been proved that violence does make a new man, you know, but the question is not just to make a new man, an individual new man through violence. Violence must be directed by a revolutionary party. That is, to me, violence is a tool for bringing up that new world, to change the whole capitalist system. I will repeat that: violence to me is a tool. Now, when you speak about whether violence is good or not, I don't feel that is the question at all. [*Sporadic applause*]

POUSSAINT: I think that's a very good comment, that we're not running a therapy on people or running a game, and that whatever you do, whatever type of action people take, you have to calculate that action on a basis of what type of results you're going to get. Now, even assuming that you believe, if you believe that violence is therapeutic, you can get therapeutic and run down the block shooting it up and get, say, one hundred black people killed or you can think about what you're going to do, not in terms of whether it's personally therapeutic or not, but what the end result of your action is going to be for black people.

Chapter 2

THE HAITIAN REVOLUTION AND THE HISTORY OF SLAVE REVOLT

C. L. R. JAMES

THANK YOU, Mr. Chairman. Now, I like to know for myself, and I mention it to you in passing, the time now I take to be five minutes to four o'clock. I will be finished at twenty-five or twenty to five, when the questions begin. I don't want to speak longer than about forty to forty-five minutes.

The history of the Haitian Revolution is not a difficult subject for me to do within a certain time. But, on this occasion, we have to take the Haitian Revolution as symbolic of the whole series of revolts of black people in the New World. That's what I'm going to do. I'm going to begin with the Haitian Revolution and after that I'm going to spend some time on the Civil War in the United States. There, again, we have black people, black slaves, moving into a great historical situation.

But before I do that, I want to say a few words about the Cuban Revolution, because the Haitian slave revolt was a revolt in a West Indian island of a certain social structure. Cuba is of the same kind and the Haitian Revolution has many affiliations with the Cuban Revolution. So, I will begin with the Cuban Revolution, then I will go to the Haitian Revolution; then I will go to the Civil War in the United States, and then I'll go somewhere, which you will know when I tell you. I'm going to keep that a secret and I hope you will be pleasantly titillated. [*Laughter*]

Now, the Cuban Revolution takes place in the twentieth century. It is the twentieth-century representative of what had taken place previously in French San Domingo at the end of the eighteenth century. The two revolutions are very closely allied. It is not so much a question of race or colour. That is what I want to emphasize. There will be, perhaps, a third of the population of Cuba which is coloured. The point is they are both West Indian communities; both are sugar plantation communities; both are, to some degree, communities that, while not advanced, nevertheless are built in the structure of Western civilization. Although many of them, many of the population in those parts of the world, are living at a level very little above the level of slavery, in social structure and, above all, in the language that they use, they have a European cast of mind. That is why the Cuban Revolution has taken place in the way that it has. That is another reason why it has not yet taken place in many of the other West Indian islands; because, among other reasons, if and when it does take place, it will take place along the structure of the Haitian Revolution and the Cuban Revolution.

So, what is there about the Cuban Revolution that I want you to know? There are a few things. Number one: after ten years, it is today stronger than ever it was before. [*Applause*] Now, that is not merely something inspiring and something that I say to lift us up. After the English Revolution, they cut off Charles I's head in 1649, and that was a decisive point—decisive for his head and decisive for the revolution. [*Laughter*] Ten years afterward, Charles I came back, 1659–1660. It is quite true and, as Hilaire Belloc has said, royalty came back, monarchy did not.[1] Cromwell had settled that for good and all. But in ten years that revolution was done. In the French Revolution of 1789 they had accomplished miracles by 1794. By 1799 they had descended into the grip of Napoleon Bonaparte, the First Consul—ten years. In the Russian Revolution of 1917, by 1927 everything that was Leninist was wiped away. The Cuban Revolution is the first of the great revolutions that, after ten years, is stronger than it was at the beginning. [*Applause*]

Now, it is very interesting to watch how that revolution has gone. When the English Revolution took place and Charles's head was rolling in the basket, or whatever it was, Cromwell and company then had to sit down to decide what they were going to do with this society that they had taken over. Whatever the program and policy, whatever the kind of party, when the revolutionary body actually seizes power, it then is faced, for the first time, with what it is going to do with it. That happened to Charles, and Cromwell was in a lot of trouble. First, he tried to continue with the Parliament, then he tried to become the Major-General. Then he tried himself as Protector, and that ended it. When he died, the whole thing was over.

Likewise, the French Revolution was in a lot of trouble until 1793, and, between 1793 and 1794, it found itself with the Committee of Public Safety and the Committee of General Security. The Russian Revolution in October 1917 didn't know exactly where it was. The workers were saying one thing. Lenin was saying, "Well, nationalize, but don't nationalize too much. Let's have workers' power, but not workers' power but workers' control," etcetera. That went on until 1921 at the Tenth Party Congress. The counter-revolution having been defeated, the Russian Communist Party settled down to find out what they were going to do with this country that they now had hold of. Every revolution tells you the same thing.

The Cuban Revolution is no different. When Castro had gone a certain distance with the Cuban Revolution, had taken power, he was talking about the need to help the peasant proprietor and the agricultural labourer, and the need to overthrow Batista. But when that was done, what were they going to do with the revolution? They didn't know. Then came the Bay of Pigs, and immediately after the Bay of Pigs, Castro announced, "Well, we are now Marxist-Leninists." They asked him, "How long?" He said, "I don't know. When I was younger, I was a Marxist-Leninist by instinct, but I didn't know it. But now we are Marxist-Leninists." [*Applause*]

No, I am not in any way disturbed that they found their way to it in that way, because in the history of revolutions, that is how they find their way. In the San Domingo Revolution, they found their way in the same manner, but it is very noticeable that in the San Domingo Revolution, ultimately, there was a clean sweep of everything and everybody who was connected with the old regime. In the Cuban Revolution of today, there is a clean sweep of everything and everybody concerned with the old regime. That is not due to the fact that they are black people; that is due to the fact that they are a West Indian community, closely allied, using a modern language, jammed together, and able to develop themselves with tremendous force. If they were in some parts of Africa, they wouldn't be able to do it that way. I want you to watch the social structure and the geographical structure of the community to understand the Cuban Revolution and also to understand the Haitian Revolution.

I can now go back to the Haitian Revolution. This revolution took place in close association with the French Revolution. The French Revolution began in 1789, but they didn't bother with the slaves. Later, when the Girondins came into power and the bourgeoisie was in power, then they began to think, well, they should help the Haitian mulattoes and give them the power, but they left the slaves alone. Then, by 1791, the slaves said, "Well, we are going to deal with it." They felt that they were following the French Revolution. But in France, they thought the black slaves had killed their masters and taken over the property. They weren't exactly correct, but more or less, they had the thing in general—the slaves had swept away the plantation owners and took over the sugar estates.

Now, to understand the course of that revolution, you have to understand that the sugar estates were one of the most advanced forms of economic structure in the world at the time. Although they are a very backward element in the twentieth century, in the eighteenth century they were very advanced and were making a great deal of money. There were large plantations in the north part San Domingo—500 slaves here, 1,000 slaves there, 200, 300—a vast number of slaves concentrated in large sugar plantations. So, altogether, they were nearer to the modern proletariat than any other social structure of plebeians or revolutionaries of the time. You must think of that as a highly organized social structure with the great mass of the slaves living around the plantation. That was the basic geographical structure. They had at their disposal the French language in which to express themselves and, still more important, they had the ideas of the French Revolution by which to develop themselves. In other words, that was a perfect situation and they developed it perfectly.

These people were backward, but as we learned this morning,[2] they had a certain integrity, a certain social consciousness of their own, that was developed apart from their masters. That was shown, not only in general and by observers who watched them closely, but also by what took place in the revolution. The revolution took place and, before long, they had made a clean sweep and were in charge completely of San Domingo.

I want to show the influence that this revolution had on the French Revolution. This morning I made it clear that the French Revolution, which was the political counterpart, as one might say, of the Industrial Revolution, marked a tremendous stage in the development of human society. What I want you to know, and what historians don't usually pay attention to—none of the great French historians, a body of people whom I respect profoundly—none of them have ever been able to treat this question of the immense value that the San Domingo Revolution was to the French Revolution. For six years the British army was trying to capture the French colony of San Domingo and they were defeated, hook, line, and sinker, by the ex-slave army.

Fortescue, the historian of the British Army, said that England's impotence for the first six years of the war, up to that time, the greatest war in history, was to be explained by two words—San Domingo. Fortescue said that Pitt and Dundas believed they only had to fight some backward Negro slaves, but after six years they found that they had destroyed the British Army. It is the greatest defeat that has ever been undertaken by any expedition from Great Britain. It is established by the official historian of the British Army that they suffered that defeat and they were paralyzed in their attempts to deal with the French Revolution by what happened with the slaves fighting under the French colours in San Domingo. That, I think, is a great historical event.

The second thing I want to refer to, as an historical development, is the abolition of slavery. Now, all of you here know a lot about Pitt and you know about Wilberforce, and you know also that the Queen abolished slavery—which she did not. When the bill was passed, she was not even on the throne of England. It was passed in 1834, and she came to the throne in 1837. But these are absurdities and falsities that the West Indian people still have. The time will come when they will clear that away. [*Applause*]

What I want you to note is this: slavery was abolished by a European parliamentary body in 1794, and the way it was abolished was this: French San Domingo sent three representatives to the French Parliament. One was a white man, one was a coloured man, a mulatto, and one was a black man. The name of the black man was Bellay. They were welcomed by the president of the assembly and, the day following, Bellay made a tremendous speech in the Chamber, calling upon the French Parliament to abolish slavery. After the speech, Levasseur (of Sarthe) got up and told the president, "We have not done properly by the Negroes and I move that this assembly abolish slavery without a debate." Slavery was abolished without a debate after the speech by Bellay, who was himself a slave who had bought his own freedom. I believe that when we are studying the Negro past, that is a piece of history that we should know as well as we know Pitt and Wilberforce and the rest of them. [*Applause*]

So, they did this work and they fought until 1798. The British Army was destroyed and they had to form a new army, and so on; the French kept on; the Negro slaves made progress; Toussaint L'Ouverture was made the governor and then he became commander-in-chief. There were many Negro generals, some of whom could not sign their name. Their names had to be written in pencil and then they traced it over in ink. (I have read the reports.) Nevertheless, they dictated first-class reports. To dictate a first-class report, you need not know how to write, you need not know how to read. I am sure that it is so today as it was a hundred-and-fifty years ago. [*Laughter*] To dictate a first-class report, you have to do something, and those men were doing something, and to see their report and the signatures in the French national archives is very extraordinary.

Well, in 1799 or thereabouts, Napoleon sent an army to fight against them. The slaves had fought against the Spaniards, they had fought against the local plantation owners, they had fought against the British and defeated a British army of nearly 100,000 men. Then Napoleon sent this expedition to fight against them. When he sent them, Toussaint was already the governor and I want to read you one or two passages of Toussaint as governor of San Domingo. (Bobby has been talking about Marcus Garvey and putting him in historical framework.[3] I'm very glad to hear this, because that is the way you understand and are able to take part in great events; in a concrete manner but, nevertheless, aware of what is taking place.) This concern with the international movement has been a characteristic of Negro slaves in the New World. This is a passage I wrote about Toussaint:

> Firm as was his grasp of reality, old Toussaint looked beyond San Domingo with a boldness of imagination surpassed by no contemporary. In the Constitution, he authorised the slave-trade because the island needed people to cultivate it. When the Africans landed, however, they would be free men. But while loaded with the cares of government, he cherished a project [James: Take note of this please when you think of Garvey] of sailing to Africa with arms, ammunition, and a thousand of his best soldiers, and there conquering vast tracts of country, putting an end to the slave-trade, and making millions of blacks "free and French," as his Constitution had made the blacks of San Domingo.[4]

There is something in the African who is in the New World that gives him this tremendous scope in any action. The originator of the movement that we know today as Pan-Africanism is nobody else than that American scholar, William Edward Burghart Du Bois.[5] He is the person who did it; started it in every way, did the historical writings, organized to suit, and organized Pan-African conference after Pan-African conference. When I see Toussaint doing these things, something strikes me, and I wonder a great deal at what is happening—I get a little clearer as to what is to happen, too.

> It was no dream. He had sent millions of francs to America to wait for the day when he would be ready. He was already 55. What spirit was it that moved him? Ideas do not fall from heaven. The great revolution had propelled him out of his humble joys and obscure destiny, and the trumpets of its heroic period run ever in his ears. In him, born a slave and the leader of slaves, the concrete realisation of liberty, equality, and fraternity was the womb of ideas and the springs of power, which overflowed their narrow environment and embraced the whole of the world.[6]

Now, take note of this:

> But for the revolution, this extraordinary man and his band of gifted associates would have lived their lives as slaves, serving the commonplace creatures who owned them, standing barefooted and in rags to watch inflated little governors and mediocre officials from Europe pass by, as many a talented African stands in Africa to-day.[7]

That I wrote in 1938. I am very proud of it. I was not afraid that things were going to take place. [*Applause*]

Then came the great War of Independence. If you want to know who the African people are in the Caribbean today and what they are capable of, we have to know what our ancestors were, what they did, because we are the same type of people. We must not forget that. It's in the history of San Domingo and the history of these revolts that you will see the potential of these people in the New World. Before we are finished, I will give a glimpse of what has taken place in Africa under very different circumstances.

Now, here is General Leclerc and his army in San Domingo. Bonaparte has sent him (Leclerc is married to Bonaparte's sister) and Leclerc is writing letters home. He says, "The first attacks have driven the rebels from the positions they occupied"; [James: You know, if you are fighting for freedom, you're a rebel (*applause and laughter*)] "but they fell back to other cantons and in the insurrection there is a veritable fanaticism. These men get themselves killed, but they refuse to surrender."[8] Those are my ancestors and I am very proud of them. [*Applause*] Here is some more. Leclerc is writing again to his brother-in-law, the great Napoleon: "It is not enough to have taken away Toussaint, there are 2,000 leaders to be taken away."[9]

You know, you go about and listen to some of these people today asking, "Where are the leaders? We have no leaders. This one is not good, that one is only there because so and so, that other one. . . . " I am positive that in Jamaica, in Trinidad, in Barbados today, there are twenty thousand leaders ready to take whatever. . . . [*Words drowned out by applause*] I'm getting near to the end of this. Leclerc finally writes: "Unfortunately the condition of the colonies is not known in France. We have there a false idea of the Negro."[10] "We have in Europe a false idea of the country in which we fight and the men whom we fight against."[11]

That was bad enough for Leclerc, a stranger, to have a false idea of the country in which he fought and of the men whom he fought against. In 1968, there are West Indians in the West Indies who have a false idea of the country in which they live and the men who live around them. [*Applause*]

Now, let me give you a final statement about the San Domingo Revolution. Lemmonier-Delafosse was a soldier who fought in the War of Independence. Many years afterwards he wrote his memoirs of the last stage of the war in which they were defeated. Here is what he says. It is a notable passage. They (the slaves) sang their songs and he says:

> This song was worth all of our republican songs. Three times these brave men, arms in hand, advanced without firing a shot, and each time repulsed, only retired after leaving the ground strewed with three-quarters of their troops. One must have seen this bravery to have any conception of it. Those songs shouted into the sky in unison by 2,000 voices, to which the cannon formed the bass, produced a thrilling effect. French courage alone could resist it. Indeed, large ditches, an excellent artillery, perfect soldiers gave us a great advantage. But for many a day, that massed square which marched singing to its death, lighted by a magnificent sun, remained in my thoughts, and even to-day after more than 40 years, this majestic and glorious spectacle still lives as vividly in my imagination as in the moments when I saw it.[12]

A dozen years before, these people had been slaves. Then they were able to fight the army of Napoleon that, up to that day, was the finest army that Europe had yet seen. But in 1920, they (the colonialists) say, "Well, we don't know if you are fit for self-government. We will have five more men in the Legislature; and then, in 1930 we'll put one in the Executive Council; and then in 1935 we'll put two more in the Executive Council. But in 1937, it isn't doing so well, we will take away all of those. So, we are training you up all the time."

Now, I want you to understand my point of view. What has been happening is this: for the last fifty years, the British government, the French government, and the rest of them have been corrupting the political consciousness of the mass of the population in the Caribbean territories [*applause*] by constantly arguing about whether they are fit enough to govern or whether they could have two men more in the Legislature and one man more in the Executive; to what extent the governor would have powers; whether he should be in charge of the police and the army; whether they could take the police but not the army [*laughter*] and all this kind of business. They have been a source of corruption of the political development of the people in the Caribbean.

The history of San Domingo shows that, after a few years of civil war, they were perfectly able to do anything that the Europeans were able to do, both as an army and in terms of government. Many of the governors of San Domingo were slaves, unable to write. Yet people who examined them said that they showed a capacity to govern which was better than the capacity that would have been shown by French peasants and other persons of a low order in France. That was because they had nothing in their minds but freedom, and they saw freedom in the terms of the French Revolution, which had helped them to liberate themselves. We need not be afraid of what the Caribbean people are likely to do. The stage of revolution that has been reached in the world at the time, and the ideas that have been developed, will be taken over by any revolution of the great mass of the population, as those ideas were taken over by the French revolutionaries in the French colony of San Domingo.

I want to stop there for a minute and go over to the United States. We have a tremendous movement in the Civil War in the United States. First of all, we had revolts—Nat Turner, Denmark Vesey, and these other revolts. Then, about 1830, they decide that the plain, straightforward revolt against the oppressors would not do, and they worked out another system. I don't think we thoroughly understand what was taking place in the United States between 1830 and, say, 1878. The American Negro slaves or Afro-Americans, whatever the phrase is (I don't want to give any offence, I'll call him whatever it is) [*laughter*], they decided that they were not going to make a plain, straightforward revolt. They were going to use the Underground Railroad and, by the thousands, escape from slavery into freedom. That helped to break up the system; the fact that in their numbers, by tens, by dozens, day after day, they were escaping.

Not only did those who left give the slave owners trouble, but they [the slave-masters] never knew whom they had, who would escape, or who would not escape. That was the situation in the country. When [William Lloyd] Garrison began in the North, there was hostility to the idea of the abolitionists' end of slavery. But later, the South wanted to make an arrangement whereby they would be compelled, in the North, to capture any slaves who had escaped, and the North revolted. They said, "To hell with you. You come for your slaves. We are not going to be any catcher of slaves for you." The result was that the arrangement which the North wanted to work out with the South could not be worked out—they could not manage it—and the abolitionist movement began in the wake of this and the constant escaping of Negro slaves.

The abolitionist movement—that is one of the great political movements of the United States. The people of the United States do not know that. As the years go by, they will begin to find out that the real beginnings of independent revolutionary politics in the United States have to be sought in the abolitionist movement. That movement was predominantly a movement of Negro slaves and free Negroes in the North. The abolitionist papers were supported by and subscribed to by a majority of Negro people. The great leaders of the abolitionist movement were not only Garrison and Wendell Phillips, but one of the greatest political leaders America has ever had, Frederick Douglass.

Working out policies, Garrison and Phillips stated, "We have our movement and the Constitution of the United States is a slave constitution and, therefore, the southern part of the United States must be split off from the north and, therefore, we will have freedom in the north when the Constitution allows us to split away because the Constitution is a slave constitution." Wendell Phillips, a most remarkable man, said further: "If that takes place and we split off from them and they are free, inevitably there will be a Negro revolt and the Negroes will take power and we'll be able to join again." Garrison didn't go so far. Douglass broke with them on that issue and founded his own paper. This split was serious because fundamental issues were involved.

Douglass said, "You are saying that the Constitution of the United States is a pro-slavery constitution. It is nothing of the kind. Both in its origin, and in the details of the Constitution, it is not a pro-slavery document." He says (I remember certain parts), "'We the people.' That's what it says. It doesn't say we the horses, we the dogs, we the cows. It says, 'we the people,' and if black people are people it means we the black people too." He fought Garrison and these fellows on that issue tremendously, and that caused the split in the movement. It was a split, you can understand, on a highly political issue. When the Civil War came, it was proved that Douglass was the man along whose lines the battle was fought.

Now, there is something which I am very sorry I do not hear more about. I want to read to you a passage from a very great historian. It is from one of the greatest history books ever written, *Black Reconstruction* by W. E. Burghart Du Bois. Du Bois quotes a passage from Lincoln, where Lincoln says,

ABANDON ALL THE POSTS NOW GARRISONED BY BLACK MEN; TAKE TWO HUNDRED THOUSAND MEN FROM OUR SIDE AND PUT THEM IN BATTLEFIELD OR CORNFIELD AGAINST US, AND WE WOULD BE COMPELLED TO ABANDON THE WAR IN THREE WEEKS.[13]

Lincoln said it repeatedly. The fact is that the Civil War and the victory of the North, which made the United States a modern country and what it is today, could not have been won without the active participation of black people, in labour and in the army, whom it was supposed to free at the time.

[*Applause*] That is the reality. I know one reason why that has taken place. Lincoln had said, "I would abolish slavery if it would help to cement the Union; and to maintain the Union, I would free half the slaves and keep half of them slaves. And if needed be, to maintain the Union, I would maintain all as slaves." That, undoubtedly, Lincoln said. But that is not the main thing. I want to go into some statements about Lincoln. You remember what he said at the Second Inaugural? It was a tremendous statement:

One-eighth of the whole population were colored slaves, not distributed generally over the Union, but localized in the southern part of it. These slaves constituted a peculiar and powerful interest. All knew that this interest was somehow the cause of the war. To strengthen, perpetuate, and extend this interest was the object for which the insurgents would rend the Union even by war, while the Government claimed no right to do more than to restrict the territorial enlargement of it. Neither party expected for the war the magnitude or the duration which it has already attained. Neither anticipated that the cause of the conflict might cease with, or even before, the conflict itself should cease. Each looked for an easier triumph, and a result less fundamental and astounding. Both read the same Bible, and pray to the same God; and each invokes His aid against the other. It may seem strange that any men should dare to ask a just God's assistance in wringing their bread from the sweat of other men's faces [James: It isn't so strange today. (*Laughter*)] but let us judge not, that we be not judged. The prayers of both could not be answered. That of neither has been answered fully. The Almighty has His own purposes. "Woe unto the world because of offenses; for it must needs be that offenses come, but woe to that man by whom the offense cometh." If we shall suppose that American slavery is one of those offenses which, in the providence of God, must needs come, but which, having continued through His appointed time, He now wills to remove, and that He gives to both North and South this terrible war as the woe due to those by whom the offense came, shall we discern therein any departure from those divine attributes which the believers in a living God always ascribe to Him? Fondly do we hope, fervently do we pray, that this mighty scourge of war may speedily pass away. Yet, if God wills that it continue until all the wealth piled by the bondsman's two hundred and fifty years of unrequited toil shall be sunk, and until every drop of blood drawn with the lash shall be paid by another drawn with the sword, as was said three thousand years ago, so still it must be said "the judgments of the Lord are true and righteous altogether."

That is a tremendous thing that Lincoln said. I'll read it again. [*Laughter*]

> Yet, if God wills that it continue until all the wealth piled by the bondsman's two hundred and fifty years of unrequited toil shall be sunk, and until every drop of blood drawn with the lash shall be paid by another drawn with the sword, as was said three thousand years ago, so still it must be said "the judgments of the Lord are true and righteous altogether."

Now, people were wondering if America was going to destroy itself because of the slaves who were persecuted. Lincoln did not begin that way. There is a letter that he wrote to a friend sometime in 1841. He said he was traveling on the boat and there was a family of Negro slaves there. He says they were being driven away from their friends, being sold to the South, and they were the funniest people you could think of. They were laughing and making jokes all the time, and he couldn't understand how people in that situation could have behaved in that way. That is a very striking thing for Lincoln to have said, because, later, Lincoln was to say, "We who made the revolution in 1776 formed a particular generation. Our children still have that tradition in them." He said, "People from abroad may come from different parts of Europe and learn this revolutionary tradition that makes the nation what it is." He didn't say, but he believed, that Negroes could not make it; that they could not take part in what he felt that the American nation was. Lincoln believed in that right up to 1862.

In 1862, the people, the colonizationists, the people who were saying that the Negroes should be deported to some parts of Africa or something, had a sympathetic ear from Lincoln. He said, "Well, let us discuss it." But later he began to see that to win the war he had to bring the Negroes in. He finally brought them in, uncertain whether they would stand to that high pitch which he felt had been established in America by those who had fought the revolution of 1776, and which had been descended to them through the years. He got to know that Negroes were able to stand it; that they were enabled by the war to stand up to all the pressures and necessities.

We have that tremendous statement, which so many Americans don't understand, "that government of the people, by the people, for the people shall not perish from the earth." What does that mean? Lincoln said, "Four score and seven years ago we founded a new society. And if now we have to see that government of the people, by the people, for the people should not perish, it means government of the people"—including the black people—"for the people"—including the black people—"by the people"—including the black people.[14]

Those later speeches by Lincoln, the Second Inaugural and the Gettysburg speech, were speeches that incorporated the mass of the Negro people, the ex-slaves, into the American community. Lincoln now had a very advanced conception of what the American community was. Following the Civil War, Lincoln thought, "Well, we must bring them in because they are perfectly able to take part in it." I would like to hear their propagandists and others of the American community make the situation of Lincoln and these others quite clear. The war was not fought for the abolition of slavery, but the war came to an end because the slaves had proved themselves fully able to stand by anybody in the American community and carry out the great principles that had been established in 1776.

That is the American Civil War. Now I go to what I have been keeping secret. I want to speak about what happened in an African state, what happened in Kenya in 1953. The Kenyan people had not been under the domination of the British for many years. They, unfortunately for them, had a high plateau with a nice piece of land and good climate, and some Europeans settled themselves there and established some agricultural plantations and said that, "Kenya is ours and we are going to live here. We are going to help the poor Africans, but this is ours and we are going to remain here." In 1953, a Kenyan minister landed at the airport in London and they asked him, "What is the situation in Kenya?" and he said, "It has never been so good. Everything is going fine and the people are quite satisfied and we are carrying on the colony as it ought to be carried on." It wasn't a few weeks afterward that the revolt broke out.

We have not been able, as yet, to get a proper account of what took place in Kenya. We are in the habit of talking about Mau Mau. Now, it is clearly proved today that Mau Mau was a creation of British colonialism. It was nothing native to the people of Kenya. It was the result of their [attempt] to try to get something with which they could fight against the Christian missionaries and the "democracy" and "advanced morals" that the British had been giving to them, and of which they were tired. The people of Kenya were not able to fight as the West Indians have been able to fight, as the American slaves were able to fight—to join an army in a modern society. They had to take to the woods and form their armies in the woods. They would hit and run in Nairobi and round about, but, essentially, their basis was what they could do in the woods fighting with a native army, made up how they could, with troops acquired cheaply from the people they were fighting against.

Then there was General Kimathi, who unfortunately was killed, and General China, who is alive today. They organized themselves and they fought the British to a standstill. At one time, the British had two divisions there, a great number of airplanes, walkie-talkies (radios)—every blessed thing that they could have to defeat the people. At one time, the British not only defeated the Mau Mau army in the field, they also had fifty thousand Kenyan people in detention camps and they had won the war. They had Kenyatta in prison, but they now had to settle and they couldn't do anything with the people in the detention camps, whom they told, "If you say you will change and will not do any old thing, etcetera, we'll let you go," and they [the Kenyans] told them, "You go to hell, we are not going to say anything. We are going to stay right here."

They [the British] were absolutely paralyzed by it. You must remember that they had won the war in Kenya. They had defeated the army and they [the Mau Mau] were hiding in the forest. And they [the British] found that they couldn't govern the people at all. So they had to send for Kenyatta, and allow him to move around and govern in Kenya. Today they are giving up the land on the plateau.

I mention this to say that, we talk about the Haitian slave revolt, and I have talked about the Civil War in the United States and the tremendous role played there by the slaves, but let us not forget Africa, Kenya in particular. On the one side, there was [Kwame] Nkrumah organizing them in the modern democratic way, and demanding democratic rights from the British government; on the other side of Africa, there was an absolutely independent revolutionary struggle that had tremendous odds to compete against, which was actually defeated in the field, but such was the power of the people that the British government finally had to give way.

I don't think we would be understanding the Haitian Revolution and the revolts in the New World by the slaves unless we understood what was taking place in Africa many years afterwards, and link the two of them together, as Bobby[15] has tried to do with Garvey.

Thank you very much, Mr. Chairman. [*Long applause*]

MODERATOR: Thank you, Mr. James. Ladies and gentlemen, I'm sure you have heard more than the usual point of controversial statements in the last speech and I'm sure that you will have plenty of questions.

QUESTION: Mr. James has made a very brilliant analysis of the Haitian Revolution and, as a black man, I am very proud that my ancestors were so great. But for the benefit of my black American and black West Indian brothers, I want to speak about the situation in Haiti now.

After the revolution, the white imperialists tried their best to isolate us because they thought it could help the slave system by which they live. In 1915, American imperialism sent their troops down there. They were trying to make some plantations, so they would have sugar cane. They killed thousands of Haitians by mating with decent Haitians because of the lady factor. When they finally left, because they could not really have the whole country like a whole American plantation—the resistance was too hard—they left a social crisis behind them. This is called neo-colonialism.

Right now in Haiti, we have a man, he's a black man, he's the ruler of Haiti. He did not just come. He's representative of the social crisis called neo-colonialism where a certain class of the society exploits or serves as the servants of American imperialism. Excuse me. I know I was supposed to ask a question. [*Laughter*] You will excuse me. I find it is very vital, you know, because [*applause*] I have spent three months in the United States and I find that many black Americans tell me that they love Papa Doc because he's a black man. I'm telling you, I'm going to identify with no black man because he's a black man. [*Applause*] I will identify with a black American because he struggles, he is fighting against white American capitalism. That means, when the Black Panthers, or whatever you have down there, start breaking down or blowing up Wall Street [*sporadic applause*], the citizens of America will, at the same time, have to send troops to Haiti because we have revolutionary parties working down there [inaudible] guerrilla warfare. It is very low right now, but it's going. [*Applause*]

We are very aware of the fact that Americans will have to send troops down there to protect the black puppets, to protect the interests of their servants. These servants are black, culturally speaking—a lot of shit about the cultural aspect of Black Power, you see. Now this is Black Power, you know—black men running the country. And the question is a statement to you. Once you want to use the capitalist system, I tell you, you are going to work hand in hand with the same men that are killing children in Vietnam now. [*Applause*] I will repeat that. [*Laughter*] I mean that, I myself, when I go in a demonstration, or do something that contests the system, the capitalist system, I know I am working for the liberation of my people. I know that I am working for the bringing up of that new world. So that, it is not just an idealistic thing because, in Haiti, 93 percent of the population, they don't know how to read, you know. They don't know about human dignity. They need help, whereas you can go into town and find those black bourgeois with 1968 American cars and tall buildings.

So, therefore, I will stress again that I identify with the struggle of black Americans and I would do anything to help this struggle as long as the black American is fighting, not just against a substance called racism that is the cause of that system; but as long as the black American is fighting racism, is fighting in my interest, and I am fighting in his interest, too. I thank you. [*Long applause*]

JAMES: I am very glad that that comrade had the determination to interpret the word "question" in a very revolutionary way. [*Laughter and applause*] I would like to tell you a few facts and one or two things that we think. I have been invited to Haiti. I was invited by the head of the military mission when they had read my book, *Les Jacobins noir*, translated into French.[16] And I was able to tell them, very politely (I'm a polite person), that I am afraid that I couldn't possibly come there under any circumstances. I would have to go and say, "Well, I'm very happy to be here and I think you are doing well enough" or something. I would have to do it. I preferred not to go. That is why I have not been able to go to Haiti. [*Applause*]

Secondly, I hope my friend there knows that the real support of Duvalier is the United States government. [*Applause*] Duvalier's government is the worst and most corrupt government in Latin America. There is no doubt about it. [*Applause*] But he is able to continue because, although he is rude to the United States and he robs tourists who go there, etcetera, nevertheless the United States continues to support him, and not to support anybody who wants to overthrow him. And the reason is very simple: they prefer a thousand Duvaliers to another revolution that might produce another Fidel Castro. [*Applause*] They can stand Duvalier, any number of Duvaliers. They have some at home too, [*laughter*] but a revolt they don't want to have. And we must be aware of this.

I have no doubt whatsoever that the American State Department and the rest of them are quite aware of what took place in the San Domingo Revolution. They are more than ever aware of what took place in the Cuban Revolution, and they are aware—they ran to the Dominican Republic quick to prevent [revolution] because any revolution that takes place in the Caribbean is going to do what the other two have done, it's going to make a clean sweep. [*Applause*] Maybe a little later I will tell you something about what one expert in Caribbean revolution has said, but the occasion has not appeared for the time being, and maybe it will before we are finished this afternoon.[17]

QUESTION: I think that we should break to attach this thought to what Mr. James just said. I hope that this congress gives the American State Department justifiable reason for being aware of what's going on here this weekend. [*Sporadic laughter*] And for the brother over there, I would like to say that we in America will do our best to keep the American troops as busy as possible. [*Applause, laughter, and cheers*] We're going to do this because we're all pretty much aware of the great significance of the revolution in the West Indies. And if you identify, my brother, with the struggle in black America, then you automatically identify with the struggle in Africa, which must be our intellectual and revolutionary focal point.

And now to pose my questions. [*Laughter*] This is not directly about Haiti, but we are all indirectly associated with one another, so my question is good. [*Laughter*] My question is regarding the ultimate goal of the African liberation struggle in the United States, and it's in four parts. [*Laughter*]

JAMES: One part at a time, please. [*Laughter*]

QUESTION: You'll find that each question refines the other until you end up with one question. [*Laughter*] Part one: What should one of the objectives of African-Americans be? Part two: Seeing that it is difficult to fight for land, what should the goal be? Part three: How do you envision the lives of black Americans once the struggle has been waged and yet won? And part four: What message would this congress send back to black Americans to give them a better understanding about the kinds of power they see while they live in an ocean of white faces? [*Applause*]

JAMES: Now the last question, what message the congress should send? Naturally, I'll leave that to the congress, so I haven't to answer that one. In regard to the rest of the struggle, I want to make some statements that refer to this struggle in a rather historical and yet concrete manner.

The first point I wish to make is, in 1935–1936, George Padmore began the International African Service Bureau. And Jomo Kenyatta came into it, and later Kwame Nkrumah came, Wallace-Johnson, and one or two others. There were never more than ten of us. Never. And most of the people we dealt with thought that we were perhaps some politically well-meaning, but politically illiterate, West Indians talking and writing about the independence of Africa: "What kind of nonsense is that?" The journalists, the members of Parliament, the heads of departments, the writers of books, the propagandists, and all of them, they knew that we were wrong. If even they paid any attention to us, it was in a kindly, paternalist, well-meaning manner: "You boys are trying but, at any rate, that is not serious." But it turned out that we were right, and they were wrong. Now, don't forget that please. You never can tell what is likely to happen. You get your analysis of the situation and you charge, and then see what takes place. As Napoleon says, "*On s'engage,*" you engage, "*puis s'en voit,*" and then you see. And you cannot really see unless you engage. [*Applause*]

The second point is this: We were talking about the independence of Africa. We had many contacts in Africa, but none of them seemed to us to be contacts that would really lead the struggle for independence. But we had to take it as it came. We were determined to go ahead, and we went ahead, and things came our way. I want to tell you something else. In 1957, I was in Ghana with George Padmore talking to Nkrumah, and we discussed the beginning of the movement and how it had got to where it was. And if anybody had told us, or we had heard him say, in 1957 that within ten years there would be thirty new African states and over 100 million African people freed, what we would have done would be to get together and get a pamphlet ready and, in a piece of agitation and propaganda say, "That man is a monster, he doesn't know what he is talking about. He's going to lead you in adventurous ways," etcetera, "and that cannot happen." And nobody believed more in the African revolution than we did. But we hadn't the conception that the movement would have moved with such tremendous rapidity as it has moved. That is something we have to remember today when the comrade asked me, what is the message? etcetera. I can only say, do what you have to do, the message will come from that. That's all. We didn't know that was going to take place.

Chapter 3

THE FATHERS OF THE MODERN REVOLT

Marcus Garvey and the Origins of Black Power

ROBERT HILL

*T*HE SURVIVING RECORDING *of Robert Hill's presentation begins with a quote from the Swiss traveler Girod-Chantrans about African slaves in Saint Domingue (what would become Haiti) that is cited in C. L. R. James'* The Black Jacobins: Toussaint L'Ouverture and the San Domingo Revolution.

They were about a hundred men and women of different ages, all occupied in digging ditches in a cane-field, the majority of them naked or covered with rags. The sun shone down with full force on their heads. Sweat rolled from all parts of their bodies. Their limbs, weighed down by the heat, fatigued with the weight of their picks and by the resistance of the clayey soil baked hard enough to break their implements, strained themselves to overcome every obstacle. A mournful silence reigned. Exhaustion was stamped on every face, but the hour of rest had not yet come. The pitiless eye of the Manager patrolled the gang and several foremen armed with long whips moved periodically between them, giving stinging blows to all who, worn out by fatigue, were compelled to take a rest—men or women, young or old.[1]

That is the driving force, not only of Garveyism and other things that I shall point out, but it is today the single most important driving force in our being here. We are breaking the silence once again. It is a difficult and painful road. You never break it absolutely. The moment you think you've broken it, it comes back to you. But we have to know that is the job that we are doing here this weekend: once again attempting to break that mournful silence imposed upon our humanity. That is the metaphysical principle of black liberation and black resistance. It is interesting, and reinforces the view, that it took a Swiss traveler to point this out. The silence was so total that we find very little recorded by the slave himself that can attest. Although they wrote, they could not attest to the objective circumstance of being a set of mournful, silent people.

Now, there is another traveller—and we in the West Indies have seen a good many of them, most of them bad, but sometimes they have left behind some very interesting things. Listen to this French man now. This French traveler says:

> One has to hear with what warmth and with what volubility, and at the same time with what precision of ideas and accuracy of judgement, this creature [Hill: He's talking about the slave.], heavy and taciturn all day, now squatting before his fire, tells stories, talks, gesticulates, argues, passes opinions, approves or condemns both his master and everyone who surrounds him.[2]

Counterpoise the mournful silence to this that the French traveller saw. He is astonished. He says, look at this heavy and taciturn beast all day squatting, and now before his fire he talks, argues, gesticulates, passes opinion, approves or condemns both his master and everyone who surrounds him. There you have the contrary metaphysics. Contained within the silence is the content of black resistance and liberation. And a French man saw it. So, now you have this silence and, on the other hand, you have the black man who is demonstrating beside his fire that he's quite prepared and he's going to stick up against it; but he's not ready yet. We now turn to when the moment of striking came upon the black man in the New World. There is a man—and I want to call attention to my brothers to this question, because it will be raised again in this conference. The man who baptised the Haitian slave revolt was a man, a voodoo priest called Boukman. And Boukman uttered a prayer the night that the Haitian revolt was consecrated, and the prayer has come down to us. Again, it is contained in *The Black Jacobins*. Listen to what Boukman says:

The god who created the sun which gives us light, who rouses the waves and rules the storm, though hidden in the clouds, he watches us. He sees all that the white man does. The god of the white man inspires him with crime, but our god calls upon us to do good works. Our god who is good to us orders us to revenge our wrongs. He will direct our arms and aid us. Throw away the symbol of the god of the white brothers, who has so often caused us to weep, and listen to the voice of liberty, which speaks in the hearts of us all.[3]

Now, those are three passages. The Swiss traveller, he detects the mournful silence that reigns. The French man says, but this is an astonishing man who can act like a beast all day but demonstrate his humanity when he is ready. And now Boukman says, and the final passage says, "listen to the voice of liberty which speaks to the hearts of us all." The silence.

Now, that brings us directly to Garvey. And here Garvey is speaking in 1921 in New York City: "Now we have started to speak. And I am only the forerunner of an awakened Africa that shall never go back to sleep." The fourth quotation. And out of all of them comes this contrary metaphysics of silence and speech, silence and voice, silence, resistance, and liberation. It is a most amazing thing when you read through the literature of black liberation and you trace certain seams. You see it constantly cropping up, that the black humanity of the New World and of Africa, but more particularly of the New World, understood quite clearly what the nature of his problem was. He understood fundamentally that it was a silence that would eat away at his soul and that today could make a proud Rastafarian drummer have to admit and confess to an African brother [that] the drum, it is small because that is the way everything that comes from Africa gets small in the New World. It is all there before you now—the metaphysics of black resistance and liberation.

We're going to have to go through some very painful work here to show you why is it Garveyism reached the point that it did, and why it had not developed beforehand. And to do that, we have to look carefully at the world in which Garvey matured, in fact, the whole historical perspective arising out of slavery and post-emancipation society. There is a young West Indian academic, Orlando Patterson, who wrote a book called *The Sociology of Slavery: An Analysis of the Origins, Development and Structure of Negro Slave Society in Jamaica*. And this is what Patterson says:

In contrast to Latin American and North America, Jamaican slave society was loosely integrated; So much so, that one hesitates to call it a society since all that it amounted to was an ill-organised system of exploitation . . . There was therefore no collectively held system of values, no religion, no educational system to reinforce the laws. Even more significant was the nature of the political system . . . The men who ruled the country and made its laws were themselves the planters who were the masters of the slaves. One can hardly be surprised, then, at the severity of the slave laws. Even where the laws, towards the end of the period of slavery, attempted to restrain the power of the master in some respect, the extent to which they could be made effective was partly limited by the extremely fragmentary nature of their [Hill: Jamaican slave] society. Like most plantocracies, Jamaica is best seen more as a collection of autonomous plantations, each a self-contained community with its internal mechanisms of power, than as a total social system.[4]

That is the historical situation. It would be very easy to demonstrate to you graphically what it amounts to. You have a national territory, and what you have is a differentiation of practically autonomous slave estates, each with an internal, self-contained mechanism of power. When emancipation comes, the barriers—and they were very serious barriers in terms of punishment of slaves who trespassed beyond their estate, who communicated with slaves elsewhere. It was a tightly held, autonomous slave society within each plantation. When slavery is abolished the barriers are lifted; there is no total social system. And what we see developing, and what I am going to demonstrate to you, is that for the first time a new society is coming into being. The importance of Garveyism is that, in the philosophy of black resistance and liberation, you find enunciated for the first time in the New World the independent black community. That is the essence of Garveyism. And today, when we look at the questions of Black Power and black liberation, the reason that Garvey could take a movement numbering in the millions, contain a whole philosophy of struggle that today still lives on and will continue to live on, could exist as a world force, as a world phenomenon at the beginning of the twentieth century in the reshaping of world history, lies precisely in the fact that the philosophy contained within itself the first independent black society in the making. It is in the power of a whole black community and society taking shape that ideas and philosophy and thought begin to spread throughout the world. Today, therefore, when we come to look at Black Power and liberation, we cannot think of that except in relationship to what black people are doing in their society. You could not have Black Power today unless the Negro, the Afro-American community of the United States, had taken on entirely new dimensions. Black Power is an attempt, in an ideological way, to attest to the creation of a whole new stage of Afro-American life and culture. [*Applause*]

Now, a subject here that has occupied a number of sociologists recently—they always seem to be the first to be occupied by these problems. They never usually resolve them, but they come up with them first. There is a growing tendency to become preoccupied with what is known as the crisis phenomenon. People now are researching crisis. A man called Alvin Gouldner has turned from very serious empirical sociology to locate the crisis situation of Greek civilization that led to the development of Platonic thought. They are now going back all over the place trying to search for crises. We are not going to humbug; we are going to look, quite clearly, at the movement of crisis in Jamaican colonial society, because that is where Garvey is coming from. One, these almost-self-enclosed slave plantations, the barriers that separate the black man from his brother in another parish, on another estate. The barriers are lifted, and the society now begins to flow into itself. A lot of material needs to be researched in this area, but I think we have enough to make a go of it. One, the ex-slaves fled from the estates and created what became known in Caribbean society as "autonomous peasant communities," independent of the estate. It got to a point where the share of the independent peasantry to the export agricultural sector was, in many important products like bananas, coffee, and cocoa and all those things, far in excess to what the plantations were amounting to. But what happens is that when this black humanity is released, it begins to take autonomous shape.

An American scholar called Sidney Mintz describes this response against the plantation and in favour of creating independent black communities as the "negative reflex slavery." I don't particularly like the term but, because it is used, let me just say this: This negative reflex to plantation slavery in the creation of independent black communities and, note carefully, peasant communities, is bound sooner or later to assume some positive character. I don't like that terminology, negative/positive, but let us just use it. The positive character of that reflex is bound to come at a moment of crisis in the development of this independent black society, where somebody has to take hold of it and express it in some ideological, philosophical manner; not only express it but indicate what you have to do to transcend the crisis in which you find yourself. And that is where Garveyism is coming from. There are two periods, three periods really, of this creation of a black society in Jamaica. A society being created in the raw. Nothing, nothing at all they had to go on. They had to create a society from start. And, I say again, I say this is the power of Garveyism. He was part of it and when he enunciated it, it went all the way around the world.

Now, the crisis of the peasantry, the first era of peasant independence, is 1838 (emancipation) to about 1846. Then, instead of independent ownership of land, you have mass squatting on estates that are broken up and abandoned. In 1865 we have a tremendous rebellion in Morant Bay led by the peasants and their leader called Bogle. There were tremendous cholera epidemics, small pox epidemics. The American Civil War was creating economic problems. There was general dislocation. The peasantry had reached a certain crisis point and the peasants struck at Morant Bay. Now, it is noticeable that when Paul Bogle came down out of the mountains in Morant Bay in 1865, when the Royal Commission came to inquire about the number of black deaths and whether the white man was justified in killing that many—not so much but maybe killed too many, this is the purpose of the commission, a tremendous royal commission that caused a serious social and political crisis in Britain, the Governor Eyre crisis—all the people who came before the royal commission said that when Bogle and his followers passed through villages, he had one thing and he kept repeating this. He told the peasants: "Join your colour and cleave to the black." Wherever peasants were, and Bogle's words reached them, it was the slogan "Join your colour and cleave to the black." [*Sporadic applause*] Bogle had a perception of what was happening. He had a perception that you now face a national society of black people. In crisis, this society had to express itself. Bogle carried the banner and the weapon. And it was in the carrying of the weapon that Bogle discovered really what he was about. And then the slogan came out: "Join your colour brother and cleave to the black."

The British sent out new philanthropic governors who were going to reform colonialism, a most impossible task if there is any one, and they start all kinds of land settlement schemes and roads and what economists called infrastructure. But the peasantry, around about the 1890s, reached the limits of their expansion and now faced a contraction in peasant society. And Marcus Garvey is born of a peasant stock in 1887. And up to the turn of the nineteenth century, this crisis is a prolonged one. It can be demonstrated statistically in an indirect way. This is the moment at the turn of the century where you have massive outward migration of black people who have no work to do in this society, can expand no more, because the political and social bases of power are still beyond their reach. I give you here a breakdown of the migration figures outwardly: from 1881 to 1890, net departures amounted to 23,791 people; from 1891 to 1910, the net departures from Jamaican society amounted to 43,438; in the period 1911 to 1920, net departures from Jamaica amounted to 77,071 people. These are just net departures. It is very difficult from the inter-censual calculations to estimate what were the gross figures of migration. These are net migratory figures. And the woman who has written a study on population growth in Jamaica in the nineteenth century as part of her economic study of Jamaica, Gisela Eisner, says that these figures grossly understate the level and intensity of external migration from the society.

So that you see two forces developing here: a national peasant society that is in a state of prolonged crisis, contraction, and the phenomenon of massive external migration. And along comes a man and he begins to look at this situation. And what is lacking is that the society has not yet been nationalised, in sorts. People are living a national experience, and before 1914 in Jamaica, nobody in Jamaica could say, and attest to this with any proof, that I was a Jamaican citizen. The whole question of nationality could not have been whole. And it is that question that Garvey and the thought of Garveyism begins to address itself to—the question of nationality—and it emerges out of a crisis of a developing peasant society.

Garvey, by any standard, was a most remarkable man. He learned a lot from his father, of course. His father was a very proud and a very famous artisan in St. Ann who owned quite a bit of land. He had a passion for learning and this peasant artisan built a house across from the main house, a little room, where he would go and lock himself in for days, sometimes weeks. And he would only feed himself on fruit. He would read and he would read and nobody could dare come and disturb him. And he took out a subscription to an English journal. They never billed him for it and then later the journal changed hands and the English company sued him for eleven years of subscription. Garvey's father not only refused to pay the subscription money back, he took it to court. His lawyer was making an ass of himself, he said; he fired the lawyer—the same thing that Garvey is going to do later on in 1924 in the United States—and he defends himself; he loses the case; he goes back to St. Ann, he tells his wife he is selling all his land because he needs the money to take the case to the supreme court, the appeal court. He loses the case and do you know that the case goes all the way to the British Privy Council and Garvey's father loses the case. But by the time he finishes this long process of litigation, they have no more land, no more resources. And here is where the factor of crisis relates itself to the person. Garvey and his mother are thrown up and have to seek some kind of refuge in the city. And Garvey becomes something that you will see again and again throughout the developing world. Garvey becomes an apprentice printer and slowly he begins to form a small group of people, he starts talking in the park. But what happened was that a most remarkable man had been liberated from the crisis and now had a certain level of autonomy within which to drive his ideas against the contraction of peasant society.

Now, Garvey is the greatest internationalist of black humanity. We don't have any more like him; I don't believe we *will* have any more like him. But notice what Garvey's internationalism is based on. Garvey is significant in calling the first strike, the collective strike in Jamaican society—the strike of the printers. The treasurer runs away with the money and the strike was broken and Garvey was again on his ass. But Garvey starts a small independent paper called *The Watchman*, gets a group of people around him. But he has an uncle in Costa Rica and, because of this tremendous outward migratory wave of Jamaican peasants going to Central America and Colombia and to dig the Panama Canal—though they couldn't get us to dig any more canals now—we are finished with that, in fact finished with all plantation life, we are now moving on to a higher stage of society—and Garvey goes to Costa Rica. He involves himself in the struggle of the Jamaican peasants and labourers. He starts a newspaper, goes to the British Consul and tells the British Consul, "You better do something for these people. If not, I will go to England and report you and get you fired." He is a most audacious man. He goes to Panama, he goes to Colombia, he goes to Honduras, and every place Garvey goes, he forms a paper, an agitational paper for black workers. He comes back to Jamaica, he starts a paper, but then he hears about a man, a man called something Ali,[5] in England, an Egyptian man. Notice, for the brothers who know it, the paper that became the most renowned agency of the Garvey movement, *The Negro World*, the quality of that paper is to be found, not in the fact that Garvey was a sensible man, not in the fact that Garvey had some ideas—it was to be found in the experience Garvey had made footing it through the woods of Honduras, Costa Rica, Panama, Colombia, and the Jamaican countryside. So that when he gets to the United States, the First World War is over and the Afro-American masses returning from the war and those at home now find conditions intolerable and move to the north. And they themselves are unburdened and in motion and Garvey connects with this, things begin to happen all over the place.

I want to make this specific point because when we start to talk about the question of international brotherhood for black liberation in the congress, you will only be mischievous if you try to make it purely an idea. It has to be grounded in the struggle of the black masses. Otherwise, you can have no international movement. Let us keep that in mind. Garvey was a man who trained himself, coming out of the Jamaican countryside in 1907, and by the time he reached America in 1917, the Afro-American masses in the United States had never seen anything like that man. An audacity, an ability to put into words thoughts that were still half-formed, to make those words ring on every continent where black people suffered, from East Africa, Kenya, to Brazil, to Venezuela, all over the world where black men were scattered, the word of Garveyism and the philosophy of black resistance formed a most vibrant theory. It was so vibrant that the colonial authorities had to ban, in many of the colonial territories, the publication of *The Negro World*. It was a most powerful instrument. I won't call any names, but I know some very, very renowned black revolutionaries who grew up in that era who were in large part educated on the weekly edition of *The Negro World*. Because *The Negro World* contained, not only in essence but in practice, the struggle of black men everywhere. You read that paper today and you are astonished. Page after page are reports and analyses on black men scattered throughout the world. That was a most remarkable achievement. But the point is, not only did Garvey have remarkable talents, not only did he come to America with some amount of experience in agitation and struggle, but he came to America after the First World War. Bolshevism was on its way to victory, bourgeois civilization and European hegemony were clearly in ruin and Garvey said: "It is now that the Negro and the world of the black man is going to take its place." And behind it all comes the driving force of the great Jamaican peasant stock. It is, when you add it up, and not in any formal way, but you drive all these contrary points into each other, you begin to get and see a sense of movement of black resistance and liberation that is not only traced metaphysically back to the Swiss traveler and the mournful silence, to the French traveler and his bewilderment at this brute, Boukman, but you begin to see a whole new world of the black man taking place. And the world is a different place because of it and the philosophy of Garveyism is today its finest consummation.

If you read the philosophy of Garveyism today, many things become apparent. One, several of his ideas read, and still read, with astonishing power. It is most amazing when a man like Garvey sits down—and I will read you a few of the quotations to give you a taste of it. But before I do this, notice that in 1912 in the United States a movement developed that bears certain similarities to the Garvey movement. It is called the Chief Sam movement. And some young American academics have recently published their work on the Chief Sam movement. It is called *The Longest Way Home: Chief Alfred E. Sam and the Back-to-Africa Movement*. Chief Sam has the base of his movement in Oklahoma. Oklahoma was then not a state, it was a territory. And the Chief Sam movement takes on added importance because of a very outstanding set of events. One, within the territory of Oklahoma, there is a town called Boley. And Boley, so far as we have been able to detect, was the only—and to this day the only—autonomous black town in a white American society. And what happened was that as the forces of Jim Crowism increasingly came down on the black man in the United States, the politicians of the Republican and Democratic parties made a deal to sacrifice Boley, and Boley as a town was broken up. Notice that it is when the black community is broken up or the black community is in a state of crisis or the black community has reached a level of development that can no longer express itself out in the open because of the limitations of white American society—or colonial society for that matter—that you begin to see all kinds of movements among the black masses. Then Chief Sam forms what is a fairly important movement and numbering in the thousands and, in fact, actually took people on two ships to Africa. But something here—I want to quote from that book—these white scholars failed to see it and that's not accidental. They say:

> Sam's organisation of the movement could hardly be called masterful. Though his local club [Hill: Note that.] proved an innovation, since the membership constantly reinforced its fervid belief in the wisdom of the African return, they developed almost without Sam's urging. His appeal was enormous; and people literally flocked to purchase his stock, never questioning its value nor the validity of the claims which he was making with reference to it.[6]

They don't see it and they have stated it. One: Boley is broken up and the Black people of Oklahoma are set loose now. Chief Sam comes along with his movement but, you know, they're not so really interested, although these people think so, in the African return, because the moment they get into the movement they organize local clubs in Oklahoma. And these local clubs in Oklahoma that were the basis of the Chief Sam movement, these men say, developed without his urging. Here's a political leader saying, "I'm going to take you to Africa," and they say, "All right, while we are waiting on the boat, to bring the boat, we will organize ourselves here," and in two twos they start organizing brand new black communities. Nobody had to urge them. This is what happens when Garvey comes into the United States. The Negro community of the Northern states is in a condition of flux. The Negro worker of the northern United States faces terror, lynching, coming back from the First World War. And the phenomenon, to this day, which is the finest edifice of black achievement, of black accomplishment in the whole of the northern United States, were the Liberty Halls that Garvey found, because it was in those halls that the black community—for the first time in the northern United States, even before their churches followed them up from the South—formed the indigenous black communities that are today breaking up American civilization. Those small embryonic communities are today so powerful and have reached a stage of development such that not even the concept and the term Black Power can adequately cope with the power and enormity of this struggle.

And Garvey was peculiarly fitted for this task because he's coming from a colonial society called Jamaica where the same problem has just—before he comes into America—exploded out into the open. He is peculiarly fitted for this task. And when Garvey comes to the United States and begins to enunciate much of his philosophy, listen to what he is saying. Garvey says, "I know of no national boundary where the Negro is concerned. [Hill: None at all.] The whole world is my province until Africa is free."[7] No black man had ever spoken like that before. "I know of no national boundary where the Negro is concerned. The whole world is my province until Africa is free." Then, at the First UNIA [Universal Negro Improvement Association] Convention of The Negro Peoples of the World, Garvey shouts, "A race without authority and power is a race without respect."[8] Such shattering thoughts that are so succinctly integrated, that relate, not ideationally to what people have as prejudices or feeling, but relate instinctively to the mass movement, the self-activity of the black people wherever there are some. "A race without authority and power is a race without respect." Do you know that today we are still at that stage? [*Applause*] Garvey could project so far into the future because he was in touch with the movement of black humanity around the world. And you read, again and again, in his *Philosophy and Opinions*, statements that astonish you with the breadth, the almost prophetic insight into the future, and the problems of black civilization wherever it is found today. Garvey makes another statement at the same convention. Garvey says:

> We do not desire what has belonged to others, though others have always sought to deprive us of that which belongs to us . . . If Europe is for the Europeans, then Africa shall be for the black peoples of the world. [*Applause from congress audience*] We say it; we mean it . . . The other races have countries of their own and it is time for the 400,000,000 Negroes to claim Africa for themselves.[9]

. . .

The Negroes of the world say: "We are striking homewards toward Africa, to make her the big, black republic." And in the making of Africa a big black republic, what is the barrier? The barrier is the white man; and we say to the white man who now dominates Africa that it is to his interest to clear out of Africa, now, because we are coming not as in the time of Father Abraham, 200,000 strong, but we are coming 400,000,000 strong, and we mean to retake every inch of the 12,000,000 square miles of African territory belonging to us by right

Divine. . . . [*Applause from the audience*] We are out to get what has belonged to us politically, socially, economically, and in every way. And what 15,000,000 of us cannot get we will call on 400,000,000 [black people] to help us get."[10]

Now, problems crop up and it is too involved here to discuss the details of the demise of the Garvey movement as a formal organization. But there's another quotation here that is most important. He says—this was his last speech at Liberty Hall before entering the Tombs Prison to await the outcome of his appeal. And Garvey said to the UNIA followers:

[M]arch "forward to the redemption of a great country and the re-establishment of a greater government." "We have only started; we are just on our own way." White men were making "a tremendous and terrible mistake" if they thought they could "stamp out the souls of 400,000,000 black men." "The world is crazy and foolish if they think they can destroy the principles, ideals of the Universal Negro Improvement Association."[11]

President Johnson and the pigs and the crackers of American, white racist society are stupid fools and crazy if they think that they can wipe out the black humanity of the United States. [*Applause*]

I could go on and on quoting from Garveyism, but I like to tell brothers, at home and abroad, if today you don't know what Garvey said, go into a little corner and catch up, because you have a lot to catch up on. If you haven't read what Garvey said today, I don't know that you can be a brother at all. I don't know because we have been fooling around, a lot of intellectual bullshit going on [*applause*] and men believing that they are making a serious contribution to black liberation and black resistance. Ground yourself in the communities of black people wherever you are, live with them, think with them, organize them, and they will point the way forward. The moment Garvey got to the United States, it was the American black people who, in their connection and relation with Garvey, laid the groundwork on which Garvey could build an organization. Once again, the self-activity of oppressed people is going to liberate them, whether you or I wish to participate or not [*applause*]—so get serious.

Now, C. L. R. James has said, in the Appendix to *The Black Jacobins*, what he considers to be Garvey's real achievement, and it is a most profound achievement. James should know, he was very much around and involved and dealing with these problems. He says:

When you bear in mind the slenderness of his resources, the vast material forces and the pervading social conceptions which automatically sought to destroy him, his achievement remains one of the propagandistic miracles of this century.[12]

And he concludes his analysis of Garvey:

Garvey found the cause of Africans and of people of African descent not so much neglected as unworthy of consideration. In little more than half of ten years he had made it a part of the political consciousness of the world.[13]

A short, stubby, rather ugly-looking—by white standards—black man. Thrust into the jungle of Kingston, the city, with his mother, in a few short years, five years to be exact, Garvey had placed the cause of Africa, African liberation, and black humanity squarely in the political consciousness of the world and there it remains today, nobody can remove it.

Again, I want to insist he didn't do this because he had some good ideas; he did this because his ideas were connected to the movement of black people, oppressed and seeking the way out to liberate themselves. [*Applause*] When you connect yourself in that way, no force, I know of none—unless these white crackers are going to blow the world to pieces—that can restrain this inordinate power of a black humanity that is going to break open wholly new paths to world civilization.

Now, there are a number of limitations which I want to point out in Garvey's thoughts. I have a paper here and I will just read it to tell you what I think is the limitation of the man's thoughts. It would not be fair to give you an incomplete appraisal on my part. I say in a paper here:

If a criticism of Garveyism can be offered at this stage, then it's chief defects [Hill: the defects of Garveyism] consisted of its acceptance of a world split up into conflicting racial identities. Garveyism, therefore, became captive to the very ideological world it was seeking to dissolve so desperately. The secular foundations of this realm of thought, Garveyism, was never able to successfully penetrate and, through their elimination, revolutionize. Since Garveyism never entered upon the criticism of the foundation of the colonial identity conflicts, it was led to abstract, pure Garveyism.

I say Garvey

fell victim to what Gouldner called "the lunge toward the universally valid," that is a single optimum solution to the problem of colonialism and black suppression. Eventually, therefore, the philosophy of Garveyism was trapped in a kind of mysticism, which is defined here as "the permanent affirmation of some abstract universal" which, in Garvey's case, was African nationality. Garvey's thoughts reached a point where, as an instrument in the resistance movement, it could not move beyond. But if Garveyism's important function was to universalize in abstract the search for some kind of nationality, then the next stage of black history, which witnessed the official presence of the black working masses, would substitute new social foundations of power to make nationality for the black people a concrete reality. Although it has been projected abstractly by Garveyism, within the next decade the whole question of nationality was brought back into the concrete Jamaican setting from which it had been derived in the first place. But now it served to enunciate and explain the purpose of new political power of the black masses. In this larger historical sense, therefore, Garveyism became absurd and, quite soon, lost its momentary autonomy in the social process. Having been earlier constituted by what Sidney Mintz called the negative response to slavery, its absorption now became constitutive and of a new and expanding structure of social change for black people. It redefined the real scope of Jamaican society and, in so doing, advanced for the first time the political society for the mass of Jamaican people. If few people understood this fact at the time, the ruling faction of the white power structure was quick to appreciate its truth because they literally threw Garvey toward his grave.

Therefore, this is no idle criticism of Garvey. It is an immanent criticism. I say that, although Garvey posed the question, and the question still remains with us, it became locked and a fixation within an abstract universal category called African nationality. Garvey never developed those ideological categories into actual political struggle. It shows itself in the United States. Marcus Garvey—and there are reasons which I think I understand for this— told the black people in America not to antagonize whitey, because whitey is going to come down on you and what you have to do is gain self-protection and self-preservation. Such an ideological movement, with the frame of an abstract nationality, it couldn't be dissolved. But no single thinker is ever able to pose categories, create them, give them content, then dissolve them when they no longer find use. This meeting here, and the black liberation movement throughout the world today, is the dissolution of those categories into actual revolutionary struggle. And that is where we are today, brothers, that is where we are today. So, no idle talk now about Garvey who was a big man with a big movement and the wondrous things he did. Look to yourself and the road ahead for revolutionary struggle. Those are the categories that Garvey gave you, now do something with them. And that is, to me, the reason why I have traveled all the way from Jamaica to come here today; to tell you we now have to recreate the international movement of black humanity. [*Long applause*]

MODERATOR: Now perhaps you can get some impression of my enthusiasm for young black scholars. I would suggest that as far as the questioning is concerned, we have, I think, about twenty minutes; that any of you who have questions, if you could line up on this side so that we can save time on calling individual questioners, in having you come down front. May I suggest that the questions be confined to the theoretical, which was stressed by Mr. Hill. He would prefer not to deal with questions of chronology, etcetera. It appears we have a question.

QUESTION: Mr. Hill, I don't know whether you're familiar with the name Pat Burns, but in case you're not, he's a radio personality who runs an open mind program, so-called, on radio CKTM. Last night I was listening to a replay of some of the choice expressions of the day on his so-called open mind program, in which some of our people came under attack; to name a few, Dr. Barbara Jones, Rosie Douglas, and Stokely Carmichael. Though I cannot go into the details of the commentary on each individual, it would appear, according to a caller, that Dr. Jones had made a remark on a rival station that 50 percent of black people in Canada were university graduates. Pat Burns made the usual commentary, of course, calling such a statement unintelligent, stupid, out of all proportions, etcetera, and promised to have Dr. Jones on his program to have her comment. A young African called up Pat Burns to find out whether he had, in fact, got Barbara Jones and what had been her comment. Pat Burns replied that, for one or another reason, he did not get in touch with Barbara Jones and he also questioned this young man as to how long he'd been here, etcetera. Finally, he asked this young African for his opinion on the Nigerian-Biafran affair. The African deemed it unfit to pass any comments just now but reflected that there is not much difference between the Nigerian-Biafran affair and what was taking place in Rhodesia. To this, Pat Burns peculiarly protested, saying that he was astonished that the African had no opinion because here—and I emphasize that—Canadians were doing all they could to help the starving Biafrans whose lives were endangered by genocide and that, in fact, in Pat Burns' opinion, the situation in Rhodesia was quite different, as there was no starvation in Rhodesia and that the black people's lives there were not impaired by genocide, as that of the Biafrans by the Nigerians. Would you care to give your comments on this? [*Laughter*]

HILL: I came to Canada on Thursday night. I come to Canada and I hear people telling me about this man Pat Burns. [*Laughter*]. I am at a loss to understand why black people are getting hung up on this whitey piece of irrelevancy. [*Applause*] What an insult it is for this backwater civilization to tell black men on the frontlines to struggle against racism, that you must have an opinion. Where were his opinions before that? To hell with Pat Burns! He's a piece of irrelevancy.

QUESTION: One of the things that Garvey also said was that we are too large, in great numbers, not to be a great people, a great race, and a great nation. If we think of ourselves, black people, as a nation, do you feel there's any need, reason, anything for a compromise between white and black to bring about any type of social revolution? [*Sporadic applause*]

HILL: That is a question of high theory, brother. My feeling is black men do what they have to because they have to do it. White men do what they have to because they have to do it. If it so happens that white men find themselves intolerably oppressed by the same oppressor that contains black humanity, well then, I don't think that we could be selfish and rule them out of the rewards of liberation. That would be very wrong. [*Applause*] In other words, for the time being, the whole question of compromise is a waste of time. Compromise comes about in action. The black people of the New World have to be at the vanguard of a new society. White men, in their same society, seem to have been relatively accommodated to their system. We expect them to move also because the president's National Commission on Riots showed the only alternative to allowing black people their freedom is a kind of urban apartheid, a very fancy name for concentration camps. Then the white man said you can't put Negroes in concentration camps or enforce urban apartheid and don't include white people too; you have to reach them, they're so close to you. So, the whole point is, we are doing what we have to do. Those who are willing to come along will do so in time. I don't want to work out any basis of compromise. Let them decide how they face the present and the future in relation to their own society. If they are willing to make a break with it, we welcome them, but we are going ahead. [*Applause*]

QUESTION: It appears that there is a growing core issue that has been raised by the discussion, namely the question of the level of social consciousness that is likely to emerge among people who are defined as black in the near future. It seems to me that, whereas it is right that there is a possibility of the development of a universal black movement, that the evidence—and my understanding of what is definitely happening in Nigeria and the understanding of nationalist developments in Eastern Europe and elsewhere in the world—the idea of national consciousness seems to be much more parochial and much more local. I was wondering how it would be or what, in fact, are the prospects for local nationalisms and local civil wars, which we witness within the context of Africa, mitigating against the kind of movement which we would like to see develop. In other words, I think there is a strong . . . [*The questioner is interrupted and told to ask a question.*] All right. I'm sorry. [*Laughter*] I would like the speaker to comment on the relative strengths of parochial and universalistic forces within ascending black communities that presently exist and how he sees these present contradictions working themselves out. [*Short applause*]

HILL: You will remember that in my opening quotation in the introduction to my address I raised the name of a man called Boukman. Internationalism and black solidarity is nothing new to us. Boukman was a Jamaican slave who went to Haiti and started the movement for Haitian freedom. Any black man should be proud and welcome to fight under the banner of any black liberation movement in the world. If Mr. Smith thinks that he can isolate the people of Zimbabwe, he ought to begin to understand that black brothers from Brazil, the United States, Cuba, the Western world are quite prepared to go to Zimbabwe and shed their blood because we're going to finish, and we mean this, we're going to finish with racism. In other words, you raised a thorny question about the Nigerian civil war and how Africans beat up each other, kill each other. But look at it. The Nigerian federal government is armed by Britain and supported politically by the United States and the Russians. [*Applause*] The Russians are in the game too, brothers. Russian planes are bombing fellow Africans in Biafra. But then look what happened: Mr. Ojukwu—because he's isolated—is now rescued by General de Gaulle. So, what really happens, once again, is that black men are fighting out an imperialist struggle. [*Applause*]

QUESTION: I would like to know something about Garvey concerning his being a West Indian as such. I don't think it is an accident of birth that men like Garvey, Mr. James here, George Padmore, and, more recently, Stokely Carmichael are from the Caribbean. I would like to know what it is about the Caribbean colonial experience that creates these men and how you explain this. Could you make some projection as to what you anticipate from the Caribbean leaders, as such, internationalists, in the future?

HILL: The first thing and the basis of internationalism on behalf of the Caribbean brothers is obviously the Caribbean revolution. That is our contribution to world-wide black internationalism. We have striven in the past, even the forefathers. The real forefather of Pan-Africanism—and I wish somebody had been allowed to speak at this congress on that question—was Edward Wilmot Blyden. Blyden was the son of some freed slaves in the Virgin Islands. That is the longest end, starting with Boukman, going right up to West Indian revolutionaries fighting, as Garvey said, "wherever the banner is raised." I'll give you another example: You hear a lot about brother Frantz Fanon, a revolutionary from Martinique. Simone de Beauvoir tells us in the final instalment of her autobiography, *Forces of Circumstance*, that Jean-Paul Sartre and she recognized instantly that Fanon was one of the most extraordinary personalities of our time. Fanon was going down very rapidly, and they invited him to come—they still thought he had arthritis—to go into a spa. Fanon got there, they met, and, after a few days and a few nights of serious discussion, Simone de Beauvoir said to Fanon: Dear Frantz, you have to let Jean-Paul get some sleep. And Fanon told her to go to hell. They went on for a fourth day and Fanon said, "All right, Jean-Paul, you look now as though you can't take anymore. All right, let us close this up." And he asked Jean-Paul a question: "Now, we've been talking for four days and four nights, no sleep. I have told you what is in my head. Now, tell me something, what do you think I am? Who am I?" Whereupon this great philosopher moved into a very involved thing, that Fanon was the voice of the Third World speaking to itself, representative of a new society, and all these things that are quite true. De Beauvoir tells us Fanon broke into an hysterical laughter that lasted for some time and Fanon said, "You men don't understand me yet. I've wasted my time." Fanon said, "I am fighting for Martinique."[14] The banner of the Algerian Revolution was only the front in which he found himself and there he decided to set down his roots with his brothers. That is not a question of whether Caribbean people are going to be internationalists or can be internationalists. The only people who still don't understand that are the Caribbean people themselves, and it's a shocking shame. We the Caribbeans still don't understand that. [*Applause*] Because the domination of our societies is still in the hands of men. . . . [*The recording ends here.*]

Chapter 4

AFRICAN HISTORY IN THE SERVICE OF THE BLACK LIBERATION

WALTER RODNEY

ROCKY JONES: It gives me great pleasure this morning to introduce to you Dr. Walter Rodney. Dr. Rodney is an African history Ph.D. major. Born in Guyana; studied at the University of the British West Indies and the School of Oriental and African History [Studies]; tutored at the University College, Dar es Salaam; researched at Ghana and Nigeria; presently at the University of West Indies; author of several publications on the slave trade and related aspects of West African history. That's who he is formally. Informally, for the last few days, he has been a brother who is well versed on our history and well prepared to share his knowledge with those of you who want to learn. While he is talking, I hope you will keep in mind that later, in our workshops, you should take advantage of the knowledge that this man possesses. Dr. Rodney. [*Applause*]

WALTER RODNEY: Initially, I had written a short supplementary paper to that which was to be presented by Mr. Richard Moore.[1] Therefore, the order having been inverted, it places me in a rather tricky position. I had intended to continue on the basis of certain things that he would have said. However, very briefly, my position is this: Moore would have spoken on African civilizations, according to the program. I myself had intended and, in fact, I will consider certain aspects of African history that would not normally fall under the rubric of civilization. And, in the process, I would have liked to question the very concept of civilization. I entitled my paper "African History in the Service of the Black Revolution," and the first contradiction, the first dilemma that one faces in attempting to utilize African history as one of the weapons in our struggle is a realization that, in a very real sense, we, as black people, are placed in [the] invidious position of having to justify our existence by antecedents, having to prove our humanity by what went before. Now, this is very invidious. Humanity is not a thing one proves. One asserts [it] perhaps, or one accepts [it]. One doesn't really set out to prove it. But, unfortunately, the historical circumstances in which black people have evolved in recent centuries have implanted in the minds of black brothers and sisters a certain historical conception and, in order to destroy that historical conception, one has to engage in this type of game of saying, "This is what the white man said but no, it isn't really so, we have a past," and that sort of thing.

Now, if we are forced into that position, it seems to me that there are two rules that we can observe to make the exercise more meaningful. The first rule is that I, as a black historian, am speaking to fellow blacks. That means that, as far as the white audience is concerned, here and in the world at large, they are perfectly entitled to listen but I am not engaged in the game that they set up by which they say to me, "You prove, black, that you're a man. Prove it to me by showing that you have civilization," and that sort of thing. I'm not engaged in that job as far as white people are concerned. I am engaged [with], I must address myself solely to, black brothers. To the extent that they have been involved and destroyed in a process, we are seeking to re-create. And, furthermore, as I said, it's "in the service of black revolution." Those whites, those few whites who may join the black revolution, will certainly do so for reasons that are far more profound than their knowledge or acquaintance with African history. So that's another reason why we don't need to address ourselves to them.

The second rule is that African history must be seen as very intimately linked to the contemporary struggle of black people. One must not set up any false distinctions between reflection and action. We are just another facet of the ongoing revolution. This is not theory. It is a fact that black people everywhere, in Africa and in the Western world, are already on the march. Nobody who wants to be relevant to that situation can afford to withdraw and decide that he is engaging in what is essentially an intellectual exercise. The African historian, to me, is essentially involved in a process of mobilization, just like any other individual within the society who says, "I'm for Black Power. I'm going to talk about the way the blacks live down in the South," etcetera. That's a facet of mobilization. The African historian is also involved in that mobilization.

Now, having said that, I would like to illustrate the ways in which, in fact—if there's to be any proving of our humanity—it will have to be done with three examples. The first is Cuba. Cuba has proven very concretely that the way of asserting that humanity is by revolutionary struggle. And when I say it has proven that, it has proven it to the black people in Cuba. Now, this is a question with which even black brothers outside of Cuba are not very familiar, and so I'll, just for a minute, indicate what the position was and is for the black people of Cuba.

They started, like everybody else in the West, as slaves. They existed as slaves longer than any other group, except the Brazilians, well into the 1880s. And subsequent to slavery, they became involved, very rapidly, in the new imperialist relationship with the United States, and this hardened the existing prejudice of Spanish slave and Spanish colonial society. There is a very useful book recently published by Esteban Montego, a Cuban slave who was a runaway and who reflects on his life in this period and gives some insights into the type of pressures that faced the black man in Cuba after slavery.[2] With the intensification [of economic and political activity] by the United States [in Cuba and] the importation of Florida-type qualities, a black man in Cuba was just dirt. I mean it was the South; it was apartheid. If you (the black man) were seen in a certain part of Havana after a certain hour you were liable to be shot, guilty of being black, you see. The black situation in Cuba was as bad as any other sector that we can point to. But within the process of revolutionary struggle, first as slaves— because they were the first revolutionaries; we black people were the first revolutionaries, the first guerrilla fighters in this part of the world, this hemisphere—and then as freed men, the black people struggled in Cuba. They struggled, of course, alongside white people who had a vested interest in struggle—white people who wanted to break the imperialist bonds. Not white liberals who are enjoying the luxuries of capitalism and give us some platitudes about behaving in the right way and so on; white people involved in struggle. It's a completely different conception of white from the metropolitan white who, whatever category he falls into, is objectively involved in our oppression and our suppression. Every white person in this room is objectively involved in the oppression of black people so long as they live in a metropolitan centre because the metropolitan centre is dominating colonial black people. It is as simple as that.

Anyway, in Cuba that's not a position. Whites fought against the system, and in that process, the black people could be genuinely emancipated.

Now, in Cuba today, barriers to entering certain buildings, certain eating houses, and that sort of thing have completely disappeared. Juan Almeida, one of the members of the Politburo of the Cuban Communist Party, is a black man who was involved in the struggle from the time of the Sierra Maestra with Fidel Castro. And the position of the black people is such, not only socially and politically emancipated, but moving in a direction of reasserting their culture (the Afro-Cuban culture), of getting official encouragement to assert that culture. And we find in Cuba today more genuine interest in the African Revolution, more interest in the African plastic arts and in African drama than there exists in Jamaica, which is a place 95 percent black, because the black people of Jamaica are still involved [in,] and are dominated under, imperialist relations. So that is Cuba and that is Jamaica.

And it means that for the African historian in Cuba, he can go ahead and research and talk about African history in a new social context. But for anybody in Jamaica, he can't seriously talk about history divorced from revolutionary struggle. He isn't serious if he's doing that. You can't say that "African history will proceed as normal. We'll just teach it in the curriculum and that will be fine. Let imperialism proceed." In any event, the system doesn't even want you to do a simple thing like teaching African history. The prime minister of Jamaica, a black man (you know he looks black anyway),[3] was approached with a request to let African history and an African language, Swahili, be taught in the schools, and he said, "No, we can't have any of that." He gave some reason—a curious reason—something about there being so many different races in Jamaica. Very curious. I mean, 95 percent of the people are black but he can't teach an African language. They teach Latin, French, Spanish, and everything else. A lot of different reasons don't seem to come into that. But it shows that the colonial structure is itself aware of the fact you can't separate a new conception of self, which should spring from historical investigation with a new actuality, from the revolutionary process to change the situation that presently exists. For the Jamaican, the system makes it impossible for him to come to this new awareness of himself because it doesn't want him to be involved in a revolutionary process.

For any historian who seeks to reconstruct the African past, to reconstruct the past of black peoples in this continent, in such a context he cannot say that the revolution will wait until people are re-educated and that re-education reaches an advanced stage, because he isn't even allowed to engage in that process of re-education. Consequently, the revolution is with us already. The history will have to be subsidiary to that, it will have to come during and after the revolutionary process. In other words, the Jamaican freedom fighter will have to be a man [who] will, perhaps in his spare time, read some African history. Che Guevara said the guerrilla should always carry something worthwhile in his knapsack. So, the guerrilla fighter, the freedom fighter in Jamaica, would read some African history, but he isn't waiting on that to move. He has to move because the only way that he can establish a relationship with his own past is, in fact, by breaking the present bonds that restrict and constrain us.

In the United States (and this will presumably apply in Canada also) the situation is rather different. In the United States the national bourgeoisie is powerful, the most powerful national bourgeois group in the world, and, undoubtedly, it will be the most powerful national bourgeois group in the history of the world because there won't be any more powerful group after the US, you know. That sort of thing is coming to an end. Anyway, this national bourgeoisie, they have the confidence that comes from their wealth. The Jamaican petty bourgeoisie is a comprador class, the neo-colonialist class. They don't have any confidence because they don't have any capital. They know they exist on handouts from the metropolitan system, so they are very shaky and very uncertain of themselves. And they will even stop you from, as I said, studying African history. But the US bourgeoisie is employing a different tactic. But the brothers and sisters, and here I am addressing myself particularly to the brothers who have come up from the United States, will have to be aware of the gambit that is in fact already being utilized with respect to African history and culture. And that is this: The national bourgeoisie in the United States appears to be giving a concession. They are saying, "Okay, fine, you go ahead and study African history and African culture," and they will give you so much African history and culture [that] you just have time for nothing else. The object is to divorce the process of thought and reflection on our past from the process of changing the present, so that you feel that you've gained something, but you end up in some remarkable contradiction. What you will find is this (in fact it's happening already): Rockefeller—who is making most of his money out of South African gold, out of the Rand, out of exploiting and participating in apartheid, the most vicious racial system in the world—that guy is going to finance a chair in African history. That's the type of contradiction. If a black progressive thinks he's doing something by going into African history, using up a Rockefeller grant, all he is doing is forgetting both the domestic and external implications of American capitalism and, in fact, supporting that system because the guys don't mind if you go into a library or museum and lock yourself up all day. That's wonderful; keep you off the street, keep you out of the struggle. We have to avoid that type of myth, that cultural revival, *per se*, is going to carry us a long way. I don't want to seem to be critical of the development of interest in African history and culture. Quite obviously not, that's what I myself am involved in. What I am trying to suggest is that sometimes, while involved in a process, we ourselves have to be very careful to delimit how far that process should go. Let's all wear Afros, let's put on African clothes. Fine. But that doesn't mean we are not going to struggle. The system still has to be broken before we can express ourselves in any fundamental way.

I had to make that type of introduction before I could go on to talk about African history as such. And when I go on to talk about that I will return to my initial submission that I would like, in fact, to question these categories of civilization. We start off with a conception of civilization and it can be proven, it can be demonstrated rather, that African history can provide us with examples of civilization in the terms the Europeans have expressed. In other words, we can go to Egypt; we can go to Kush, that's in the Sudan; we can go to the western Sudan, to Ghana, Mali, Songhai; we can take the central Sudan, Bornu, and Kanem; the Hausa states; Mossi, coming further south; we can go across to the eastern part of the continent and find the early Bachwesi empires and the later developments of Bunyoro, Baganda; we can go further south into Central Africa, the Luba-Lunda Kingdoms; we can take the development in southern Bantu in the eighteenth and nineteenth centuries in the Shona sections in the centre and over in the far east, that's the Zulu rising. We can build up a picture that conforms to a European conception. In other words, we can play the game of proving to white society that "you were wrong when you said we had no history, that we had no civilization. Look [at] what we produced."

But I'm only going to deal with one aspect of that, and that's Egypt. Everybody knows about Egypt. I don't have to delineate the Egyptian civilization. If you want to read about Egypt, you have to go and check some books on the Middle East or you have to go and find some guy who calls himself an Egyptologist. You never find any assessment of Egyptian culture, any serious assessment, within the African continent. Not never. Of late it is changing. But the traditional approach, the years of study of Egypt, have taken place in a context of [the] Middle East, Mesopotamia, background to European culture, that sort of thing. Africa just doesn't come in.[4] Very curious. To begin with, we have a simple geographical description. European refers initially to either what is actually within

Europe or what proceeded from Europe as a geographical entity. American the same, Chinese the same. But curiously, Egypt is well entrenched in Africa, but it never appears in any assessment of African civilization. In other words, what I am trying to say, why I am taking this single point, is to show the ways in which the issue can be evaded. White society can either say you have had no history or, where they see an element of civilization in their terms, they can say that was not yours, either by saying it outright or ignoring it.

In the case of Egypt, a second argument is advanced: the question of colour. If you press the first argument I made, then a white [person] will say, "Well, you know, the people in Egypt were white so that really it has nothing to do with Africa, which is a place for black people." In that sense, one will have to go back and try to determine what was the racial composition of dynastic Egypt. And, as far as we can tell, the Egyptians represented themselves as red- or copper-coloured, as distinct from lighter-skinned white peoples living outside of Egypt and as distinct from darker-skinned black peoples living outside of Egypt also, to the south. Their own conception of themselves was certainly not white. Furthermore, the whole history of Egypt is one of southward expansion and of contacts, sometimes not very pleasant contacts, in the form of slave raids with the south. So it is clear the whole Egyptian population must have been infused with a large quantity of black blood, if we want to take it in racial terms.

We can go further than that. For the whole of the eighth century BCE, the Egyptian dynasty was actually in the hands of the Nubians, in the hands of the Empire of Kush. In other words, for that period, black men were ruling the society. I found no evidence that the society itself was racially conscious. I'm only making this distinction in terms of race because we are attempting to break down certain myths. And the myth is quite simple. In other words, if we look at Egyptian society, we see that it certainly was not white, we can take the medial position that it was brown and that it had very large elements of black, including a whole black dynasty. This is just to illustrate the ways in which, even within the terminology that Europeans have established, one can indicate that African history exists, that African civilizations exist, that the black man can look back on this and gain the necessary revolutionary inspiration. But I want to move on from there because I don't feel that we should accept these categories that have been established by European writers. These categories are established simply by looking at European society as it has existed, extracting out the elements that they consider to be meaningful in that society, and then judging the rest of the world with these standards, as though these are universal criteria. It is what I call "cultural egocentrism." These fellows have no concept of judging any culture by attempting to get out of their own. They base themselves solidly in their own limited perspectives and then judge everybody else by that.

In Africa, even apart from the state systems I have merely enumerated and that, presumably, Richard Moore will talk about in more detail, one could find a whole variety of people, millions of people, living outside of the normal political state. And in European terms, they were not civilized, because to be civilized you had to be living in this large political conglomeration, you had to be writing, preferably (this is one of the criteria which is normally adduced for civilization), and you had to be engaged in a political and administrative process that is rather similar to that, let's say, of the modern United States. In other words, the greatest expression of human progress is in terms of the size of the state, in terms of the size of the armies that the fellows can send against each other to kill each other out and the like. I mean it really is amazing because, even within white society, those people who question the society—and there have been many in the post-war epoch who question the very basis of the society—would wonder if, on sheer size and population and so on, the United States is the most civilized country in the world, if we use those criteria.

We know that it is the most barbarous because of the way in which it has exercised its power, because of the way in which it has stifled its own population. And that is not only the black population but the white population. We have to challenge those criteria, and when I look back at African states, at African society in the broadest sense, I would, in fact, like to throw out the word civilization. I think it is a very arbitrary word, I don't think it gets us very far. I mean, we use it as a prop so that we can advance our thoughts and at a certain stage it will abolish itself, as it were.

I abolish it on a whole variety of grounds. I mean, one could add, for instance, that we as black people—and this is a question that came up yesterday in an embryonic form when C. L. R. James was speaking—must define the world from our own position.[5] So I want to talk about civilization and I'm a black man and I've been subjected to slavery. And I can't look around and say European society was civilized. I can't say this. I can't participate in what the French call *la mission civilisatrice* when this is what colonialism was for them. "If that is civilization," was it brother LeRoi who said it?[6] "then give me back the jungle." That is a definition we as black people cannot accept at all. And once we throw aside that definition, we have to start working with other things. We have to forget the sort of formal approach and start trying to determine what is meaningful in social relations and what were the features of African social relations that were most meaningful. And that's what I'll talk about for a little while.

I think that, just as we can say, in the small societies, before the European arrived in Africa, certain states and certain political developments were in existence, similarly, we can emphasize the culture-history; we can try to determine, in the period before the fifteenth century, what were the lines along which African culture-history was developing. And here we must understand that Africans, for the most part, were living in small societies, some of them so-called stateless societies—just a family, an extended family; no superstructure of the state, no huge territorial delimitations. But, whatever the situation in which they lived, whether it was an isolated family unit, whether it was a clan arrangement, or whether it was a state, it seems to me that certain principles can be extracted [as] the dynamic principles of African culture. And this is what represents the civilization—having eroded the erroneous concept surrounding it—of Africa in that particular period. I'll try to select just a few [of] the most outstanding (in my estimation) of these principles.

One of them is hospitality, the way people related to each other in terms of hospitality. Another one is the way in which the people of a certain age in this society were treated. Another is the whole question of law in African society, the way that the law was administered, the whole ethos behind the law. I think I would like to take those three points and start to have a look at them now.

I start with hospitality. In the African systems, Europeans who arrived in the fifteenth century or Europeans who arrived subsequently within an indigenous context saw the Africans living by themselves. It's amazing the regularity with which they stressed the nature of African hospitality, the extent of African hospitality. This was not just, as it were, an individual response of Africans. It was rooted in the nature of their social organization. The extended family, for instance, was in itself an agency of social relief. It was in itself an agency that would deny the existence of the extremes of poverty and abandonment in African society, which we find in modern capitalist society. Because, as an extended family, it meant that the responsibility was theirs. All members of the family share a responsibility for others. This is the nucleus of the whole concept of hospitality.

One can go further and take the principle of the family when it is projected into the clan arrangement. A clan, in a rough sense, is a whole collection of families. It's a set of people who share a common ancestor [and] common totems, [as] sometimes the term is used. Now, within that clan there are numerous people who don't know each other. They just know they belong to clan A. They've never seen each other. Their relationship in terms of physical and genetic proximity is very vague. They acknowledge an ancestor who is very remote, on the borders between history and legend. But, nevertheless, a clan brother is a brother and he's treated as a brother whenever the occasion arises. In other words, I belong to clan A and I come from 300 miles away and I meet another clan brother; he has certain responsibilities toward me—to house, feed, clothe me. The system provides for that hospitality.

We can go further. Take the structure of authority, whether it be the chief, or a king, or a ruling group. They too have certain very clearly defined responsibilities with respect to the action of giving, the key being hospitality. So much so that I came across a very interesting incident of a small chief in a Sierra Leone system who they were about to elect into a king and the guy says, "Well, sorry, I'm not going to take that job. I just don't have the funds to carry out the type of hospitality which is normally expected from a ruler." That's his job—to keep an open house. Guys just turn up there and, as I said before, a brother is a brother, a sister is a sister.

Now, I don't know how it will appear to you, but when I started off and I looked at this, to me, this is a more profound aspect of relationship than how big the state was and how many armies were jumping across to kill each other. This was an aspect of interpersonal relationship. This was a quality of life that doesn't exist in our society. It couldn't exist in capitalism, which is based on profit motive. This is not to say that there aren't individuals within the capitalist system who are hospitable. All over the world one finds hospitable individuals. Here I'm talking about a hospitable society, not the odd individual. The whole society is geared toward a reciprocal relationship with those around. And this, to me, is very, very striking, and it seems to me that, as a principle for human organization, it is one of the facets about African cultural development to which greater attention should be paid.

Let me talk about the old men: age. Again, we'll start with capitalist society. The old people in the capitalist society have no value. Capitalism wants labour. You've finished working, well that's tough. In more recent times, you get a pension, but the system doesn't have any further value for you. In West Indian society, in the period of the slave trade, the planters used to make a concrete economic calculation. They had this discussion going. The discussion went along these lines: "Shall we let these blacks work for us for a long time and get old and try to get the maximum period of work out of them? Or shall we work them to death in a limited period of time and get new blacks?" And most of the planters, in fact, felt that it was more advantageous to avoid the problems of having old people in the society. What's an old black going to do? He can't produce. He can't work the eighteen hours a day the plantation system required. So it's better not to have old black people in the society. And capitalist society all over, not just on the question of race, adopts this attitude to elderly people.

African society is fundamentally different. Throughout Africa, the principle of gerontocracy prevails. The elder, by virtue of his age, is vested with certain authority and certain power. This is basic because, for them, wisdom is a reflection of an experience and, by that very fact, all things being equal, the older the man in the society, the more his experience in the problems within that society, the more his reflection on them, and, therefore, the greater his wisdom. There is more to it than that: it means that the older man has had an opportunity within that society to acquire [a] certain formal education, because African society had its aspects of formal education. There was a period of intensive education when a man or a woman, or should I say a boy or a girl, was about to be initiated into the society, to become a man or a woman. That was always a period of intensive education. And, subsequently, as individuals moved from age group to age group, or from one level in a secret society to another, or from one age sect to another—all these being institutions that related people on the basis of age—he was also privy to additional knowledge, so that he was going through a process of learning. When he reached a certain stage, he was supposed be an historian, lawyer, guardian of the constitution, and the president of the state. He was supposed to be a tutor to the young king when he came up, to the king's sons that is, or nephews, depending on the system, and, in effect, these elders were given responsibility. They were free, of course, because of the hospitality, from the task of winning a living, and the system asked them to be alert.

This is the difference. I've seen a lot of old people—in England in particular it struck me. It is not as bad in the West Indies. Our black people still manage to survive, even in old age. But I looked at English society and it has completely destroyed a certain sector of the society. These women who reach a certain age, they can't relate to anything else. They perhaps go to a little bingo party and then after a while they can't even totter out to that. And then you just herd them into old people's homes. They have no function. They do nothing, so they rapidly degenerate and become cabbages, because your mind, if you don't keep it going, is going to degenerate. And this is our society that we live in now. African society catered for a completely different conception. The man is always growing, the man is always learning, until he dies. And that is why field researchers have found that when you go into an African society, you can go and find any old man. Find him, he might be sixty, he might be seventy, and with perspicacity he will point out to you elements of the culture and recall episodes of history going back more than a hundred years—in other words, more than his lifetime. He has been trained by the society to function in that way. Now this, to me, is tremendous. A society that takes you from birth and carries you all the way so that life has meaning to the end. Well, you judge that for yourself.

I want to talk now about the attitude of the law in African society. This is my third episode, my third area of illustration. The law in African society was, of course, customary law, rather than recorded law. In recent times, that customary law has become the subject of serious scholarship, and numerous treatises have been presented on African law. The principles are very complex. To begin with, we must understand the framework in which it functions, a framework, as I see it, of social order, social stability. So that immediately limits the areas in which the law is going to operate. Let me illustrate. And this, again, is using European evidence. All the things I am saying I can quote *ad extentum* from European sources. It is a useful technique. The man says, "No, that's not so." Then you say, "Well, this man said so, it wasn't me, you know. White people went and saw this." This is European evidence. They go to African society and they're amazed at the type of social security that existed there in the fifteenth century. All this stuff I'm talking about is cultural history, the period before the European arrival. Some of it carries over, but I'm talking about traditional African society.

All of the travelers into the western Sudan, time and time again, they reiterated, "This is tremendous. How can we travel such huge distances from one end of the Empire of Mali to another and we don't find any robbers, we don't find any vagrants? If we lose something, when we turn up at the court of the king, we find that thing has been transmitted there to be given to us." It was amazing to them because they were operating from the background of brigandage in Europe, highway robbery. I mean our society—well, capitalist society—is a robber society, so this explains the whole thing. [In] the whole development of capitalism—piracy, brigandage on highways, etcetera—the security for goods and persons is a very late development in European and capitalist society, and it has come about through the establishment of massive mechanisms for keeping people in their places; in other words, a police force and army. But in African society this wasn't so. It wasn't the police who were all around to see that goods and persons were secure. It was the social constraints. People just didn't do that. Mungo Park went to the Gambia.[27] He saw a little group called the Djolas. He said these are a bunch of savages. Yet, he himself had to concede. He says, "I left my goods there for months unattended and when I went back, there wasn't a pin removed." And this is a generalized type of remark that is made about African traditional society; a socially induced security. Everybody moves around and the like. Now, that's the norm. This doesn't mean that there is no crime whatsoever. I'm just suggesting the area that, in that society, was exemplary in its freedom, especially in comparison with Europe.

Now, insofar as there was crime, it had to be dealt with by the law. And the principle of the law was not to deal retribution to an offender, which has largely been the principle of European law until recent times, [wherein] the whole penal system is still being questioned. But, fundamentally, it hasn't changed. The law is to deal retribution, the law is a means of controlling certain individuals. And this is, of course, particularly relevant to us as black people in white society. But, that apart, what was happening in African society was that an offender was asked to make restitution, either to the individual whom he offended, or to the state if his offence was against the state, [or] against the society as a whole. It was a question of restitution rather than retribution being meted out to him. It meant that if he stole, the object was to replace what he stole, not to put him in jail. I have never, ever read of a jail in traditional African society. I have never read of stocks and fetters and chains before the slave trade. This was the African traditional society that didn't jail people. It said to them, "You replace what you have taken."

Again, the contrast with Europe is clear on all these points, and what I am developing, therefore, is the idea that there are principles of human activity that we need to look at, which are quite distinct from the so-called principles of civilization, and that when we look at that, we begin to see how tremendously meaningful African life was.

Now, we as black brothers, we look around—in the West in particular, and even in Africa this happens because Africans too have been subjected to the processes of white cultural imperialism—and you want to engage in the exercise that I mentioned at first, that is, trying to destroy the myths the whites have prepared. Even though this places you in a defensive position you have to do it for your own benefit and for the benefit of your brothers and sisters. And you look at the western Sudan, and that is great. You see in the fifth century— and, no doubt, brother Richard Moore, [who] is here now, will talk at length about that—states that are developed in a period comparable to the European Dark Ages and Middle Ages. I shan't go into that, as I said. But there is a trick in that, when you are finished saying we have states, we have civilizations like the European, the guys are then going to say, "Well, what happened afterwards? We developed, we produced the modern state." And that leaves you in a rather bemused position if your initial premise was that human development can only be expressed in its highest form in that type of structure Europeans call a state and within the terms that they consider civilized.

At some stage you have to supplement your awareness of the great achievements, of the striking achievements of African society. I know this from personal experience. I go to a black and you can see anguish in him. He says to you, "I want to know something about the great achievements [of] Africans. Tell me something striking." So, you start to tell him about Lalibella and about rock churches shorn out of sheer rock in Egypt. You tell him about the pilgrimages of Mansa Musa to Egypt. A hundred years after, people in Egypt were still recalling it. He carried so much gold that, years afterwards, the Egyptian economy was still disjointed. You tell him about the sculpture of Benin and Ife and suggest to him that these things are the marvel of the modern European world. But then you go further. I would go further. I'm suggesting to the black brothers and sisters that we need to go further than that in illustrating these principles that I indicated earlier. For an actual political purpose related to the revolution, we have to indicate that this cultural basis existed quite independent of states because, if not, there are certain types of contradictions into which we fall.

Here, I have in mind the way in which the white world normally plays up certain aspects of African contemporary development as relapses into barbarism. You say that what's happening in Nigeria, what happened in Congo, this is a sort of atavism—the blacks have gone back to the primeval savagery once the restraining hand of white civilization has been removed. And to counter that type of nonsense one doesn't only have to point to the development of so-called civilization. One also has to show these aspects of everyday life that were meaningful long before the Europeans arrived, and if we were to pursue the process, we could see how, in fact, these things were distorted during the era of contact with Europe; how they were distorted, particularly in West Africa, during the era of the slave trade.

My final reflections, before I give over to this brother, concern some other questions that brothers, in my part of the world anyway, have been asking. They say, "Well, if you recall African history and you recapture African culture, to what extent is it possible to practice this today? Is it just a question of doing this as a sort of catharsis to throw out what the Europeans said or is there a possibility of using these principles in constructive contemporary action?" For Africa, the answer is clearly yes. In African society, any serious attempt to revolutionize the society will have to take serious cognizance of these principles. And the best example is the work being done in Tanzania today and the type of analysis being carried out by that remarkable man, Julius Nyerere. Take a document like "Socialism and Rural Development," which is something blacks should all read.[28] He is attempting to select the elements of culture in Tanzania, the process of cultural history before the Europeans arrived, and as it was affected by European arrival, and then from that, to try to come to terms with the modern situation. You can extrapolate, you can see the process. It's not just going back and taking out, harum-scarum. It has to be dialectical, you have to see what still exists in the contemporary situation that comes from the traditional roots. And, in that sense, the analysis of culture-history is extremely relevant to the present revolution.

Now, I wouldn't go that far for the New World. I would not be able to say what the shape of this society is going to be. It's a very tremendous question, but one that I don't really need to ask. White people always keep asking, "After Black Power, what?" This is not really for all of us to determine. That's another epoch. It's like Marx writing about the class struggle and he says, "After all that is finished, the history of humanity will begin." Well, I see it that same way. When we have achieved what we want to achieve, the history of humanity will begin. Humanity will work out its history. We are concerned now with the blacks. The blacks have to get something done and I don't think, really, that we can use African history in the Western world in the sense that Nyerere used it. I think we can only use it in the first sense, as a sort of catharsis toward action. We probably could do more with our own history, the history of black people in the New World, as a basis for working out what is a revolutionary strategy in the New World and what will be revolutionary in the new situation. But that is another matter.

For me then, African history, as carried out by the black brothers and sisters, will have to be a process of coming to grips with all aspects of African history and with trying to determine what the categories are into which we should fit things, as distinct from saying, let us start and try to determine whether we can reconstruct African history along the same terms in which European history has been reconstructed. Because that analysis, where you utilize only the European criteria, is itself the same process of bastardization; the guy oppresses you and then he selects your terms of reference [for you]. Even when you're fighting him you use his terms of reference. But what I am trying to suggest here is that we have to break out from those terms of reference. Thank you. [*Extended applause*]

ROCKY JONES: You see, that's a brother with total involvement. He was not prepared to speak for that long when he came. He was rapping off the top of his head. He had a message, and he said it. That is total involvement.

Chapter 5

THE
CIVILIZATIONS
OF ANCIENT
AFRICA

RICHARD B. MOORE

ROCKY JONES: I hope that, when the time comes for the roll to be called down yonder, I can present as impressive a battle record as the next speaker. He is the author of *The Name "Negro": Its Origin and Evil Use*, published in 1960. He is the author of *Basic Views on Image and Independence*.[1] He has presented articles to *Freedomways* magazine. He has written articles, "Caribbean Unity" and "Pan Africa and Du Bois"[2] and many more that have appeared in *Freedomways* magazine. He has been a lecturer and consultant on African and Afro-American history to Uniondale public school system in Long Island, New York. He is involved in the Afro-American project of history and culture of the board of education of New York; founder and proprietor of the Douglass Book Center in Harlem, New York. He has transferred a collection of books, etcetera, on African and Afro-American history to the government of Barbados. These books are now being used for the Centre for Multiracial Studies in Barbados under the joint auspices of the University of the West Indies and Sussex University. Brother Richard Moore. [*Applause*]

RICHARD MOORE: Brother chairman, fellow sufferers from colonialism, and fellow seekers after truth, justice, and a better society.

I'm to speak to you on African civilization according to the assignment given to me. But I am, like my younger brother,[3] in disagreement with the term "civilization." He's never been able to find it, and I recognize that this concept of civilization connotes, as it has been used by European colonialists, a vague but superior manner of acting or way of life, especially if it is recognized in contradistinction to that which is regarded by them as barbarism or savagery. The western European is thus supposed to have achieved civilization, whereas other "off-coloured" people, be they considered yellow or black—particularly the black—have never achieved civilization, according to that view.

Now, is it possible for these benighted blacks ever to attain civilization if left to themselves, such is the set and deep-seated opinion and feeling of European colonialists and European-American racist overlords? Quite evidently, this usage of the term civilization is misleading and false. The term civilization has no definite and scientific content. Of course, there have been some students, like [Lewis] Morgan in his *Ancient Society*,[4] who have attempted to put some scientific connotation into this term. But their proposals have been inadequate and, what is more to the point, they have never gotten through to the people, even to the generality of scholars in their own or cognate field. So, to this day, among European wielders of power, various spokesmen, and even among some unwilling imitators or unconscious followers, civilization is the unique accomplishment of the superior European, as distinct from the barbarism and savagery of Asian and African peoples. Let me point to one example so you will understand that I am not Don Quixote chasing at windmills.

No less a person than the world-renowned British historian Arnold J. Toynbee, in his *A Study of History*,[5] has declared that of the several civilizations that he has perceived and recognized as such, none has been created by the black race. Now, it should be noted that in order to make this frequent condemnation of what Toynbee is pleased to call the black race, this spokesman of the British power structure finds it necessary to exclude from this black race the Dravidians, whose race is indeed the figment of his own imagination, because there is no such thing in life, in nature, as race in fact. There is only a race in the consciousness and idea of man. And race is a trap that very shortly we will have to dispense with if we are to find a basis for survival. For, with the development of racism, we are threatened with such human conflict, and with the means already developed for human destruction, such as atomic bombs and the like—who will be left? What race will be left? It seems none; therefore we had better begin to put our emphasis not upon race but upon the human species.

Toynbee had to explore the Dravidian people, most of whom are much darker in colour than this speaker or most of us in this room, perhaps any of us in this room, and then he went on to sever the Egyptians from the black race. So please mark that the Egyptians were a people who, in the main, came from the south of Egypt, that is from inner Africa. According to their own tradition they came from the south of Egypt and developed and maintained for thousands of years, four millennia at least, the most complex, luxurious, and happy way of life that the world has ever known. The Egyptians, then, were undeniably an African people of the most highly developed and astounding culture known up to their time, and who still compare favourably with any so-called civilization that has since been achieved. In light of the foregoing, then, permit me to flout and to bypass this racist trap called "civilization" and so deal with culture that is common to all mankind and that in no knowledgeable sense can be held to be basically different or inferior to what some Europeans blatantly boast of as their superior civilization.

Indeed, this attempt of modern, so-called civilized Western man to inflate his achievements at the expense of the accomplishments of early man must be seen as not only groundless, but utterly ungrateful, since those first early germinal culture inventions were not only far more difficult to accomplish but also represent the indispensable foundation of all the achievements of modern man, however great and marvelous. Most of us, it is to be hoped, will now be in a better position to survey the record of human culture and to appreciate the significant contribution of African people, beginning with the earliest known developments in antiquity.

As a result, for our development in what is known as the Judeo-Christian culture, most of us have been brought up on the legend of the Garden of Eden. This story of the Garden of Eden has been embellished, but nobody knows or could say exactly where this Garden of Eden was. Although, because of the story of the ark, it was guessed that after this flood that had destroyed everything except those that were in the ark, the ark is supposed to have rested on Mount Ararat. But that is a guess. It certainly is absolutely unproven. And then, certain scientists have assumed that man developed in Asia. But Darwin, the founder of the modern theory of evolution, pointed to Africa as the homeland of man, not as a statement of fact, but as an assumption, as a hypothesis that, according to modern developments, especially in the fields of archaeology and paleontology, has been proven to be correct.

Now, of a certain Archbishop Ussher in England, who worked out a fabulous chronology. If you open your Bible, especially the King James version, in the margins at the beginning of Genesis you will see the notation 4004 BC. According to this chronology that Archbishop Ussher gave us, man was created 4,004 years before the Christian era. In fact, Ussher even went on to tell us the exact moment, the day, and the hour at which all this happened. All of this is mythology and assumption with no basis whatsoever in fact. We come near to fact because of the discoveries that have been made rather recently by archaeologists, paleontologists, and anthropologists. We have the discoveries of Dart, Robinson, and Broom, for instance, of near-men—creatures who were very much like men but not yet men—that were made in South Africa.

And, following those discoveries, we have the clinching discoveries made by Dr. Louis S. B. Leakey at Olduvai Gorge in northern Tanzania of Zinjanthropus who, by the potassium-argon process, were shown to have been 1,750,000 years old. The name Zinjanthropus is coined from zin, an Arabic name meaning South Africa, south-eastern Africa, and anthropus, a Greek word meaning man. So, these fossil remains of man were called Zinjanthropus by Dr. Leakey. A number of pebble tools on the living floor were found near these fossil remains. And together with certain physical characteristics, the conclusion was made by Dr. Leakey and other scientists that Zinjanthropus was the first man. But this was based mainly on the tools that were found nearby the Zinjanthropus.

And meanwhile, Jane Goodall made some definitive studies of chimpanzees in Africa and discovered that the chimpanzees made tools. Tool-making could no longer be held to be a unique characteristic of man, since the chimpanzees also made a kind of tool. So, as a scientist, Dr. Leakey faced up to the situation and Zinjanthropus was put back in the classification of what are called the Australopithecines or near-men, but not men. However, Dr. Leakey went on to find other fossil remains on that living floor in Olduvai Gorge. And we must point out that Olduvai Gorge is part of that Great Rift Valley, which is the result of age-old volcanic eruptions in which the earth was torn asunder, and so, in Olduvai Gorge, you have what is almost like a layer cake, with the oldest layers being at bottom and the most current layers at the top. And on the lowest floor, called bed one, these findings were made and there Dr. Leakey discovered the remains of man, the oldest man known today, and called him Homo habilis. Homo is man, as you know, and habilis is clever. So, Homo habilis is clever man.

There we have these facts that indicate that Africa was the cradle of mankind, according to our knowledge today, [for] all of you, I don't care what your so-called colour may be. There is no such thing as a white person anyway. You are pinkish [*laughter*] or pale or yellowish or what not, but not white. Nobody is white and nobody is black like black shoes. See, we have developed these loose colour designations because of the racist domination of our culture and the dichotomy, which results from it, of division into so-called whites and so-called blacks. But all of us were nurtured in this cradle of mankind at Olduvai Gorge in Tanzania.

And here I wish to quote the statement of Dr. Leakey himself in his book, *The Progress and Evolution of Man in Africa*, published by the Oxford University Press. On page three Dr. Leakey states, "Africa's first contribution to human progress, then, was the evolution of man himself."[6] All that we are came out of Africa. Africa has made us, Africa has nurtured us. And not only man but man's culture. For man, as he becomes man, develops culture, a way of reacting to the universe, a way of fabricating and making things, a way of conceiving the universe. And we're beginning to discover that Africans developed philosophy—that is, some of us who have been brought up on the tradition that philosophy began with the Greeks.

Now Dr. Leakey continues:

> Leaving aside for a moment the progress made by man himself in Africa, let us look at what happened to development of his culture. Once man had taken the first vital step and had begun to make Oldowan tools, cultural progress seems to have been very slow for a while. At first indeed we can find little indication of any marked change in the cultural pattern.
>
> Nor is there much evidence that the earliest men in Africa carried their culture from this continent to other parts of the world, although there are some indications of a relatively early migration of the Oldowan culture into Portugal, while the earliest Asian Stone Age culture, the Soan, may possibly be a direct descendant of the Oldowan of Africa.[7]

It is clear then that the oldest known human culture is the Olduwan culture developed in Africa.

> . . . since there is available clear evidence to show that the Olduwan gave rise to the first stage of the Chellean and that, thereafter, the Chelles-Acheul culture developed all of its major stages in Africa, we may, I think, safely assume that the men who made the Chelles-Acheul culture, like the makers of the Oldowan, also originated in Africa.

Here we should point out that the so-called Chelles-Acheul has been named from the first site in which it was discovered by modern men, namely in

Chelles and Acheul in France. But as Leakey points out, subsequent discoveries have shown its development in Africa:

> Secondly, we know that throughout this Middle Pleistocene epoch, waves of migration were carrying the hand-axe culture from Africa to Europe, as well as to some parts of Asia. World progress, then, at this period also had its roots in Africa.[8]

Dr. Leakey then continues:

> There are people who believe that the "S twist" ovate constitutes some kind of projectile and that Europe can, therefore, be credited with the birth of the idea of making "weapons to attack from a distance".
>
> Whatever may eventually prove to be the truth about how "S twist" ovates were used, it nevertheless seems likely that the first true weapon for attack from a distance was invented by the makers of the hand-axe culture in Africa. This weapon was the bolas, which was evolved long before the "S twist" ovate. Once the bolas was developed, early man became a much more proficient hunter than he had been and we find the remains of many large animals on his living floors.
>
> Another important aspect of early human progress in the African continent was the invention and the perfection of the spear-head of stone—a type of weapon which appears much later in Europe and Asia. During the early part of the Upper Pleistocene (well before the laurel-leaf blades of the European Solutrean) the makers of the Sangoan culture in Africa were producing beautiful spear-heads of stone. These we find already well developed in Middle Sangoan times.

"It was shortly after this time—at the beginning of the Upper Pleistocene," according to Dr. Leakey, "that Africa ceased to play the dominant role in world progress, after having led for something like 600,000 years."[9] But Dr. Leakey is mistaken in that respect. Africa continued to play quite a role in the progress of mankind after that period, as has been indicated by Dr. J. Desmond Clarke in an article, "The Prehistoric Origins of African Culture," which he contributed to the *Journal of African History*. I cite:

> Artifacts of comparable age and form have been found at a few other sites, notably at Ain Hanech in Algeria, at Casablanca in Morocco, in the Albertine Rift, and at Kanam on the Kavirondo Gulf of Lake Victoria

(which yielded also an enigmatic hominid jaw fragment), as well as in residual gravels in rivers and marine high terraces. It would seem that if it is indeed in the East African tectonic region that tool-making first developed, it was not very long before such a fundamental advance in technology spread widely throughout and beyond the continent.[10]

Dr. Clarke also said,

By the beginning of the second glaciation in the northern hemisphere, there is substantial evidence that tool-making had spread throughout all the semi-arid regions of the continent and had overflowed into other parts of the Old World. The artifacts are still predominantly choppers, chopping tools, and work flakes, but they are now more shapely, show greater variety, and are generally more skillfully made, though still remaining remarkably crude in appearance. They represent the earliest stages of what is known as the Chelles-Acheul or Handaxe culture, the later name being derived from the commonest type of tool, roughly the shape of a hand when seen in silhouette, though the earliest examples are very crude and rare.

An evolved pebble culture of this time occurs outside Africa in the Jordan Valley [Moore: You know of course that the Jordan is a continuation of this rift development of which I spoke and the Jordan Valley is just east of Northern Africa, of Egypt for instance]. Closely related forms may be seen in the industries from the Choukoutien Cave near Peking and from South-East Asia. In Europe also it has been claimed that a pebble culture occurs with Heidelburg man in Mauer in Germany. In Africa, Europe, the Near East, and India, the Handaxe culture passed through remarkably similar evolutionary stages, and it seems probable that the populations of those continents [Moore: Please mark this.] were not as isolated as was at first supposed and that changes in culture as well as in the genotype were the outcome of free movement, exchange, and intercommunication.[11]

So, what is the gravamen of all that? It is that there is no such thing as a pure race; that man has been mixing and mating for centuries and that the idea of a pure race is pure moonshine. This is the scientific fact that emerges from this discussion.

There is one more quotation that I would like to make from Dr. J. Desmond Clarke and it is the following:

... the Middle Stone Age proper evolved from the Sangoan and Fauresmith after about 35,000 B.C. and ended about 8-10,000 B.C. There has for long been a tendency in Europe to refer to Africa after the end of the Middle Pleistocene as a cultural backwater. This was based initially on the fact that the earliest sapiens stock in Europe is associated with what we know as blade and burin, or Upper Palaeolithic, industries, which rather abruptly replaced the Neanderthal populations and the Mousterian culture there about 35,000 B.C. In Africa the prepared-core technique, Mousterian if you like, continued for further 25,000 years, and by inference drawn from the European association it was, therefore, considered that in Africa the Middle Stone Age was made by late surviving Neanderthalers. Radiocarbon and later discoveries show that this is not the case, and there is no evidence of any such time lag in the genotype as has been postulated. The reason for the survival of the prepared-core tradition is obviously that it was the most efficient for producing the specialized equipment that was required by a hunting people in tropical and sub-tropical environments.[12]

I think this indicates, then, the immense contribution made by Africa—that of man himself, that of early human culture in the very early period of the development of man. Let me indicate also that it is known that several land bridges connected Africa with Asia and with Europe and, therefore, it was very easy for man to migrate from Africa into Asia and Europe.

Now, the cradle of mankind, at Olduvai Gorge, as far as our knowledge now goes, is near the Great Lakes in East Africa, which are at the head waters of the Nile River, which flows for some four thousand miles until it debauches and flows into the Mediterranean Sea. Man doubtless has traveled in various directions and certainly down the banks of the Nile into Egypt and across the Sinai, the Isthmus of Suez, and the Sinai Peninsula into Asia. Moreover, there were two land bridges now sunken under the ocean that connected Africa with Europe. One of these connected what is now known as Tunisia with Sicily and with Italy, and the other land bridge was at the western end of the Mediterranean, across what is now known as the Strait of Gibraltar, a bridge that connected what is now known as Morocco with what has come to be known as the Iberian Peninsula of Spain and Portugal. Hence, man moved through all these bridges into Asia and into Europe.

African culture spread widely and certainly flourished and flowered in Egypt. But it has been the preposition of most European scholars to extract Egypt from [Africa] or it was impossible to them to concede that a civilization of the character of that developed in Egypt could possibly be developed by anybody but themselves. And so they had to take Egypt out of Africa and annex it to Europe. Does this sound fanciful to you? What did Hegel say? Hegel, one of the greatest of modern European historians and scholars, said: "Africa is still on the threshold of humanity, outside the historic compass."[13] And Hegel said Egypt is not African. It's not African, it's European. And this has been the refrain of most European historians. But Egypt is African. Geographically, Egypt is an essential and integral part of Africa situated in the northeast of the African continent. And the culture of Egypt is demonstrably, chiefly African. In the legend of Egyptian people, their tradition is that they came from the south, which is toward inner Africa. And students like Gerald Massey—a great English Egyptologist who has been disregarded by the general run of academic scholars in England because, in the first place, he knew too much and said too much for their liking—Gerald Massey amassed tremendous evidence in his tomes, *The Book of Beginnings*, *Natural Genesis*, and *Ancient Egypt: the Light of the World*. Go to the libraries and see if you can find these books and dig into them and you will see the evidence that Massey amounts there from mythology, from astronomy, from various sciences and disciplines, which showed that the culture of Egypt was essentially African. And I don't need to dwell on the accomplishments of Egypt because those I think are pretty widely known.

Most of the artifacts, the things that we use today in our culture, are developed from norms, from patterns that were created in Egypt. Chairs, for instance, and tables. Architecture, as you know, was developed and brought to great heights in Egypt. The Greek pantheon is a copy of basic Egyptian models. I haven't time to go into this at great length but let me point out that the greatest known thinkers of Greece—and not so much Greece either because most of them came from Ionia, which wasn't on the Greek mainland at all (it was in Asia Minor)—studied in Egypt. The first philosopher, Thales, was trained in Egypt; the first great law-giver Solon was likewise trained in Egypt; Pythagoras, great philosopher and musicologist, was also trained in Egypt. So too were Anaximander and Plato, by whom the modern world swears. Plato got his basic knowledge from the priests of Egypt, the thinkers of Egypt; and no less a person than Democritus who, according to European records, was the first European to talk about atoms, atoms which have become such a significant thing in modern life since we've learned how to smash the atoms. Well, we may smash ourselves in the process but, nonetheless, Democritus, who wrote about the atoms, was also trained in Egypt and doubtless he was taught about the atoms when he learned of the philosophy that was connected with the God Atum of Egypt. I'll let you think about that and maybe you'll have some questions to ask me about it. But there it is. [*Applause*]

Now, we also speak of the superior religion of Christianity, and we assume that this is European or at least Asian. But where indeed was the alembic—you know in chemistry they have an artifact that they call the alembic, where substances are brought together and fused and new things develop in the alembic. Well, the alembic was at Alexandria in Egypt, hence the Judaic thinkers and certain Greek thinkers who came in later, but basing themselves upon the African thinkers, the Egyptian thinkers, they formulated the basic philosophy for Christianity and then, following them, came three fathers of the Christian church: Tertullian, Cyphrian, and Augustine. These three are unquestionably among the greatest founding fathers of the Christian church. They were Africans and their basic philosophy was garnered from the African traditions.

We know of the development of culture to the west of Egypt, through North Africa, what is now Libya, Tunisia, on to Morocco. We know of Carthage, which was founded as a colony by the Phoenicians, but which was based in the main upon African elements. And we have knowledge, perhaps the greatest military genius that the world has ever produced, namely Hannibal of Carthage, who performed that feat of scaling the Alps with elephants and who was defeated by Rome, finally, only because of treachery at home, chiefly among the Phoenicians and some of the Numidians. But we have these cultural developments in North Africa, so there is a tremendous development there about which we need to inform ourselves.

We will pass south now through the Sahara Desert: It wasn't always desert, you know. Prior to the Ice Age the Sahara was green and fertile. And we have found—at least Henri Lhote has found—at various points in the Sahara paintings, very old paintings, which indicate the culture existed in the Sahara before it became desiccated. And there are pictures of chariots driving through the Sahara, horse drawn chariots. There was then this great culture in the Sahara and south of the Sahara in the savannah area, which has been called the Sudan by the Arabs, Bilad as-Sudan, meaning land of the blacks, but not Negroes. Bare it in mind, Arabs did not know anything about Negroes. They simply used black as a colour designation and not as a racial classification. So there has been communication between North Africa and Africa, which is called Africa south of the Sahara, unbroken, really, for centuries. And in the Sudan, there developed, from the third century onward, kingdoms and empires, the first being Ghana, after which the present Ghana has been renamed. And here I would like to digress for a moment to indicate why names are important, because I meet people who confront me with the most stupid kind of statements. A quotation from Shakespeare: "What's in a name? A rose by any other name would smell as sweet." But the thing that distinguishes the rose is its smell, right?

The name is associated with the smell, which is the dominant thing. But when a name is given to human beings by slave masters for the purpose of maintaining their slave system, these names become symbols of actions, of attitudes, of thoughts, and finally of destruction, oppression. And we have the development of names like Negro and people say, "What difference does that make? Why do you make so much stress upon a name?" A name is a handle. It is a symbol which tells people how to treat you, and Negro tells them to treat you like a slave, like an inferior savage and beast. [*Applause*] And a whole system of psychology has been developed, and every time their Negro becomes a little bit weak in its vicious connotations, they inject some more of it, [*applause*] as during the Reconstruction period when those southern former slave holders wanted to maintain the institution to the extent they could; they wanted to drive even the few Afro-Americans who were in politics out of politics, they wanted to drive them out of office, and they wanted to disfranchise them, to take the vote from them. Negro, then, got another vicious injection. Negro became synonymous with beasts.

If you doubt me, get a copy of *Race, Class, and Party* by Lewinson.[14] You will see reproduced one of those cartoons, which were widely spread in their newspapers, of this Negro and a brute, a beast who had to be destroyed. What irks me with some people is that they can insist on names of honour and dignity for themselves and they want to push this confounded vicious slave terminology on us. [*Applause*] Well, I can tell you that this book, *The Name "Negro": Its Origins and Evil Use*, has done its work.[15] And the young people now, they've got it in their own consciousness. You better not call these young Afro-Americans or Afro-Canadians or whatever they may be, you better not call them Negroes. [*Applause*] So much for this name business, we get back now to the culture.

You can understand now why, for instance, when the people [in] the area that had been designated the Gold Coast by the British colonialists, because it was a coast on which they got gold, when they became free and independent they immediately changed that name and took the old honourable name of Ghana. [*Applause*] And I say one of the key things that people of African descent in the so-called New World will have to do will be to reject this slave name Negro and to adopt Afro-American, Afro-Canadian, indicating our African origins of which we have no need whatsoever to be ashamed. [*Loud applause*]

In the Sudan, south of the Sahara, there developed these fine cultures. And perhaps some of you will be surprised to know that when a Muslim traveler known as Ibn Battuta went through the Sudan in the fourteenth century he wrote, "men have no reason to fear robbers or violence," a condition flourished then, a condition of real culture, of high culture. Our young friend[16] has made some reference to that this morning, I don't think I need to develop it. But we had such high culture in that area that there developed in the capital city of Timbuktu at the University of Sankore the studies of religion, philosophy, law, and surgery and medicine to a high point of development. They performed operations on the human eye in Timbuktu, in Ghana in the fourteenth century.

[*In response to an inaudible question from the audience Moore replies:* "Of course it's in Africa." *Again, in response to the same person, Moore says:* "I'm reminded that Timbuktu is a glorious city of Africa. Of course, it was the capital of these states: of Mali, of Ghana, and then of the Songhai Empire. You may pursue this study further. There is a good study made of them in *The History of West Africa*[17] by Basil Davidson or in similar books."]

Now, the basis of the commerce, of the trade and commerce of these kingdoms, was on the exchange of salt for gold. Salt was mined in the north and exchanged for the gold that was produced toward the south. And it was a very ingenious system of development, highly developed statecraft is indicated. If we look into West Africa a little bit for the development of culture, we find a very early development of what is known as the Nok culture, which seems to be the forerunner of the cultures developed at Benin. There were developed highly structured forms of art, especially by the lost wax process; the French call it the *cire perdue* process. So, you have these bronze sculptures of great beauty that were made in Benin, and sculptures in Yoruba, which have now been rediscovered by Europeans and they have influenced such modern painters as Picasso, Modigliani, and others. These cultures existed for centuries in this area.

If now we go to the Congo, we find, prior to the Europeans, a high development of culture in the Congo. A recent book, *Daily Life in the Kingdom of the Kongo* by Georges Balandier, indicates the character of this culture, this culture that existed before the Europeans got to the Congo.[18] Moreover, let me introduce you to a German anthropologist who made many trips into Africa, who did considerable fieldwork in various areas of Africa. His name was Leo Frobenius. Unfortunately, his major works have not been completely translated into English, but his work on the history of African civilization has been translated into French,[19] and from the preface of this, a translation of a part was made by Anna Melissa Graves and also by Dr. Du Bois. And you will a find a statement of this in the book *The World and Africa* by Dr. Du Bois, in which Frobenius tells us that when the Europeans arrived in Africa and landed at Vaida, they found streets well laid out, bordered on either side by two rows of trees, people garbed in beautiful robes, and in the Congo, similarly clad in silks and velvets made from raffia. And in Mozambique, a similar thing; each pipe, each cup, each spoon decorated[20]—truly human culture. This existed in Africa for centuries prior to the arrival of Europeans.

Frobenius laments, the Europeans destroyed this culture considerably as they penetrated into Africa. And what was the main modus, the main means by which this destruction of African culture was accomplished? It was the slave trade, and the slave trade was possible because of guns, superior weapons in the hands of the European intruders and invaders. There is no question about this. The slave trade tore millions of our people out of Africa. Think what would happen to Western society, to the Americas for instance, if fifty to sixty million people were torn away, taken out of these cultures during a period of a century or two. There would be the same kind of decline that took place in Africa. And remember that for every slave who got through to work on a plantation in the New World, there were at least six, seven, or eight who perished in the process of capture and transmission, and the middle passage, that horrible passage on board the slave ships.

It must be noted here because there has been an attempt on the part of [people]—well I don't want to characterize them too harshly, but I will say that they are "misleaders"—to put the onus for the slave trade on the African kings. I'm not relieving African kings of their responsibility, but their responsibility was minor. The major responsibility was on the Europeans who very frequently would only give firearms in exchange for slaves and, since firearms had become the necessary means for maintaining the independence of the state, in order to get the firearms, African kings gave the Europeans the slaves in exchange. And this, I believe, is one of the greatest tragedies of history: the slave trade and the European invasion, the colonialist suppression of the African peoples.

With this decline of African culture there was not a complete succumbing, fortunately. Certain African modes and customs were maintained. Our young friend [Walter Rodney] I think has told you of some of them. The attitude toward the aged for instance, toward elders. You know, when I first arrived and listened to the statements in the opening session of this congress, I became quite disturbed for a while. I felt superannuated—no longer any place for an old man like me. But this morning, I'm encouraged by the statement of our young collaborator who indicates that the African culture emphasizes the significance of the old in their culture.

And I would adjure our young Afro-Canadian or Afro-American brothers not to be too precipitous, not to assume that all who preceded them were Uncle Toms. Because we are not, we haven't been. [*Applause*] Yes, many of us [are] overborne and there were some Uncle Toms to be sure, although this isn't quite the term. The horrible character was not Uncle Tom; Uncle

Tom was whipped to death because he would not reveal the place at which a slave was hiding. He was whipped to death on that score. Rather it was Quashie who whipped Uncle Tom to death, he was the creature who ought to be reviled. Anyway, the fact must now be made known that Africans did not succumb to European domination, to colonialist exploitation, except when overborne by *force majeure*, and that here in the New World they revolted; Africans fought against European enslavement in Africa and on ships. You should know of the revolts, for instance, on the Amistad led by Cinque and others, and that was only one of many. The first Africans brought to the New World were brought in 1502 to what is now called the Dominican Republic, and a few years later there is a record of a rebellion at the mill at Diego Colon. And the Africans were said to teach bad manners to the indigenous population, misnamed Indians by Columbus. What were the bad manners? They taught them to fight, to revolt against their oppression. [*Applause*] So, Africans came into this hemisphere fighting and we've been fighting ever since. [*Applause*]

And this struggle will not cease, because there is something within the heart and mind of people of African descent, as there is in all human beings, to oppose enslavement, to oppose indignity, to demand human recognition and human status. [*Loud and extended applause*] I think this is a point at which I might conclude these remarks on African culture, to indicate that this culture has made tremendous contributions to the development of mankind and that through the last five centuries this culture has very largely been overborne, [but] that it now rises again. Even the British prime minister spoke about the winds of change that were blowing through Africa. We know, of course, of the development of a vicious and pernicious system of neo-colonialism which is at work to undermine and to destroy African independence. [*Applause*] We have seen it at work in the Congo where the Republic of the Congo was dismembered and destroyed and the great leader, Patrice Lumumba, foully murdered. [*Applause*] A man who had quite a part in this foul tragedy is now head of Columbia University, [Andrew W.] Cordier. [*Applause*] This is the man they think will settle the situation [at Columbia]. They propose to settle it with bloody terror. You can kill a certain number of people, but you can't destroy the will to freedom in man.[21] [*Applause*]

We have seen it at work, too, in Algeria, even after that long travail of the Algerian people, who for eleven years fought against French imperialism, giving the best of their sons in that struggle. We saw Ben Bella removed [and] we haven't heard anything more about him. Why? Because Ben Bella had offered troops to aid the liberation of the people in Angola and the Mozambique. Ben Bella had to be removed and was. We have seen also that as soon as the great African, pan-African genius Kwame Nkrumah [*applause*] turned his back on British-trained military figures, figures indeed because they were manipulated, carried through a coup and then they turned over the major industries that had been developed by the Ghanaian people and for the Ghanaian people, in their effort to achieve African socialism. They turned over those great industries and the Black Star Line and the Volta River Project to alien European and European-American interests.

We have seen this operation of neo-colonialism in Africa and we see that in the people of Angola and Mozambique, and what has been falsely called Rhodesia, but is properly called Zimbabwe. [*Applause*] And Zimbabwe is an indication of the great cultures developed in Africa, for their stone structures held together without any cement—tremendous structures. One of them has been called the Acropolis. Now, you don't call a structure the Acropolis, you don't give it the name of this great European thing if it isn't significant. We've had these great cultures there, but the people of Zimbabwe are held under the iron heal of the murderous Ian Smith and his regime. [*Applause*]

And, worst of all, we have the most abominable and atrocious system of oppression that has ever cursed mankind—apartheid rule in South Africa—dominating the majority of African people in their own land and denying them even the right to use the name African. They are called perhaps Bantu and Kaffirs, and the Afrikaner, as he calls himself, has stolen the name of African for himself. He is now the Afrikaner, the man of Africa. And we see Luthuli, the president of the African National Congress who was given the Nobel Peace Prize for his non-violent attitude, we saw his body was found on a railroad track, murdered by the apartheid beasts that now rule and desecrate South Africa. Culture requires the removal of the bandits who suppress culture and the time has come for men of good will everywhere to take a position against this system of colonialism, of neo-colonialism, and of the suppression of man by man. [*Extended applause*]

ROCKY JONES: There is nothing I need to say We're going to allow audience participation, but believe you me, it's going to be different this morning than it was before. There will be no one allowed to advance any type of thesis whatsoever from this mike. You may come up, you may ask a question, and then you go back and sit down. The floor is now open.

MOORE: I'm ready for you. Come along.

QUESTION: It is very unwise of me to come along and ask this question after the last speech, but I just want to ask the last speaker whether he's aware [of] a form of writing, in existence before the invasion of West Africa. Also, whether he's aware there is a form of money that was being used, and that the use of money was not taken to Africa by the Europeans. Third, the point about the slave trade: Most of the slaves were got from certain parts of Africa but I wonder whether he was aware that further on somewhere in the West African coast there are still in existence slave posts and dungeons where these people were kept until they were being shipped and, therefore, that the impression that the bulk of slaves were sold by their own relatives was a distortion of the truth.

MOORE: Yes, we are aware that there had been forms of writing that existed in Africa and were developed there. In fact, the writing that is now used by Europeans, the alphabet, is derived from the Phoenician alphabet, which in turn was derived from the Sinaitic writing script, which in turn was derived from Egyptian hieroglyphics. And if you wish to get documentation about this, you might consult *Egypt of the Pharaohs* by Allan Gardiner,[22] and a book by Albright,[23] on the cultures of the Near East. Moreover, the Vai, in what is now called Liberia, developed a system of writing of their own; this was subsequent to the arrival of Europeans but it's their invention. As to money, of course money was known and used in Africa long before the coming of the Europeans. This was implicit in my statement about the trade, the commerce existing between North Africa and the African empires in the Sudan. Cowries, cowry shells were one form of currency; gold, gold ingots were another form of currency. The Ashanti had their own weights for measuring and weighing gold and all this is a matter of record.

I might point out that Frobenius made it clear in his statement that the notion that West African culture derived from Muslims is false. And, as a matter of fact, in most of the West African states the rulers were only nominal Muslims and many of them were not even Muslims at all. They still adhered to the ancient African traditions of religion.

After the slave trade, certainly there are certain forts and fortresses, which still exist. One of them was taken over by Kwame Nkrumah and, in fact, he established his residence within one of these fortresses. I think I made it sufficiently clear that, while African kings were involved in the slave trade, they were not primarily responsible for it, although they had a degree of responsibility. I might indicate that one of the greatest slave traders in East Africa was an African, Tippu Tib, who was a Muslim and, therefore, we can't swallow this notion that the Muslims are so pure or purer than the Christians. Six of one, half dozen of the other, in so far as we are concerned from the historic record.

And the philosophy of Africans is more and more coming to be recognized. For instance, a French anthropologist among the Dogon people in West Africa conducted conversations for a long period with an African sage—one of the wise old men of that area is called Ogotemmeli.[24] And from him he received a statement of their philosophy that is [part of] the development of that culture. Moreover, Father Tempel, a priest in the Congo, has also come to know of a certain philosophy of Bantu-speaking people and he has written a book or a pamphlet on it that has been published by Presence Africaine,[25] so there are all these evidences of significant phases of African culture that we can't subsume in a single lecture but will become apparent to you as you continue some inquiries into this matter, and I hope you will do so.

QUESTION: I'd like to know what you think about the situation we as black people have found here in this black congress, gathered with the picture of Brother Malcolm X, and those going against the grain of [inaudible] philosophy, everything it is based on. We at the congress gathered [inaudible] to discuss black liberation.

MOORE: I'm very glad that you put that question, because it is, in the first place, important to understand the workings of this colour division to which I referred earlier in my discourse. Not every person who has a pale skin is an enemy of ours. [*Applause*] Some of the most indomitable fighters for the liberation of people of African descent have been Europeans or of European descent, like John Brown.

SOMEONE FROM THE AUDIENCE: That's the only one?

MOORE: No brother, [there are] many others: William Lloyd Garrison, Wendell Phillips, and thousands who aided in the underground railroad to pass fugitive slaves, at the risk of their lives and their fortunes, from one spot to the other. I am not saying that we cannot meet among ourselves, if we so desire, to discuss certain things. But this is a public congress. This is not now a conclave for the purpose of, let us say, developing an inner program. This is a public congress for the purpose of making clear to the world at large where we stand, and so we welcome people who are interested enough to come and hear, and those who want to fight with us—more power to them. I can't go for this racist nonsense that you've got to consider every person with a pale skin an enemy.

Look man, let's get down to brass tacks. Whom do you consider Tshombe, an enemy or a friend or a soul brother? Tshombe is one of the most dastardly enemies of the African people who ever came down the pipe. [*Applause*] And Tshombe certainly isn't any white person. Tshombe is black. The colour of skin doesn't determine how you think and how you feel, and we have to understand that we have to unite ourselves, of course, as people of African descent who have special oppressions, but we have to maintain the possibility of entering into alliances with those who are willing to fight with us even part way. Even part way, even part way. [*Applause*]

QUESTION: The point we are trying to make here is that when a white man sees a black man he doesn't consider the black man's philosophy. He could be a socialist, he could be a communist, all the white man sees is black and that's where we are at. But when we see a white man, we have first to consider his philosophy—we don't ask whether he is communist, socialist—the point is, once he acts liberal we accept him. Well, days for that are over. When a white man comes to our meetings our philosophy is—and when I say "our" I mean we of the Black Liberation Action Committee—to get him out and when he wants to fight, then he can organize with the white people and fight against white people because it's white people who need fighting against. [*Applause*] So when we have a black congress, I expect that the hall will be filled with more black people than white people because it is not the white people who need to get together, it's the black people. [*Applause*]

MOORE: Well, my young friend, expectations are one thing and achievements are another. And if there is a minority of people of African descent in our audience here, in participation in this Congress of Black Writers, where does the fault lie? You see, we can't condemn those who are interested enough who are not of African descent. In fact, what am I talking about not of African descent? You are all of African descent. You don't know it, but all that I said this morning indicates that you are of African descent. [*Applause*] So, we have to teach you.

And the point is that I'm not sold, as the vernacular has it, on the idea, I don't believe we can adopt a philosophy that puts us in opposition to every person whose skin is paler than ours. After all, we are a minority in this culture and we have to be sure to organize ourselves on the basis of people who have a special disability but who have the right to organize, and this must be recognized by all other people. We will do that and must do that, but, at the same time, we will not consider every person of paler skin an enemy, we will deal with them as they deal with us, as human beings who are concerned about a better future for all of us. After all, we don't live in this world by ourselves and, while we need to consider our own position, develop our own philosophy, and have our own leaders, we are men among other men. And we have to deal with them in order to obviate, for all of us, the holocaust of total destruction that faces us. [*Applause*] And that's it.

ROCKY JONES: Because of the time element involved we can't accept any more questions so I'll allow the brother to have the final word.

WALTER RODNEY: I think this is crucial, so I'll have to say a word or two. The trouble is that I have a slight disagreement with this brother.[26] That's fine, that's a brother. Really, what we ought to be doing—and that's why I'm with the brother there—fundamentally, we ought to be talking among ourselves as blacks. It doesn't really matter, then, what types of disagreements [we may have], we formulate things among ourselves. We are creating something, we are talking to each other. For years, black people haven't talked to other black people, they've talked to whites and say, "Look, here am I. This is what I am." Even the history bit was addressed originally to whites, saying, "I'm not all that bad. I've had a history." That is out. We are talking to each other. [*Short applause*]

That's why I started out by saying I find myself in the objective position where whites are present but I'm talking to blacks, I would like to communicate, I would like to get a dialogue [with blacks]. And if whites are here, well, for the time being, that represents the fact that this particular situation in Montreal hasn't developed to the point, because if it was held in Washington, I don't think they would even have gone, you see, but this hasn't developed. However, I'll make a general statement about this white friends and white enemies. At least I'll have to put my position over.

I feel that it isn't that every white man is an enemy, but every white man is an enemy until proven otherwise. [*Applause*] This is the point so that, as far as I am concerned, I look around me, I see enemies. They are involved in my objective oppression. Let me give a concrete illustration.

I come from Guyana. Alcan Jamaica and Alcan from Guyana, these are Canadian-American companies. They take our bauxite, they process it, they provide a standard of living at Arvida[27] and in Canada that is five times, six times, ten times as high as the standard of living of the black workers in my country. Every white Canadian who lives off the profits of that company is my oppressor, objectively. [*Applause*] Now, what happens is this: A white is going to look at me and see me as I see myself. I am going to define it. This is crucial, and we can only define this among ourselves, first and foremost, because there is too much intervention, all the while, you're too aware that the man is present.

For me, I think I'm happy that I have got beyond that. You know I see you people and I don't see you. I see some black faces and I'm talking to them. But not all of us have reached that level of development, so it interferes, you know, a lot of static gets in the way. And that is why we, perhaps, have to resort to the elementary device of retiring to caucus and say, "Well, look, let us examine things now." You see, we have to define the position. It is no use talking about a white friend or a white ally. To ally with what? To aid what? We must define what is to be done. When we define it, we can see if there is an ally. If, for example, we say, "What we need is to fight, what we need is to obtain guns"—this is what Cleaver told them, you know. When the white guy got up, Cleaver just shocked him. He says, "How can we help the black people?" You know this meager and pious attitude, and Cleaver told them, "Well, go get some guns and shoot up some white people." And so the guy nearly wet himself.

We must define. This may sound crude, but it is a concrete reality. I mean, take the Rhodesian-South African situation today. There is clearly no other avenue but struggle in southern Africa. Let's just forget this continent for the moment. I've been to [see] some white liberals who are against apartheid. When they analyze the whole situation, when they see the absolute necessity for the black people to struggle, they don't carry out the logical conclusion and say, "I personally will prepare to fight and shoot whites for black humanity and for our common humanity." They don't carry out . . . that is the logical conclusion that you should reach to. And now, until [a] white is engaged in that process with me, he's an enemy. [*Applause*]

A white man in this society—let me talk to whities now, if we have to talk to whites—what I say to you is this: You sit in this society and if you want to ally with me you have to say for yourself, "Look, I don't like this society. This society derogates from my dignity as a white man. I suffer in the process. I am castrated. I cannot be creative in this type of philistine society. I want to break with Canadian and American imperialism." Free yourself, you know, brother. I could call you brother now, that's biological in the widest sense, you know, [*laughter*] and we all descend, we all come way down from Olduvai Gorge, so let's say brothers now. We haven't talked about soul this time, just brothers, right? [*Laughter*]

If you want to get with us, you have to see yourself. Forget us for the moment, forget us. See yourself. Look around you and look around the whole world and see whether you think that, as a human being, you are maximizing your potential, whether there is something inside of you which is a little better than the rest of the mammals, the other species, whether just by creating these concrete structures, you have maximized it, if that's enough. You ask it and if you decide that you want to tear it down then you will move with us. And when I see the evidence that you are tearing it down, I say, "That's a friend." But otherwise, sorry. In fact, I'm not sorry. You're an enemy. That's how it is, you know.

So, I have to disagree, as I said, with my brother. Unfortunately, I have to disagree in this type of context. I would prefer to do it among other black brothers, so we see together where we are going. But if it has to come out, that's how it is. For a lot of us that's how it is. All right. [*Extended applause*]

ROCKY JONES: Okay. We've got a real dilemma. On one hand, I have got the steering committee and the organizers of the conference telling me that we've got other speakers to follow and I've got to break it up so that we can reconvene in fifteen minutes. On the other hand, I've got all kinds of participants in a conference saying they want to talk. As chairman that puts me in a very awkward position and I think it should be up to this body to resolve it. Is that fair with you? I want to ask this body: do we continue this discussion or do we close it off now?

A RESPONSE FROM THE AUDIENCE: If we close now, this question is going to come up in every caucus, in every little meeting we have; at every little discussion this question is going to come up over and over and over, so we had better resolve it today sometime, because we are having a whole day again tomorrow.

SECOND AUDIENCE RESPONSE: There is an instrument whereby we get together in caucus, during workshops, and at black caucus every evening after each day. I presume that at such a time this type of closed deliberation will be quite appropriate. But we do have a program and unless you are prepared to push this right until five, we'll have to stop.

ROCKY JONES: Can I just see the hands of all those people who want to stay now? That's it, we're breaking it up. We'll reconvene back in this room at twenty minutes past, which is going to give you a fifteen-minute break, because we're way behind.

Chapter 6

BLACK HISTORY IN THE AMERICAS

RICHARD B. MOORE

'VE BEEN IMPRESSED in the place of Mr. LeRoi Jones to deal with this topic. I'm afraid I'm a poor substitute for Mr. Jones. In the first place, our age levels are a little different, and I suppose our approaches would be a little different. But, in any case, the subject is the same. Now, it has been customary for historians in the United States to begin what they were pleased to call "the History of the Negro in the United States" with the arrival of twenty "neegars" at Jamestown, Virginia, in 1619. However, this is certainly a misstatement of the historical fact. In the first place, America cannot be limited to the United States of America. The term America actually relates to both continents, North and South and Central America, and to the islands adjacent there, too. So, we have the arrival of people of African descent, perhaps with the navigator Alonso Niño on the flagship of Columbus, Santa Maria, in that voyage of so-called discovery of America. Some people are always discovering something that doesn't need to be discovered, because it was there and there were people there long before their so-called discovery.

Shortly after the arrival of Colon—who is called Columbus in English—in 1492, Africans were brought into the so-called New World to what is now the Dominican Republic. An edict to allow this was issued by the rulers of Spain, Ferdinand and Isabella, late in 1501. But it appears these first Africans arrived in early 1502. They were brought in ostensibly to toil on the plantations and later I shall deal with their reaction to this.

Now, I will point out that in the settlement and discovery, in the settlement and colonization of America—of the Americas to make it clear—people of African descent were present in all the major developments. Africans were with [Vasco Núñez de] Balboa. They largely were responsible for the ships Balboa used. They were with [Hernando] Cortez, and, in fact, one of these Africans brought into the Americas the disease of small pox, which had developed among the Europeans, which was an uncowered contribution to be sure. But another of the Africans who were brought in grew the first wheat in the western hemisphere, and wheat, you know, is an important staple element in the human diet, certainly in the diet of European-Americans.

Africans were with [Francisco] Pizarro in Peru (in what is now Peru). In North America, one of the outstanding discoverers, so-called, was Estevanico, or Little Steven, who was the slave of [Alvar Núñez] Cabeza de Vaca and who was with an expedition that was shipwrecked and somehow they managed to survive (I think four of them, including Estevanico, survived), and, finally, Estevanico was sent ahead of an expedition from Mexico to what are now known as the Zuni Indians, indigenous people. And so, he became what has been called the discoverer of what is now Arizona and New Mexico.

In the trek westward there were numerous Afro-Americans who played significant roles, like James P. Beckwourth, who discovered the best route through the Sierra mountains onto the west. There was York, a powerful African who, by his physique and his mental equipment, was quite effective in gaining the friendship and respect of the indigenous people. In the founding and settlement of the west, there were figures in the north-west, for instance, and in California [William Alexander] Leidesdorff developed the first horse racing and made quite a number of contributions in San Francisco. An engineer in southern California made significant contributions there. And so, in this whole process of the settlement and colonization of what is now the United States, Afro-Americans played a significant role.

In the fields of invention and science, significant contributions have been made by Afro-Americans. Many of you are familiar with the contributions made by Dr. George W. Carver in discovering over 100 uses for and derivatives from the peanut. But not so many are acquainted with the work and contribution of Banneker, Benjamin Banneker, who in the pre-revolutionary and revolutionary period of the United States was a scientist of repute. He made the first clock striking the hours in North America; he published almanacs for some eleven years; he was among the scientists who surveyed and laid out the capital of the United States; and when L' Enfant, who was the chairman of that commission, left and went back to Paris in a huff, it was Benjamin Banneker who was able to carry through the work of surveying and planning what is now Washington, D.C. The capital building of Washington, D.C, the dome, involved the work of a highly skilled artisan who was an Afro-American.

There are a number of other inventions but let me mention just a few. One of the most significant inventions in America history, unquestionably, has been the invention of the vacuum pan, which was invented by Norbert Rillieux, an Afro-American in Louisiana. He had gone to Paris and studied at the Sorbonne, had taught there, and he developed this process, a chemical-engineering process, for reducing sugar. Prior to that, it was necessary to use large gangs of labour to ladle the juice of the sugar cane from one station to another, until finally the process of refining was complete. This vacuum pan eliminated all that labour and revolutionized the methods of producing cane sugar. It also revolutionized methods in other industries, such as glue and so on, so that this was a significant contribution.

Likewise, in the field of invention, we have the contribution of Jan Matzeliger, who invented a shoe-lasting machine, a machine for attaching the sole to the upper of the shoe, a process that involved much skilled work of artisans. And this invention of Matzeliger became the foundation of the United Shoe Machinery Corporation, and the shoes you wear today are made on a machine, the basic patent and invention of which was that of Jan Matzeliger. He died rather poor, however, although fortunes were made in the business of manufacturing shoes as a result of his invention. There are many others that I don't have time to mention, so I will shift now to medicine and surgery.

I suppose many of you have been concerned recently about the operations that are being made on the human heart, the transplanting of the organ of the human heart in South Africa. It's interesting to note that one of these transplants involves a heart that was taken from a so-called coloured South African and transplanted into the body of a white South African. And we learn, too, of the transplantation of kidneys from coloured South Africans to white South Africans. So, it begins to appear as if a new function has been developed for people of colour, so-called, namely to furnish organs for the superior whites. [*Applause and laughter*] Well, this bears looking into and anything is likely to happen under apartheid. However, it was Dr. Dan, Daniel H. Williams, who performed the first-known operation on the human heart in Provident Hospital, a hospital that he himself had organized and developed because, due to the prejudice that existed in Chicago, it was impossible for Afro-American physicians to be allowed to practice in hospitals dominated by the European power structure. So, Dr. Williams developed the Provident Hospital and at this hospital he performed the first-known successful operation on the human heart.

In the field of bacteriology, there is the development of William Hinton, who developed a test for syphilis superior to the Wasserman test, and, in a similar field, we have the significant contribution of Charles R. Drew who developed the blood bank—the method of preserving human blood so that it would be available when needed for transfusion to patients who needed it. This was an important and significant breakthrough in medical knowledge and technique.

Dr. Drew developed the blood bank and it is interesting to note that, although he was head of the organization for the development of the blood bank, the American Red Cross prohibited people of African descent from giving blood that might be used for transfusion to European-Americans, who had some notion, you see, that blood had something to do with sex and if they got what they would call "black blood" into their veins, something might happen to transform them! [*Laughter*] This of course is fallacious. Blood has nothing to do with sex *per se*. The organisms that have to do with that have nothing to do with blood, except that the whole body is nourished by the circulation of blood. But in spite of this, Dr. Drew continued to develop the blood bank system that made it possible to save the lives of hundreds of thousands of soldiers in World War Two, and of other human beings.

It really is worth thinking about that this man, Dr. Drew, who made such a significant contribution to the saving of human life by the creation of the blood bank, was allowed himself to bleed to death in the South when, as a result of an automobile accident, he would not be admitted at the nearest hospital because of the prejudice against colour that exists in the United States, and particularly in the South. Here are some contributions then that are quite significant. [*Someone in the audience*: "And Canada?"] And Canada? That is what we call an addendum. But I want to pass on to what I think are the more significant—or before I reach that I must deal with—contributions in literature, in music, and in the arts. (You are more or less familiar with some of these.)

You know, of course, that Afro-Americans have contributed music beginning with the spirituals, ragtime, jazz, and bee bop and what not. But of course, much of this has been taken over by European-Americans, so much so that Langston Hughes had to write the line, "You took my blues and gone." Now this contribution in music, of course, is parallel to the contributions of dance and rhythm, and we have in literature, from the beginning of the United States—even in the pre-colonial period of the United States—the writings of Jupiter Hammon, Phillis Wheatley, and, of course, we have the poets later like Paul L. Dunbar and Claude McKay, who might be called a herald of the cultural renaissance of which Harlem was the focal point during the 1920s. Claude McKay wrote, among other fine poems, that great stirring poem "If We Must Die." Incidentally, this poem was used by none other than Winston Churchill in an appeal for support of the war against the Nazis. Churchill didn't have, what shall I call it? He didn't have the breadth, the largeness of soul even to indicate the name of the author of the poem. But he did use it effectively in his appeal in respect to that war. I suggest that you familiarize yourself with that poem. You will find it in the book *Harlem Shadows* by Claude McKay. Writers like Langston Hughes, Rudolph Fisher, and others developed in that period, and in literature we have had the contributions of Richard Wright with *Native Son* and *Black Boy*, and many other writers with whom some of you are doubtless familiar.

But the contribution that I think has been the most significant of Afro-Americans in American history has been the contribution in the struggle for democracy. Now, democracy is something talked about in America. In fact, it is projected as the unique and specific contribution of America to the world. And democracy is understood to mean the rule of the people, but somehow during the long span of the history of the United States, democracy has been more honoured in the breach than in the observance. And so, the record of the Afro-Americans in the struggle for democracy becomes one of the most significant contributions to American life and history. And this, as I pointed out when I spoke before, began back there in 1511, when the slaves revolted on the plantations of Diego Columbus and went off and joined the indigenous people, who are miscalled Indians, and united with them in a struggle against slavery. They formed a number of communities that were called Maroons—(*Cimarron* in French and then the English called them Maroons)—in which they established themselves, developing communities.

Outstanding among these communities was the community developed in Jamaica. The Maroons fought and compelled the British government to enter into a treaty with them, recognizing their independence in those communities. In Guyana, which was dominated by the Dutch, a similar development took place and the revolting Maroons established themselves in the hinterland in communities such as the Djuka and the Saramaka and they developed communities that they ruled with their own statecraft. They used cultural traditions and cultural elements that they had brought with them from Africa; they used this to maintain themselves. In fact, when some Europeans managed to get into these communities—and they couldn't get there unless they were taken by these Africans, because they alone at that time could forge the rapids of the rivers—the Europeans had no craft and no method of doing this.

Now, of course, Europeans can get into these communities from the air by airplane. At that time, however, the revolted people of African descent in Guyana forced the Dutch to recognize their independence and to give them a supply of firearms once a year. Quite interesting, isn't it? Well, they maintained their communities for a long while. There was a similar community developed in Brazil, in Palmares. And there again, you see the methods of statecraft of an African character used to weld a community, to govern it adequately, so that these contributions indicate the significant struggles made by people of African descent in the Americas.

When we come to the American revolution of 1776, it is not known that the first bloodshed in that revolutionary struggle was that of Crispus Attucks, an Afro-American. And some five thousand Afro-American soldiers fought in the revolutionary conflict, even though, at first, they were not wanted by the European-American revolutionaries. As a matter of fact, the founding fathers of the United States Republic decided not to admit Afro-Americans into the army and this was only changed after the British general issued a proclamation promising freedom to all people of African descent who fought in the British army. And thousands of people of African descent who wanted freedom fought for the British. A number of them were later brought by the British to Nova Scotia, here in Canada. But this forced the hands of the American revolutionary leaders and so they themselves then had to enlist Afro-Americans in the revolutionary war and, at Bunker Hill and Concord and various other battles, the Afro-Americans distinguished themselves valiantly in this struggle. In the War of 1812, when it was necessary to fight against the British invasion of that period, most of the sailors, in fact a large number of the sailors, were Afro-Americans. In the battle of Lake Erie, they fought with [Commodore Oliver] Perry and others.

Now, the abolition struggle, the struggle to abolish chattel slavery, was a conflict that achieved its significant dimensions only when Afro-Americans entered it. This fact is vouched for by Henry Wilson in *The History of the Rise and Fall of the Slave Power in America*. In those three massive tomes, Wilson gives the history of that struggle and shows that when Frederick Douglass—who had escaped from slavery in Maryland and who joined the abolitionist in Massachusetts—this was the emergence of the slave himself in the abolition movement. And henceforth, new vitality was to be perceived in this movement and Douglass and many other abolitionists played a significant role. In fact, Douglass went to England, achieved much distinction there, and they sought to keep him in England. They said it's impossible to let a man like this go back to America where he might be re-enslaved, recaptured as a fugitive slave and sent back into slavery. But Douglass would not remain in England. He said, "I must return to America to fight with my people for the liberation of my people." And so he did. Hence, Douglass was purchased by a group of English abolitionists, mostly women, so the master would no longer have the legal right to recapture him. Douglass was also furnished with funds to aid in the establishment of a newspaper in upstate New York, in Rochester. And it was Douglass who brought forward the policy at the outset of the Civil War: "Free the slaves and arm the blacks."

Lincoln and his government thought they could maintain the situation as it was, with slavery existing in the South, and so Lincoln tried to avoid anything like abolition. But Douglass and others kept pressing for this policy and finally it became clear to Lincoln that to win the war against the South, it was necessary to arm the Afro-Americans, and Lincoln did. And some 200,000 brave, black, Afro-American soldiers fought in the Union army and were the decisive force in the Civil War. It was their contribution that made it possible for America to conquer the secession of the slave-holding cabal that would have sundered the United States and rendered it impotent, as no longer a powerful nation. So here was a significant contribution to democracy.

But during the Reconstruction period, the first governments established involved some Afro-American political leaders and the vote was given to a number of Afro-Americans. But then a campaign was developed by the former slave holders to disenfranchise the Afro-Americans and they did succeed in doing this to a large extent. They utilized all kinds of measures to accomplish this. Even today, in spite of all the decisions of the United States Supreme Court, there are large areas in the South where Afro-Americans cannot vote, although it was them who laid the foundations of democracy in the South. (At least that time it was all male suffrage. We've gone a step further and we've got women suffrage as well nowadays.)

The Afro-American, then, made significant contributions in this struggle all along the line. And now, in the present period, with the development of the struggles led by Martin Luther King, initiated by Rosa Parks in Montgomery, Alabama, and carried forward, the effort is made to really achieve democracy in the United States of America. And I take it that there are similar developments on a smaller scale here in Canada, where I understand there's a special kind of prejudice operating against people of African descent, especially in employment. For a long time, I understand, it was difficult for Afro-Americans to get employment here, except as porters on the railroads. This struggle has significance, not only for people of African descent, but it has significance for all Americans, because you can't have democracy and have human rights if they are not guaranteed to all human beings at the same time. This is a *sine qua non*, the indispensable condition for any kind of genuine democracy.

Until now, we have had only a projection of the ideal of democracy and some struggles to achieve it. Among those struggles, the Afro-Americans have been outstanding in their contribution and I take it that in this present period they will continue in this struggle, for Afro-Americans have decided that unless there is democracy for them, there will be no democracy for anybody. [*Applause*] The contribution then leads, not to the further division of people, but toward a basis upon which people can unite. We ourselves will unite and then we will unite with those who are ready to unite with us. And it is on this basis that we have to go forward into the future. The African people need support from us here and they have to get it, not only from the Afro-American populations—whether in Canada, the United States, Latin America, or the Caribbean—they also need support from the overwhelming majority of European-Americans, whether in Canada or the United States or elsewhere. And no general goes to war with the least possible forces. It is statesmanship to fight when you have mobilized the most powerful force that you can assemble. Afro-Americans are not going to fight and die alone. [*Applause*] They are going to carry forward this struggle to the bitter end and they will help to build at last a society that will wipe out all racist distinctions and treat human beings as human beings should be treated. [*Extended applause*]

MODERATOR: Ladies and gentlemen, the floor is now open for discussion. Mr. Moore is willing to answer your questions.

QUESTION: Mr. Moore, you have described the Afro-American contribution to democracy, but I would like to hear you describe, in that same fight for democracy, how capitalism has made America reject democracy or prevent democracy, and how Afro-Americans are contributing to democracy right now by fighting capitalism. [*Short applause*]

MOORE: Well, it would appear that it is necessary to develop an anti-capitalist manifesto. Of course, it is obvious that, just as the institution of chattel slavery was basically responsible for the oppression and exploitation of people of African descent when it dominated the situation, the economic system of capitalism that succeeded chattel slavery is likewise responsible for the oppression and exploitation of people of African descent that followed; and not only responsible for such a situation, but also for the oppression and exploitation, albeit to a lesser degree, of people of European ancestry as well.

Now, the question involved here is whether it is possible within the framework of capitalism to achieve human rights for the most oppressed minority group, that is the Afro-Americans. I don't know that we need to try to settle this because it's a moot question. So far as I'm concerned, I think we have to recognize that the struggle has to be conducted against those who are the chief beneficiaries of the system, and that certainly means the big capitalists who are going to use all the forces they can to maintain a system from which they benefit. And one of the chief forces they have used and that they are going to use is the instilling of race prejudice in the minds of European-Americans. That's one of the chief forces, because they must divide in order to rule. This has been the basic strategy of empire from the days of Rome on down: *Divide thee ad inferna.* This struggle, then, has to be conducted and eventually—eventually—it may lead to an essential change in the economic and social system. And we can recognize that everything will be done—as Hitler did in Germany, as Mussolini did in Italy, as has been done in Africa, in the South, everywhere—to maintain the whole structure of economic, political, and social suppression. That structure cannot last forever, nor for long. (*Short applause*) But it will not cease to be simply because of wishful thinking. It will have to be changed by those who have a stake in change, by those who have the need for change. And, therefore, the most oppressed are the ones who have the greatest need for and stake in change.

What is the far future going to be? None of us knows. But one thing is certain: if we look at what is developing in all of Western society today—the revolt of the students, black and white, the strikes, the unrest, the malaise in the society—you will know that we are living in a similar period to that in which the Romans lived and of which [Edward] Gibbon wrote in *The History of the Decline and Fall of the Roman Empire.* [*Applause*] To save mankind from the utter collapse of this system people must be ready to move in and to introduce a method of human organization and control. I'll leave you to think [about] what is the best method for that. [*Applause*]

MODERATOR: Well, from the response we had after Mr. Moore finished speaking, it seems we are more or less in consensus, which is fortunate on the occasion because I am directed by the committee to adjourn the session now and allow forty-five minutes for lunch. I'm told we are running very late. Just before we go, Mr. Moore has just one more word.

MOORE: I made an important omission in my presentation and that was under the pressure of what I thought was time. Some allusion has been made to it, some reference was made to it by an earlier speaker, in fact, who dealt with the Haitian Revolution.[1] I should have pointed out that one of the most significant contributions made to democracy in this hemisphere was that of the Haitian Revolution, because the revolution of 1776 in America, on the mainland, did not free the slaves, as we know. It left the institution of chattel slavery dominant in a whole area of North America. But it was this successful revolution, carried through by the Haitian people, that laid the axe at the root of the institution of chattel slavery in the world, and it was soon followed by the abolition of chattel slavery in other areas, because of the success of the Haitian Revolution. It might well be that a similar contribution will have to be made in the present period. [*Applause*]

Chapter 7

RACE IN BRITAIN AND THE WAY OUT

RICHARD SMALL

JAN CAREW: Now I introduce to you Richard Small, who has come over to enlighten us on the up-to-date situation. [*Applause*]

RICHARD SMALL: Thank you, brother Carew, sisters, and brothers.

We have to deal with the subject of "Race in Britain" and I prefer to think of the title as "Race in Britain" and not "Racial Discrimination in Britain" because I think that we should be able to take it for granted that racial discrimination exists in Britain without having to be lectured on that and to instead deal with the much broader question of race in Britain. The second thing I would like to say as an introductory remark is that the most I can do in this kind of session is to give some kind of notes about what has been race in Britain, what is race in Britain. Instead of dealing with the way out in any kind of specific detail, to pose some questions that face us about the way out and to hope that those questions can be taken up in the kind of gathering where we can discuss the way out in detail instead of this kind of gathering, not only where the press isn't present but also where people who have to engage in the work of finding the way out are alone by themselves.

To look at the subject of race in Britain itself, I think we have to realize, first of all, that Britain and race, the two words and the two things, have been intertwined over a long period of time, not just simply since the

1950s, with the inflow of black immigrants into Britain, but going back perhaps to 400 years of Britain's contact with black parts of the world. It's important to realize that because, if you don't, then you limit the question of what is Britain and race simply to what has been happening internally in Britain and excluding Britain's external relations with other parts of the world, which really is the foundation of the present situation in Britain, where the black people are a kind of chickens coming home to roost, the kind of completion of the circle of a certain history of Britain, a certain part of Britain's history.

The next thing that is unusual, perhaps, about the situation in Britain—that is the internal situation—is that it's not just simply a question of black people, of African people, people of African origin, but it is also a question of the presence of Indians and Pakistani people living in Britain. And to give you some idea of how it is a factor, both in the internal politics and the external politics of Britain, to give you some idea of the dangers of our limited [understanding] of the situation in Britain, I want you to take, for instance, a newspaper of just two or three days ago, the paper that I bought just before coming on the plane to Canada. And the two main stories were, first of all, the Conservative Party Conference where the principles of Powellism[1] were being discussed, the principles of how the Conservative Party should deal with black people in England. And, on the other side of the page, with equal space, was the question of [British prime minister Harold] Wilson's talk with [Rhodesia's prime minister Ian] Smith in Gibraltar about Zimbabwe. And unless you begin to see, unless we appreciate the connection between those two situations, between the external and internal, then we are going to blind ourselves to an important part of the question, and perhaps end up concentrating on just a little part in the way, no doubt, that they would like us to concentrate our energies.

So that is the first point, the internal and external factors of Britain's relationship with black people throughout the world, black people who include both people of African origins, West Indians, etcetera, and people of Asian origins—Indians, Pakistanis, and, of course, the East Indian people of the West Indies.

Now, this relationship is so intertwined simply because of the history of Britain. And that history of her relationship with black people throughout the world goes back, perhaps, to sometime in the sixteenth century when two Johns, John Hawkins (and I forget the other one), first brought black slaves from Africa. First of all, they took them to England, then later on, with the development of the sugar industry in the West

Indies, there was the wholesale transportation of people from Africa to the Caribbean. And that became an important internal question in Britain at that time because this country which liked to present herself and, even today, presents herself to the world as the country guided by such great morals, had to deal with the question of how a country that claimed to base itself on the equality of man, coming from the principle of Christianity, etcetera—the presumed principles of Christianity—could deal with people of the world in the way in which she was dealing with black Africans taken to the Caribbean. And that was a very important discussion in Britain and it ultimately ended by their resolving the problem by saying that the people of Africa, black people of Africa, were not in fact full human beings and therefore could not expect the equality and equal treatment that all peoples of the world deserve.

They rationalized that question, they justified that question, by making out that black people were inferior. And that whole philosophy, that whole view of us, permeates through to today in many of the things that they put forward, not just black people in Britain, their rights and their civil liberties, but also in the way she deals with the question of Rhodesia. You simply have to listen to the discussion about that, the discussion in which Rhodesians mean the white people and Africans mean the black people; when they talk about control of government, they assume that it should be white people who should control it in Zimbabwe and not black people, the people who, 300 years ago, were regarded as being subhuman.

And then the next important historical point in my view in this question is the whole matter of the abolition of slavery in the Caribbean, because it has been presented to us in the West Indies and throughout the world that some kind of moral imperative drove Britain to agree to abolish slavery and the slave trade in order to free people. And the fact of the matter is that it was not for moral reasons that it was done, but because they were aiming at undermining the slave plantations of Haiti and also at opening up possibilities for Britain in India, removing the concentration that had been placed on the sugar industry in the West Indies and transferring those interests to India, to the exploitation of another set of black people. On this occasion, they claimed that they were going to India, not only to civilize it, but to modernize it.

And again, we are facing in Britain the result of that kind of attitude in the way in which they deal with the people of Asian origin who have migrated to Britain. One of the things, for instance, that is done at present is to try and divide that black community by explaining to black West Indians that, in fact, there is a difference between West Indians and Asians.

They tell us that we can speak the language, but the Indians can't, that we have some kind of British background and, therefore, are more acceptable, but the Asians come from an alien background and, therefore, cannot claim the same rights that we should claim. And so today, those historical roots are still playing their part in the question of race in Britain.

Now, the next important point, I think, in this historical business, which begins to show the relationship of Britain to the rest of the world on the question of race is the question of the world wars. Because again, we have to delve into our history and get a new conception of what those world wars were fought about. We have to get that new conception because Britain thought that it was important to win over the support of black people to fight for her country by saying that the fight was for freedom, for democracy, etcetera. In order to get black troops to fight and defend that empire she claimed it was for freedom and democracy. And some black scholars are examining the question of what in fact were Britain's interests? What were those wars fought about? And from the work that has been done, it is becoming quite clear that one of the decisive factors that led up to that war between Britain and Germany was the question of the division of Africa—who should take the spoils.

And again, in the Second World War, the necessity to get in black people to fight to defend this empire—the fight to defend India, to defend the Caribbean—arose. The kind of arrangements that were made, for instance, about Chaguaramas,[2] which became an important factor in West Indian politics, was not for the freedom of black people in the West Indies, but to protect what they consider their strategic interests. But there is another side to this that we should consider, which, again, is important, I believe, for our conception. By the very fact of fighting in those wars, by the very fact of Britain being forced to claim that she was calling and fighting for the freedom and democracy of people, she posed the question about freedom and democracy, not in Britain, but freedom and democracy in the West Indies, in Africa, and in India. And you will see a direct relationship between those people who went to war to fight for this freedom and democracy, and the struggle for independence that was launched in India, in Africa, and in the West Indies. In many cases, some of the people who raised that question in a very practical way were people who returned to their own countries at the end of those wars.

And the next connection is very important, because in the same way that black people were called upon to fight for this freedom and democracy during the war, they were similarly called upon after the war when the job of reconstructing Britain's economy had to be done and when she herself was faced with the problem of a shortage of people to build up those industries once more. And it is very important to see this constant connection between her policy of subjugation of the rest of the world and the counter result of it, which was a movement for the fulfillment in a real way of those ideas in our own society. That is not to say that it is Britain that is responsible for our independence. I am not arguing that. What I am pointing out is that the very process of trying to control the world has led up to the breakdown of that very empire.

Now, after the soldiers had fought in the Second World War, many of them returned home to their own countries and, in particular, to the West Indies. And there in the West Indies during the war, as in every other part of the British Empire, there had been a slump—many people were out of work and continued to be out of work even after the war had finished. Britain was trying to build herself up and she turned, as a matter of deliberate policy, to invite those people back. And it is still part of the British government policy to have recruitment exercises in Barbados to get people to come and work in certain industries, in particular the transport industry, when at the same time she's talking about black people overcrowding the country.

The next link I want to make is this: black people have been coming into Britain, or had been coming into Britain up to 1962, on the basis of the right of entry of Commonwealth citizens to Britain. But it is very interesting to discover what created that right of entry, because, after all, in a country that has passports, there is no right of entry. Why this special right for members of the Commonwealth? And this, once more, is linked with her imperial past, because at the very time when she was attempting to expand the empire, at the very time when she was attempting to build her empire in parts of Africa, Asia, and, in particular, the West Indies, she was faced with the difficulty of getting people to go there. And one of the concerns that people had, that is British white people had, about going there was that if they went there they would lose their British nationality. They therefore took the unusual step—not so unusual if you think of it in terms of empires because I believe that Romans did a similar thing—of granting anyone who lived in that empire the right of citizenship in Britain, therefore the right to return as equal citizens in her own playground, Britain. Of course, she did not expect that black people would exercise that right; it was designed for white people, for British people. So, once more, the chickens were coming home to roost; the result of the policy of imperial Britain was having an impact that was completely unexpected. Black people were moving in on the basis of this right and they were moving in order to reconstruct this society that had done so much to destroy [other] parts of the world in order to control [it].

And so, by 1961, the racialist debate had reached the stage at which the Conservative Party introduced the racialist Commonwealth Immigrant Act. It was an important marking point in history because, previous to that, the British, in their own way, had been able or had attempted to disguise in a very polite way the kind of racialism that had spread through the society. They had tried to make out, for instance, that black people in Britain did not have as hard a time as black people in America. But the debate about that Act was very important because, for the first time to my knowledge, there were people on the floor of the House of Commons making the most undisguised racialist speeches that you could expect. There was a most weak presentation by one of the government ministers, Butler, and after that it was taken over completely by people like Powell and Cyril Osborne.[3] Those of you who have lived in Britain would know what those names represent. The Act was opposed by the Labour government, they claimed, upon moral grounds—that they couldn't support an Act that was conceived by a racialist thought. But by the time they came into power, they not only announced that they would cut the number of entrants into the country to 8,500 but, later on, they spread all kinds of stories about [an] invasion to suggest that black people were flooding the country. They had to deal with this challenge that was being presented to them, not only from the Conservative Party, but from elements within their own ranks who were saying that it was time to deal with the presence of black people there.

You will notice that so far I have been talking about the Commonwealth Immigrants Act, cutting down on immigration, etcetera. One of the euphemisms they have developed is this very euphemism of the Commonwealth immigrant, which is their way of saying black people. The stage today, however, has been reached where they openly talk in terms not of black people, but of coloured people. And we have rapidly reached the stage today where the Conservative Party, bit by bit, has been putting forward more and more racialist proposals and the Labour Party, equally following behind them, only a few steps away, have been accepting those proposals and introducing them. You will no doubt know, for instance, about the immigration act that was passed when the Kenyan-Asians started to come to Britain. Again, that was the chickens coming home to roost. As a result of the division in the colonial empire that she [Britain] had created between black people in Africa and the Asian businessmen, whom they had attempted to satisfy and to make more happy and at ease,

there was a great deal of suspicion of those people [Asians] when independence was being demanded. A special category of citizenship was given to
them [Asians] and, under that category, they were able to come into Britain. But the moment they started to move in, the Act was passed. And that
Act is the furthest they have gone so far in statutory racialism, because it
makes a distinction between actual citizens of the United Kingdom, those
whose parents were born in Britain, and those whose parents were not
born there. The situation, then, is fairly clear.

Let us look then at the actual situation of the figures. The first thing
is that there are about one million black people in Britain. That figure
varies according to what propaganda they want to make, but it is likely
to be put a little higher than that if, say, a man like Powell wants to scare
people. And it is estimated that by 1985 there will be about three-million
or three-and-a-half-million black people living in Britain. Let us now
look at some other figures that give us some idea, because what I want to
move to now is our actual position there and what we can do. What I have
tried to trace so far is the history of the thing and the existence of racism
in the society. What I want us to look at now is what do we have that we
can work on?

The first thing we have is at least one million black people. The next
thing that we have is the actual position of those black people in British
society. Because, you see, the very fact that the movement into Britain
was a movement to work in industry means that they are placed today in
very strategic positions in industry. They are placed in areas where there
has been fairly low unemployment, where it has been difficult to find people to do the work, and where they have gone in to do the work. That's
the first important point. And the second part of that is, in particular areas
in Britain, the black population is not spread out evenly and, therefore,
there are particular concentrations in particular places. There are concentrations and they are placed in key industries. Not key necessarily, I'll
give you a list of the important industries in which they are placed.

For instance, two-thirds of the black population in Britain work in the
manufacturing industries and it is estimated that 46 percent of hospital
doctors in Britain are black. In addition, of course, the London transport and various other transport services are to a large extent dependent
upon the labour of black people. And if you look at what Powell has to
say today, he's saying this: even if you stop immigration completely today
and allow no one else in, that is, either workers or dependents of workers, the situation is nevertheless going to be intolerable because they are
concentrated in what he calls the very heart of the country. And he even

goes further and says that if the situation continues, they are going to change the character of Britain. And there is something of the character of Britain that needs to be changed. [*Applause*] So, there is this history and this position in which the black population are placed, and there is this growing campaign against black people in Britain, so much so that it has now reached the stage where Powell says that they have to be sent back home. And there is even a conservative fellow who says that "we believe in the policy of repatriation and, in addition, we think that we should pay the people who are going home a certain sum of money as compensation, as damages for the loss of the right and the prospect of living in Britain."

Now, what has the black community done? What positive things have they been creating that can give us some indication of the way out. And again, this whole thing is linked historically because, first of all, Britain was an important centre for the revolution in Africa. A great number of people who fought for independence in Africa based themselves in Britain. It was a very convenient place because of the very nature of the empire: when people had to deal with the questions of their freedom and their rights, they had to come to Britain. Everybody had to come to Britain from Asia, from Kenya, from Ghana, from the West Indies, and, therefore, London was a very important crossroads, not only for the rulers of the empire, but for the destroyers of the empire.

The next thing that has been done that can give us an indication of what we can do is what happened in Notting Hill during the riots of 1958.[4] Because, as a result of those attacks that were made on the black population, certain organizations, certain new methods of working, developed. It may have been something perhaps as simple and as temporary as the kind of procedure—a bit different from what Jan Carew was telling us about— where, seeing black people standing at bus stops, black people would say, "Where are you going? Can we take you there? Can we drop you home?" The protection of the police did not exist, the protection of the government did not exist, and black people had to protect themselves. You will see that kind of activity coming up again in this present day, where patrols have had to be organized against the police, where, for instance, people have stoned Indian homes and then when the Indians go to the police and report it and ask for protection, the police say it is not their responsibility to protect houses. And as a result of that kind of attitude, patrols, guards of the houses in particular areas like, say, Islington, have been organized for the last three or four years.

And at the same time, there are all kinds and varieties of organizations in Britain. Most important are the types of organizations that have been brought over from our countries of origin; for instance, among West Indians, the church. I place importance upon that and do not apologize for it, because it is very easy for people who claim to be militant to dismiss the kind of internal organization, the sort of social organization of the church, as being some reactionary type of activity. I have heard parsons make speeches about the situation of black people in Britain that extend far beyond anything I have heard coming from Black Power or militant leaders. Therefore, that is a very important aspect of our organization, an important aspect of our society that we must look at. You do not accept every church, but there is a certain kind of cohesion that can be built from it that is important for our unity and, secondly, sense of unity. Other kinds of simple organizations like the pardner,[5] for instance—the credit unions, which have been brought over from Jamaica—exist. Organizations like barbershops and the shop itself [also] exist.

Now, there are certain limitations, there are certainly things that have to be built upon. But those things exist, and we should see their importance. I give you an example. There was an area, somewhere in the Midlands, where Indian workers went out on strike and, because of the sense of community that existed, the Indian landlords and the Indian businessmen gave credit during the period of the strike to the people and the families of the people who had gone on strike. And in that way, they were able to defeat the management on the issue. And it's very interesting to see how the British react. They were faced with a very highly developed sense of organization that they could not beat. And their answer was—some of the papers, at any rate—was [to argue] that these Indians were introducing alien attitudes into the society that were unhealthy. In other words, the sense of community, the sense of brotherhood, the sense of unity was alien and to be discouraged. In actual fact, the Indians were making a combination of their own kind of social activity and the social activity of going on strike, which has been developed in Britain among the black population, in order to achieve their rights.

So, that is some idea [of] the stage things have reached. And what I want to deal with quickly now is the question of the nature of the black population. I think it is important to discuss that because it is, first of all, an immigrant population and I think, on the whole, particularly in countries like the United States, what has happened is that when an immigrant population comes in, for the first generation, people are very passive and they accept very easily the kind of injustice and the kind of discrimination that the so-called host society metes out. That has not been the case in Britain among black people and it is one of the things that accounts for the kind of hostility that is meted out to black people. "You see these blacks are too audacious, they are too self-confident. They are not putting up with the kinds of things that are being done to them." And to a man who believes that Britain is his home and nobody else's, they are being out of place, they shouldn't be doing that, they should take the licks. And I want to suggest one or two things, I believe, that explain this attitude among the black population.

I believe, first of all, that one of the important factors, one of the extremely important factors, is that people from India, people from Africa, and people from the West Indies have come out of an immediate experience of the fight for independence in their own homes. The last twenty, thirty, forty years have been a struggle for freedom in Africa, in the West Indies, and in Asia, and people who are either directly involved in that struggle or who lived and saw that struggle going on are not going to go to another part of the world and accept the same kinds of injustices that they were fighting ten or fifteen years ago. In other words, in believing in their own freedoms and rights, they have disregarded the attitude that says that nationality is what determines rights, the attitude that says only people who are born and are citizens of this country are entitled to rights. In other words, there is a conception of rights and of freedom that goes across boundaries, that says we do not put up with injustice, either at home or abroad. I believe that is an important factor. [*Applause*]

And that has been general to the whole black population, the whole immigrant population. I believe, however, that there are some things specific to the West Indian population, which constitutes at least half of the black population in Britain. It is part of the kind of conception that this conference has been aiming at, a conception of black people, and particularly of West Indian people, who for the whole period of time that they have existed as a people, as a Caribbean people, have been directly involved in some form of struggle for their own freedom; that the day that you took a black man from Africa and brought him to the West Indies— the day that he put his foot on that ship, the day that he landed in the West Indies, the day after slavery was abolished, up to this day—black people in the West Indies, the West Indian people, the people of Asian origin have been fighting, in some way or the other, for their freedom in the West Indies, and will fight for it in Britain.

And the third thing that I believe has formed this kind of personality is the general world situation, the situation in particular of black people throughout the world—of black people in the United States, of black people in the West Indies, the black people in Africa, and the black people in Asia—who today still have to be fighting for their freedom. But that struggle is still a part of our world [and] constantly informs, inspires, and encourages black people in England to get their rights there. And there is one other important factor that we should bear in mind. You see, an easy explanation of the attitude of West Indians has been that, in Britain, they have been more militant, more demanding, because they have been the most disappointed. The argument goes like this: They were taught to believe in Britain as the mother country in the empire, but they have come to Britain and have been disappointed and therefore have rebelled the most. That, in my view, is a lot of sociological nonsense. The explanation, in fact, is this: that the West Indian did not come to Britain in order to satisfy some longing for his home, in other words, to meet some long-lost mother. Black people, West Indians, came to Britain as a part of a whole process that has, all along, all this time, been an important part of the West Indian history. Britain was not the first place that black people came to. Britain has not been the first place that West Indians have traveled to. West Indians, from as early as 1853, have been traveling out of the West Indies to other parts of the world in order to build that world. In 1853, it was a case of going to Panama to help with railway construction; a little later, it was a case of going to Panama to help with the building of the canal; in Costa Rica, it was in order to help with the building of railways and of [cultivating] bananas; in Honduras, it was a question of going there to open up the land and to plant bananas; in Cuba, it was a question of going there to take part in the expansion of the sugar industry and the sugar economy that was developing toward the end of the nineteenth century; more recently, in Florida, it has been a case of going there to take part in the farm worker program. And then Britain herself was again in crisis [and] called for people to work in those industries and to build that country and live there.

So, we must not forget the other side of the question, which is, why have black people found it necessary to move out of the West Indies? Why have they felt that the West Indies cannot be made their actual physical home? I don't think it is necessary for me to answer that at the moment, but I want to give one example of the kind of attitude that exists today and, in my view, has always existed in the mentality of black people and, in particular, West Indians.

Around the time when the Conservative, the Labour government (they both mean the same) passed the legislation in order to stop black people from coming in, to reduce the numbers, a public meeting was held and a doctor who is very prominent in the activities of an organization called CARD [Campaign Against Racial Discrimination] was addressing the meeting and he challenged white people, in particular the Labour government, by saying that he wants them to disprove that black people had not built more houses in Britain than the amount of houses that they live in. That's very important. One of the arguments they have used in order to cut back on immigration has been that there are not enough houses. But at the same time, the building industry in many parts of Britain exists upon black labour. And he was challenging them to prove that black people had not built more houses than they live in. But he said that he couldn't prove it himself. He was just assuming that they built more houses, he didn't have the figures. And at the end of his speech, a man at the back of the audience got up and he said, "You don't have to assume. I know because I built it. I built that bridge over there, I built that pub over there, and today I cannot go into that pub. But I built it."

And that is the story of the role of black people in Britain. That is the story of the role of black people in all those different parts of the world that I listed that black people have migrated to. That is the story of slavery, that not only did they build the West Indies and cannot live there today, but that they built Britain, which they are today being told they cannot enter and exist as human beings. And nobody is going to put up with that. Nobody is going to put up with that for long and I believe that gives some idea of the kinds of sensibilities that have been driving the black population in Britain along.

I want to point out one of the things that makes that population quite unusual. And it is continually surprising to me. That is the attitude of young black people in Britain. Again, one could assume that perhaps the older people would be a little more alienated from British society and that the younger people themselves, having been brought up there would consider themselves black Englishmen. But, as brother Darcus[7] told us yesterday, there is no such thing as a black Englishman. The attitude of black people in Britain toward British society is one of complete disassociation, one that says that we demand our rights as black people and that we will not put up with anything less than that. It is, in my view, quite an unusual attitude because they have not, in any way, compromised their position and, at the same time, they do not have any view, necessarily, of leaving Britain. They have a view of themselves as living in a country from which they demand rights and they are not necessarily calling themselves black Englishmen.

Now, the question we have to answer, which we can't answer here, is one of the way out. And the way out has to be seen on two levels in my view. It has to be seen, first of all, on the local level, that is the situation in Britain; and it has to be seen on the international level. I think the important point that we can discuss later is the question of whether you want one monolithic black organization in Britain. I don't believe that is the answer. I think there are all kinds of factors against that. The next thing that we need, that exists to a certain extent, is an extension of international links: to establish the sense of confidence that you can get and that is there already, to a certain extent, but that can be built upon; that what you do in Britain is not limited to what is happening in Britain but is part of a worldwide movement. That is very important. It is very important, for instance, to get information coming in on what black people in the other parts of the world are doing.

And it is important also for this reason, and I go back to where I started: The international nature of British racism that accounts, not only for the hostility toward black people in Britain, but also for her policy in Rhodesia, for her policy in South Africa, and all parts of the world where black people exist needs to be countered. And we black people in Britain, our destiny is as tied up with that as it is with anything else. But a defeat in Rhodesia is a defeat for us. Everybody knows that the day that a compromise is made in Rhodesia, as sure as it will be by any British government, is going to be a setback for us and we are the only people to deal with that. It is ridiculous, for instance, demanding that Britain must send troops to Rhodesia, to Zimbabwe, to free Africans; as ridiculous as it is to believe that when people in Ghana, people in Tanzania, people in Kenya, anywhere like that, were fighting against Britain and her colonial policy, that Britain herself was going to send troops to free those black people. It is as ridiculous as that. And so, it is important for us to understand that it is black people in Africa who will free them, that the freedom of black people in Africa is important to our freedom in Britain, that the two are linked and we must play our part in that. [*Applause*]

What is important, therefore, is a conception of what has been called the Third World, which disregards national boundaries, which does not limit ourselves in any way to a particular area but has a view of the world that crosses over all of this and allows ourselves some root, some way of making our own way in Britain. And, therefore, this conference is important, but the most important part of it is not here but what we discuss about what can be done, which has the worldview as our total view. Thank you. [*Long, loud applause*]

JAN CAREW: Thank you very much for a very enlightening talk on the situation in Britain. We will now ask for questions from the floor. Brief and to the point questions, if you don't mind, and then ask brother Small to answer as many of them as he sees fit.

LLOYD BEST: Mr. Chairman, ladies and gentlemen. Let me warn you from the start that I am not going to be brief at all. I want to speak at some length if I may [*discussion in the audience*]. Nor am I merely going to ask a question. I want, in point of fact, if I may be so arrogant, to try and introduce into this conference some dimensions that I think have been sadly lacking, and have certainly worried me deeply.

The first thing I want to introduce into this conference is the dimension of caution. I have a feeling, somehow, that we have been operating, in the two days that I have been here, with formulations that appear, to me at any rate, to be excessively simple. We are, therefore, making false diagnoses for the most part. We are dealing in propaganda and we are making, consequently, prescriptions that have no operational significance. Time and again, questions have been raised from the floor about what we are going to do about the very difficult situation in which the whole world finds itself. And it ends up in thrills, nothing specific, nothing concrete. I want to suggest some analytical reasons for this because I think the conference, so far, has been operating on intellectual levels that are absolutely scandalous. Most of the talks are pure propaganda motivated by indignation and hate, and a good deal of racism [*rumblings from the audience*].

I know what I have to say is very contrary to the mood of the conference, but think it is our duty to impose some kind of rigor and some kind of standards on what facts are. I know it's very unpopular, but somebody has to say these things.

Now, let me begin at the beginning. Most people are simply dividing the world into cowboys and Indians, shall we say. That is to say, people are accepting the simple notion that the world can be analyzed in terms of black and white. [*Short sporadic applause*] Now, I am a person who has dealt with issues of this kind for many years and my record on the question is there for people to examine. I'm not afraid to say things here that will, of course—as they have been described already—be described as Uncle Tom statements. Because I refuse to fall into the simple trap, which is in fact. . . . [*Someone screams from the audience,* "Is this a question period?" *and there are murmurs from the audience.*]

JAN CAREW: Can I put it to the floor, ladies and gentlemen? I for one am quite willing to hear any opinion on any subject relating to the conference, [*strong applause*] but naturally we cannot do this without some kind of consensus. I will ask Mr. Best to be as brief as possible, but I think he has got something to say, even for us to disagree with. Then the meeting can be a bit livelier. [*Applause and more murmurs and lively discussion with the audience*] We are not going to stick to any rigid parliamentary procedure. We want a conference out of which we can get some. . . . [*Applause and more comments from a particular individual in the audience.*] Well then, you can leave.

BEST: I think we have the time, I hope we have the tolerance. [*More shouts from the crowd*] May I proceed Mr. Chairman?

CAREW: Ladies and gentlemen. Once more, can we put this to a vote? Do you want to hear Mr. Best go on or not? [*Applause. Carew says quietly to someone,* "I think we have to end it, man."] I will then suggest, ladies and gentlemen, as a compromise, that we do have a question period and that if there is time after the question period, we can have Mr. Best continue. [*Short applause*] Could we have some questions now? [*Carew states off the record:* "Because the meeting is going to end in chaos."]

Could we have some questions? First question, and I'll ask Mr. Best to stay here and we'll continue on with this a bit later. [*Short applause*] So, would you mind questions from the floor? Are you asking a question? Then come up here. If you want to ask a question, please come up and ask it.

QUESTION: I'd like for you to tell us how you think the conference is going so far, your opinions on it?

CAREW: You'd like whom to tell you? [*Inaudible response*] Well, we are directing questions at the speaker, so you know it is completely out of order to ask him. Would Mr. Small like to answer that? How do you think the conference is going?

QUESTION: I'd like to hear Mr. Small's opinions on the conference as of so far.

CAREW: We have one question. Would you mind if we dealt with that first? Would you like to answer that question, Richard?

SMALL: Yes, I'd like to answer that question very much. It is exactly what we are seeing here now; that this, as I understood it, was a conference that was called to give a conception of what black history has been and, to follow from that, a conception of what black people can do. But it has been impossible in meetings such as this to discuss that. The reason for that is quite clear. We cannot discuss that here, and that is why I started off by saying that the points that I raised were, first of all, to give factual information about the situation in Britain. Second, to raise questions that we need to deal with about how we can get out of the situation that we are in in the world, and that we cannot do it with an audience that is predominantly white; that we need a black audience [*applause*], black people who will decide what black people will do. [*Loud applause*]

CAREW: Mr. Hill.

ROBERT HILL: Mr. Chairman, thank you very much. I want to ask Mr. Small a question so that probably what he said could be better clarified in terms of his suggestion that the black people of Britain relate themselves more concretely to the global struggle of black humanity.

Now, people didn't go to Britain because they wanted to see the Cliffs of Dover. In fact, just about two months ago, there was an English professor by the name of Dr. Wilson who came to Jamaica. He said he had to come to Jamaica in his capacity as chairman of the Birmingham Race Relations Council or Race Relations Welfare Board. He said that people had come to Britain, had been allowed to come to Britain, who knew absolutely nothing about British society and it seems rather likely that if you want to go to a place of which you know nothing, that would suggest a certain level of mentality of the black man, which I cannot accept. But he said that part of the problem of black people living in Britain was that British society was not prepared to accept them. Neither did it know too much about West Indians coming. He had, therefore, come back to Jamaica to try and catch up on his knowledge and the knowledge of the British experts who have to deal with this technical problem, as they like to see it, and he said that he had come to try and learn something about West Indian society, so that when he went back to Birmingham he could understand why black West Indians behave the way they do.

He said, however, one thing is quite certain. Birmingham, which is one of the most developed industrial complexes in Britain, if not in Europe—he says without black West Indians today, Birmingham as a city is inconceivable as a production centre. In other words, what he is saying is that black men had come from the colonies, knowing nothing about British society, not wishing, as their first wish, to live in Britain, were forced by economic circumstance to go there—he says they didn't know anything but, on the other hand, that if you took those West Indians out, you could not have Birmingham as a city.

It seems to me [that] the type of West Indian who went to Britain is not the colonial that the English have in their minds. And, in relation to the question that Mr. Small raised, what I want to find out is this: Do West Indians in Britain see themselves as a continuing permanent segment of British society or are there developments to indicate that these people within British society might be considering the real problem, which is go home and struggle for liberation in your own country? [*Short applause*]

SMALL: There are of course some people who see the situation as leaving Britain and going to the West Indies, and some black people, who are not even from Africa, who see the situation as going to Africa and fighting there. Yes, that is true, but that is not a large segment of the community by any means. I think that, on the whole, the people's attitude to this is not a clearly worked out thing that says that we'll either stay here or we will go back to the West Indies to fight. It is a very simple human attitude. We are here and we want to make a life while we are here, which is a completely justified attitude. It is certainly much more moderate than the attitude of white people who, not knowing anything about Africa, went there and settled, lived there, not knowing about Africans, still not knowing about them, and, in fact, claiming rights over the Africans. There's a very small body of people in Britain who argue in this way: Britain went to Zimbabwe and she has settlers' rights, she's on the A role. We black people in Britain have come to Britain, we are settlers. Perhaps we should also be on the A role and the native people be on the B role. [*Applause*]

CAREW: Mr. Best, you can ask your question now. [*Simultaneous boos and applause*]

BEST: I am not going to allow Mr. Small to get away with avoiding the issues. I want to ask him a direct question. Why is it that he cannot propose to this audience what black people can do to solve their problems? He keeps saying that he cannot do this because we haven't got the right audience. Now, I don't understand that proposition, so I want to ask him to give us an explanation here as to why he cannot make a statement about what black people in this audience can do to solve the problem?

SMALL: The answer to that is very simple. I have certain ideas. I didn't come to this conference and believe that my ideas would be accepted. I wanted to hear the ideas of other people and I wanted to hear the ideas of black people. I believe that our experience in Britain in particular illustrates this, and it's similar to the experience throughout other parts of the world where black people are: Black people in Britain, particularly after Notting Hill, started forming organizations that were supposed to be multi-racial, that were based upon the idea that if you drank tea with people you could get to understand them better. We found out, not through any kind of theoretical position but simply from practice, that this was a waste of time, and increasingly, black organizations, black activity in England, has been black. I am not saying that the situation is rosy, that everything has been solved. There are some serious problems. I don't want to discuss it in this place with the audience that we have, [*applause*] the press that we have, with this microphone here, and with people taking photographs. [*Applause continues*]

QUESTION: I have just come from ten days on Parliament Hill. There were many people who came and approached me, there were many people who didn't. I didn't draw a line around myself to say who could come and who could not. I am at this congress because, although it says, "Congress of Black Writers," no one refused my fare when I came. I understood this was open to the public.

CAREW: Do you have a question?

QUESTIONER CONTINUES: Yes, I must just say two words. I also, in Vietnam, found I was in a country where a people of a different skin and a different culture were fighting. I was there to help. I knew I could not fight their war for them. I think our position is the same here. I want to say, as white people, we have our struggles and problems; we don't come here to tell anybody else what to do, but this is our struggle too. And, again, I must ask, are we doing ourselves a favour by drawing a circle around ourselves or are we helping the enemy? I think there are people all over the world who are a part of the world's battle to succeed and I think, with due respect, and certainly I say it from the bottom of my heart, because I wouldn't for one minute diminish the struggle of the black people, but those who are here, like myself, are here only to be in the nature of some help and have no other intention. And I would ask the speaker, can this not be accepted without causing a rift in this congress or need it be the problem that is being presented? [*Applause*]

SMALL: All congratulations to a lady who thinks it necessary to fast on behalf of the Vietnamese. All congratulations to white people who think it is important that they should do what they can do to overthrow the society that is keeping down black people. All congratulations. But she didn't help plan the Vietnamese war. She went there to help. [*Applause*] She went there to help. Fine, that is good. The simple answer to white people at this stage is—and it is an answer that's been given time and time before—if you want to fight racism deal with the racists. [*Applause*]

QUESTION: I almost blew my top just now when I heard him introduce Mr. Best again because I don't think I want to hear Mr. Best. Now, the fact is this conference has a day to go. This conference has a day to go and there are many important speakers speaking tomorrow. If Mr. Best is dissatisfied with the intellectual level, or whatever, of the conference, he could speak to the leaders of the conference and let them try to steer it in a proper direction tomorrow. I do not believe Mr. Best should come here and wash our dirty linen in public. [*Applause*] Speak to the people involved and let them right the conference. We have a whole day to go. I don't want to hear Mr. Best and I'm sure many people feel the same way.

CAREW: Are you asking a question?

QUESTIONER: That is a question and an answer if you want it that way. [*Sporadic applause*]

CAREW: Please, could we have questions?

QUESTION: If he can make a statement, why can't I just make a statement?

CAREW: Well, make a statement, but ask a question or make a statement in question form. [*Carew laughs*]

QUESTION: Ladies and gentlemen. I am an African, I'm black, as you can see, and I want to live as a human being. There are internationalists, all right, there are individualists, all right, there are well-wishers, there is everything. But the fact of history, even white man's history, is, if you want respect, if you want to be like anybody, you must be equal. You cannot hurt a person unless he's afraid of you. I don't mean power-wise. You must make him believe that you're as capable, as intelligent, and as productive as he is. What is help? In America help has existed for a long time. What did they do? America, as one person said, could take the Russians. When Khrushchev said, "We'll bury you!" they could say, "Come on!" But they couldn't say that to Carmichael. So, the question is not a rift between white and black. The question is the equality of white and black. The question is not whether the white people can free South Africa, but whether the white people can understand that South Africa, Rhodesia, or Zimbabwe, as we call it, the people here, everybody could live together happily. The whole issue is, can we understand each other on the foot of equality and not as somebody trying to help because he's . . . Why don't we help the white people?

When the black people want to discuss a black problem, the best thing the white people can do is discuss the white problem. When they want to discuss the white/black problem, they must be on the same footing. And don't believe in helping, believe in equality, on an equal footing. Don't believe in internationalists, they are liars. There is no internationalism unless there is equality. Thank you. [*Applause*]

CAREW: No comment from the speaker. [*Laughter*]

QUESTION: Thus far, the conference has been extremely abstract, and the speakers have been speaking of black unity. [*Carew:* Questions, questions.] Right after I make my statement—which will transcend national boundaries, and I have several questions that I would like to ask. First, I would like the speaker to explain the complete acquiescence of the African nations to the situation in Rhodesia and South Africa [*shout from the audience*]. Let me finish, please, then he can explain.

Second, I would like them to explain their acquiescence on Biafra. This is a perfect example of class struggle and genocide and African nations have stood by and watched. There has been no interference. [*Shouts from the audience continue.*] Whether or not Britain, Russia, or the

United States are supplying arms or want it, whether or not it is imperialism, African nations could interfere to stop the starvation that is taking place in Biafra. [*Audience:* There is not starvation there.] Well if you have seen the pictures that I have seen, there is starvation.

And third, I would like to know, since they have been talking about the Third World, where they place China in relation to Africa? China is a yellow nation; she is neither white nor black. Where does China stand?

CAREW: I have the profoundest sympathy with the gentleman's question, but they are way out in terms of reference in the meeting unless Mr. Small wants to deal with them.

SMALL: I don't want to deal with them, I want to say this: What I said before I believed in. I will not answer questions like that because it is wasting the conference's time. [*Applause*] I have a view, I have a view about the African situation and they are toward, not Rhodesia, Zimbabwe, [*applause*] and I have a view about Biafra, but I am not going to take part in discussions with people coming up here to try and distract us from the questions we need to deal with. [*Applause*]

QUESTION: Ladies and gentlemen, my name is Fred Oliver. I'm from New York. I came to this congress with the understanding that there was a certain format, a certain way of doing things that was ascribed to, and now I find that I was mistaken. I would like to ask the committee—the committee, because I feel that they are the people who are responsible here. Are they not responsible for the format of this congress? Are they not responsible to see that the format is confined to the outline that was set up? I would like to read them their own editorial that was published. It said: "The most noticeable characteristic of modern white oppression has been its guilt-ridden conscience. Not content to confine its vicious pursuit of material riches to the level of physical conquest, it has always sought to justify its oppressive control over other races by resorting to arrogant claims of inherent superiority and attempting to denigrate the cultural and historical achievements of the oppressed peoples. The machinery of oppression has thus been not only economic and political, but cultural and intellectual as well." And I feel that what is transpiring here now follows exactly in this line. [*Sporadic applause*] One more word please. [*Some commotion*] One word. We are here as black people in order to formulate our own ideas, our own goals, and we must do this without interference, without being subjected to the outside interference, if you may, that would come about by discussing these issues in the white audience. Thank you. [*Applause*]

CAREW: No comment from the speaker. Next question please.

QUESTION: I'd like to ask you this question. Do you think it is at all possible that because one portion of society, and that being the black portion of society, isolates itself from the white portion of society, are you not in fact playing into the hands of the American ruling class? Isn't this the thing that Hitler played on? Isn't this the thing that the American ruling class wants you to do, to isolate yourself from us and then they can set about to annihilate you? You are a group, a minority group. [*Shouts from the audience*]

CAREW: Thank you very much. Mr. Small will answer it.

SMALL: That is exactly what we have to deal with. He tells us that we are a minority group. [*Applause*] He tells us that black people in the world are a minority group. Now, that is fantastic. I give you this secret. The first thing we have to learn is that we are not a minority group. And we are going to have to start acting on that. But we can't discuss with you what we as a majority think we can do in order to remove a minority, which includes the people who are oppressing us, from off our back. [*Applause*]

CAREW: Thank you very much, ladies and gentlemen. The next item on the program begins at 8:30 at the Student Union Congress Festival. Thank you.

Chapter 8

MOVING AGAINST THE SYSTEM

New Directions for the Black Struggle

HARRY EDWARDS

WALTER RODNEY: The next speaker is an activist brother who many of us know. Presently based on the west coast, organizing within the Black Panther movement, Brother Harry Edwards. [*Applause*]

HARRY EDWARDS: Brothers and sisters, friends, local, national, and international Gestapo, [*applause and laughter*] and I also detect an unhealthy sprinkling of niggers and honkies in our audience.

I want to make everybody feel welcome and I think that since you paid your tuition to get in—and I understand that they did make whites pay an out-of-residence fee—I think everybody should feel welcome. I don't believe in, you know, discriminating. [*Applause and laughter*] I'm not going to be formal. I'm not an artist and, despite my three Ivy League degrees, I'm not going to talk in some kind of language that is going to go over the heads of the people who are sitting here. I understand I have twenty minutes, I'm going to try to cut it down to fifteen because there are more experienced and wiser brothers who are going to speak after me that I'm quite certain you would be much more interested in hearing.

You know, the truth is a bitch. I appreciated what the brother [referring to Ted Joans' "The Truth"] said about the truth because the beautiful thing about it is it doesn't hurt anybody except the criminals, the people who are wrong. Malcolm told the truth and they wiped him out, but a funny thing about the truth is that you cannot kill it. The brother has been dead now for almost four years and today he is stronger than he was at the time that he was killed [*applause*] because the brother told the truth.

Now, you always run into people who don't like the truth because it undresses them, it tells off on them. But, here again, you have nothing to fear from it unless you are wrong, and I think that if the shoe fits, then I think you should put it on. We are, today, at a stage in liberation struggle where I think we have to take assessment of where we're going, where we have been, and what directions our strategies must take us in. And so, what I'm gonna try to do in fifteen minutes is to try to bring some perspective on exactly what direction I feel the movement should go in, what direction, what things I feel are important.

We're at a stage in the liberation struggle when we should have moved past the part of concentrating our efforts upon individual oppressors. And this is something you run into time and time again. In over seventy-five lectures in the past year, time and time again, you have these brothers who get up and the first thing they want to do is lambaste honkies—individual honkies at that. I think we should have moved past that stage. Whether we are in Europe, Africa, North America, Latin America, or any place else where this white man has taken over and oppressed and enslaved, we must begin to see the necessity to concentrate our efforts upon the system. And this is a very important concept, because here we have to understand that we are not dealing with an individual, psychopathic, inhumane beast such as Adolf Hitler. We are dealing with a system that turns out Hitlers and they are not all white. [*Applause*] We are dealing with a worldwide system that turns out Hitlers in the same sense that it turns out Chevrolets, Jaguars, hydrogen bombs, and rifles. [*Applause*]

If we look at the differences in the impact of the two strategies, perhaps we can get some notion, clearer notion of precisely what I'm talking about. We have to look at these strategies by example: the attack upon the individual and the attack upon the system.

In the first instance, we see where the hippies, which is short for hypocrite [*short applause*]—and this is something I think may bear going into—and the yippies attack [Lyndon Baines] Johnson; for four years they attacked Johnson, an individual cracker. So, Johnson was removed, and the system very quickly cranked out three other Lynching Beast Johnsons [*applause*] who will be no better, who will be no better and no worse than the original. [*Applause*]

The system cranked out Wallace, whose whole philosophy is law and order, translated into another way to commit genocide against black people legally; [*applause*] the dishonourable Hubert H. Honkey, [*applause and laughter*] who is again talking about law and order—how to keep the black man down on the very bottom; and Nazi Nixon, whose central thesis is law and order. And you only have to look at a couple of their campaign advertisements to understand this. Here the hippies and the yippies did not attack the system, they attacked an individual. [*Short applause*] This is no good. That was in 1956 when people were talking about attacking individuals, attacking [*inaudible*] Maddox to get him to eat some chicken, attacking a hot dog stand, attacking a school bus, attacking an airplane, attacking a toilet. Those days are gone. Today we've got to attack the system that produced and perpetuates these inhumane.... [*Words drowned out by applause*]

The hippies attacked the individual by dropping out. The yippies attacked the individual by running their own candidate, a hog, not realizing that even with their candidate, nobody in the country, except the racists, had a choice this year because we had a whole family of hogs in the White House for the last five years, so that wasn't even a choice. [*Sporadic applause*] Here, the authority of the existing system was not even challenged as far as its legitimacy, much less in its right to commit the kind of atrocities that it is committing today on the domestic and on the international level all over this world.

In the movement that centred upon the athletic arena—in the United States and also, to a large extent, on the international level, particularly when it regarded the question of South Africa—the strategy was entirely different. We did not concern ourselves and waste our energies with trying to get rid of an individual cracker, an individual racist, or an individual cog in a wheel that is grinding out racists every day. We moved against the system in its athletic and social and economic spheres. The use of black athletic talent was challenged; the legitimacy of the use of black athletic talent by the system was challenged under the circumstances that existed in the United States. The US will never again be able to assume, *carte blanche*, that black athletes will serve as propaganda fodder, as economic capital, and as twentieth-century gladiators for the corrupt and genocidal system that exists in the United States. [*Applause*]

Moving against the system has several distinct advantages over moving against individuals. In moving against the system, we first eliminate the tragically comical obsession that Negroes have with white folks. What is one cracker, more or less? What is one honkey, more or less? What difference does it make whether a cracker is in the room or not?

I think that one thing we have to recognize—and if you can't deal with the truth then you're in the wrong place, you're listening to the wrong cat—we have to recognize that as long as there are more than three of us in a room and all of our faces are black, the white man is there somewhere because his eyes and his ears and his mind and his mentality are there. We have to recognize this. When we get ready to take care of business, we are going to have to break up into ones and twos and go on and take care of business and get away from this notion that, somehow, by keeping the white man out, by keeping his physical presence out, that he doesn't know what's going on. [*Short applause*] Honkies are at once the tools and the chief beneficiaries of the system of oppression.

We are the victims of the system. Therefore, if we are going to take the thing on a priority level, on a level that is geared to bring about the greatest result and the greatest impact at the least cost to black people, then we must move against the system and over honkies, and not vice versa. And here, too, we stand an excellent chance of gaining allies. White folks in this struggle must be used. There are those white folks who are waiting and willing and begging to be used. [*Short applause*] There is not a Negro factory in this country that produces weapons; there is not a black ammunitions factory in this country; but there are honkies who want to be used in this regard because they too have begun to awaken to the carnivorous nature of the systems that control what is called the free world. [*Applause*]

In moving against the system, we also eliminate the tendency that exists among Negroes to choose between the lesser of evils—to choose between whites who are on the ascendancy to positions of power, as if one was any better than another. In moving against the system, we recognize that, regardless of who he is, if he is upholding or participating in the perpetuation of the system, he is as guilty as any other criminal, he is a genocide artist and he should be treated as such, regardless of whether he's "Dixicrat," "Repulsican," or anything else. [*Short applause*] To use one of Wallace's phrases, once we begin to understand that it is the system that we must first control, that we must first remove, that we must first destroy, we'll be able to see that there is not a damn worth of difference between people who are in positions that work to perpetuate the system. We are no longer put in the position of choosing between a pound of strychnine and fifteen ounces, between a [Richard] Nixon and a [Hubert] Humphrey, or between an [Ed] Brooke and a Humphrey, or a [Richard] Hatcher and a [George] Wallace. It doesn't make any difference; they're all in the system, they're all serving to perpetuate the system in the United States.

By also concentrating on the system, we can impart added emphasis to the philosophical and action qualities of the concept of blackness. I think this is something we should all understand. We are no longer susceptible, under these circumstances, to people like [Carl] Stokes and Hatcher and Ed Brooke being put up as supposedly black leaders, as evidence that America is working diligently and sincerely to solve the problems which are oppressing black people in that country today. In other words, we are able to see more distinctly that the nigger cobra inside of the house is to be and should be dealt with at least as much dispatch as the honkey whoop at the door. Because if the nigger cobra bites us in the house, to hell with the honkey whoop at the door—we're dead already. I think this is something we have to understand. [*Applause*]

We must, in other words, begin to clarify, systematically, who we call brother. This is something that the Vietnamese people have succeeded in doing very well. They killed at least as many yellow Uncle Toms as they killed honkies over there in Vietnam, because they understand that it is the system and those who perpetuate the system who must be moved against. In dealing with the system, we can also see that rhetoric becomes quickly recognized for what it is—the rantings of people who, in many cases, lack either the intelligence, the desire, or the guts—or all three—to get involved in action aimed at removing the oppressive structure from the backs of black people. To lambaste honkies is a fruitless waste of time at this late date. Talk should be aimed at educating black people to the system as the enemy. Racists are born every day. If we were to move against racist individual honkies—and since we don't control any bombs or any airplanes, despite the fact that there is one black airline pilot for American Airlines, I don't think that the likelihood is very great that there will be a hydrogen bomb dropped from a 727 Boeing passenger jet—we would have to move against them individually. And in doing that, we couldn't even beat the birthrate. There would be more racists born than we could deal with every day, and not only this, but we wouldn't have time to think about black people because we'd be fighting honkies twenty-four hours a day.

So, I think the rhetoric today must be aimed at black people and must be geared toward educating them to the fact that the system is the enemy; that it is useless to talk about integrating with a system that is geared toward the total destruction and a genocidal elimination of black people on the face of this earth. [*Applause*] Finally, by concentrating on the system, we realize that two systems cannot occupy the same social, economic, and political space simultaneously. Racist and humanitarian systems cannot exist simultaneously in the same social, economic, and political space.

Therefore, since the racist system, the system of oppression, is the one that's in existence, this means that those who really understand and who are sincere must begin to move to destroy that system.

One of the systems has to go. Night-time has to go and daylight to come on the scene. If black liberation is to succeed, the systems that perpetuate this racist and inhumane situation must be destroyed. And this cannot be done with rhetoric; this cannot be done with bullshit. It takes action. In the US, it will not suffice to attempt to replace the words of Jefferson, Lincoln, and Washington and other similar racist honkies, with the words of Malcolm, King, and Lumumba. We must first destroy the racist systems founded by these crackers and, upon those ashes, build a system of humanity that Malcolm and King and Lumumba were granted time only to conceive and not to construct. Black people must not only seek other alternatives to the systems that exist, but we must create those alternatives by any means necessary.

Thank you. [*Applause*]

Chapter 9

FRANTZ FANON
AND THE
THIRD WORLD

JAMES FORMAN

WALTER RODNEY: . . . There's a second dimension. Forman, as a writer, as somebody trying to analyze the process in which he himself has been involved, notably in his work *Liberation Will Come from a Black Thing* and the more recent, which is just about to come off the press, *Sammy Young*, an analysis of one of the first martyrs of the black liberation movement of our epoch.[1] I will give you James Forman. [*Applause*]

JAMES FORMAN: Brothers and sisters, delegates and participants.

I was asked to speak on "The Third World and Capitalism," which is the subject originally designed for this afternoon.[2] I'm happy to see pictures of brother Frantz Fanon on the wall behind you. These are pictures that you don't ordinarily see. We have to begin distributing more and more pictures of Frantz Fanon.

I would like to talk about Frantz Fanon within the context of the subject this afternoon. But I think before we begin speaking, this is a brother who was slain, died of leukemia but he was killed in action, and he has to be remembered as Che Guevara must be remembered, as Malcolm X, Martin Luther King, and all the other black martyrs. So, I think we ought to stand for just a minute, a few seconds, in reverence of these martyrs of the black liberation struggle who have been slain. Would you stand, please? [*Audience stands in silence for approximately six seconds*] Thank you.

Frantz Fanon fought and died for revolutionary socialism throughout the Third World, especially in Africa. He fought in the Algerian War for a beachhead that could spring forth a continental revolution in Africa. He died, not in the same manner, but with the same aspirations as Che Guevara died in Latin America. He preached against narrowness and pitfalls of a purely nationalist revolution that won a flag, a new style of dress, and underneath the dregs of humanity remained the same. He understood and tried to warn of the dangers facing Africa from the lack of ideology. He stated that, as he traveled throughout Africa and observed the various customs and the discussions in ruling political circles, he was convinced that the greatest danger facing Africa was not colonialism but the absence of an ideology. He was saying, in other words, through the will of the people, that one could rid themselves, people could rid themselves of colonialism, but the lack of ideology would force a lot of divisions in Africa. He sought with his writing skills, through lectures, discussions, and examples, to urge an ideology that would clearly fight against the bourgeois nationalist governments that we see installed throughout Africa and the Caribbean. He sought an ideology that would appropriate all the richness of Africa and the Third World for the masses, the wretched of the earth.

In September 1956, Fanon addressed the First Conference of Negro Writers and Artists in Paris and delivered a paper on racism and colonialism. He had decided at that moment in 1956 that all his energies had to be devoted to the Algerian War of Independence. He decided he could no longer work as a hospital administrator in the French colonial medical services at Blida Hospital in Algeria. He would cast his lot with the Algerians. Twelve years have passed since that date. Today we must state five obvious facts:

Fact number one: Racism, capitalism, colonialism, and imperialism dominate the lives of the people of the Third World—the people of Africa, Asia, Latin America—black people in the United States, and other colonized minorities that also live in the United States.

Fact number two: Lacking a unified socialist ideology, we see blacks against blacks, Nigerians against Nigerians, Africans against Africans, Kenyans against Kenyans, armed struggle inside liberation movements, bourgeois nationalists running most black governments, quarrelling and fighting over the crumbs from the table of imperialism, while three continents go underdeveloped, unliberated, and the richness of these continents primarily still in the hands of white Western imperialists.

Fact number three: However we may twist our words and regardless of our personal subjective feelings, the truth of the matter is that we cannot end racism, colonialism, capitalism, and imperialism until the reigns of state power are in the hands of those people who understand that the total wealth of any country and the world belong to all the people. Societies and countries based upon the profit motive will never ensure the new humanism or eliminate poverty and racism, for which Fanon argues in all his writings and about which brother Harry Edwards has just spoken.

Fact number four: However we may twist our words and regardless of our personal feelings, the stark reality remains that the state power necessary to end racism, colonialism, capitalism, and imperialism will come only through long, protracted, bloody, brutal, and violent wars with our oppressors.

Fact number five: If liberation movements from the very beginning are not dedicated to revolutionary socialist principles or do not evolve into movements for socialist principles while the fighting is going on, it is not evident that those who fight will assume state power and implement decisions that appropriate the wealth of the countries for the entire people. Rather, to the contrary, the absence of [a] revolutionary socialist ideology within certain ruling circles of countries in the Third World is directly related not only to the fact that many rulers have settled for a new flag, a new style of dress, a seat in the United Nations, accommodation with the former colonial power, but, more importantly, they had no intention in the first place to make a people's war and to have total economic and political independence. [*Applause*] This is due to four factors: (a) lack of ideology, (b) negotiated independence, (c) opportunism, and (d) failure to develop a people's army.

a) Lack of ideology: If the political and military leaders do not have the perspective and do not learn from study, experience, travel, or however that it is impossible to liberate one's country unless one appropriates all the wealth and places it in the hands of the wretched of the earth, it follows that they will not implement decisions based upon this fundamental socialist principle.

b) Negotiated independence: Many people have had this principle in mind as they were waging a struggle for independence. But failing to win independence by defeating the enemy through armed struggle, it was necessary to negotiate with the colonial powers. This is a reality of Africa and the Caribbean where negotiations with the former colonial powers went on. In this process of negotiating, the colonial powers granted political independence—granted political independence—but maintained economic influence, control, and investments because it was cheaper to grant political independence and keep the economic control—this is what we hear from neo-colonialism—than it was to engage in a series of rebellions and perhaps wars such as the Algerian War. The mere act of negotiating independence meant that the controls necessary to appropriate the entire wealth of the country did not fall to the political leaders. In many instances those political leaders selected to head the country were themselves a guarantee that the entire wealth of the country would not be appropriated. They were well chosen, carefully selected, their politics acutely screened, and the colonial masters knew that they could negotiate safely without fear. Many people on the speaker's stand, for instance, cannot get into certain countries within the Caribbean. That's a fact. [*Applause*] There are exceptions to what I am saying and these exceptions vary in degrees, but as a general rule, if we survey the politics of the Third World and look at the ruling establishments of most countries, we must come to these conclusions, for we will see and we have learned from experience that the process of negotiating independence and not winning it by armed struggle has built-in limitations. France maintains the right to send troops, for instance, to its former colonies in the event of disturbances, riots, or rebellions. The Red Berets of France can go to Gabon, Chad, at any time they so desire, as the United States is trying to send its Green Berets throughout the world.

c) Opportunism: Opportunism becomes a factor when the bourgeois nationalists allow themselves and are allowed to be hand-picked as the representatives who will negotiate for those who may have launched and carried on an armed struggle for many years. They have become the spokesmen for those who picked up spears, knives, guns, hand grenades to fight the colonial masters but whose class is not represented in the deliberations. Thus, we often hear that there will be a second revolution in many countries of the Third World, especially Africa, revolutions where state power will be seized by peasants, proletariats, but not the bourgeoisie. [*Applause*] In some instances, political leaders have understood and struggled against the pitfalls of negotiated independence. They have recognized the limitations of their independence, which was negotiated with former colonial masters; they have declared themselves committed to socialist principles; some have nationalized more of their economies than others.

d) Failure to develop a people's army: But we have seen coups d'états resulting from not arming the population and creating a broad people's militia that would fight against colonial efforts to topple a progressive government or leader. It's happened in many countries, you can fill in the examples. Lacking broad support that is well-armed and capable of defending efforts to break the chains of negotiated independence, the kind of independence that we have seen granted to many of our countries, political leaders often find that they are helpless, they have no power, when they contemplate total nationalization of the resources of the countries.

Delegates and participants, in addition to all the implications of what I have said thus far, there are seven points particular to the life of Fanon that black writers and all revolutionaries should examine, for they point in a direction that we should move.

Number one: Fanon was a man of action, an activist, a militant. His life was engaged in the struggle against injustice. It is not just sufficient for the revolutionary artist to preach against injustice. He must become activated in an organization, in a group, in a political party, in revolutionary movements that are seeking to change injustices, seeking to bring about social change.

Number two: Fanon saw the need to consistently wage an ideological struggle. *The Wretched of the Earth* was written in three months after he knew he had leukemia. Three months before he died he wrote *The Wretched of the Earth*, knowing full well that he had leukemia and that he was going to die. He was writing and synthesizing experiences that served as a manifesto for liberation fighters based upon experiences of some thirty-six years, of moving about throughout the Third World, from the realities of Martinique, which are the realities of racism and colonialism, through North Africa during the Second World War, throughout Algeria, and throughout other parts of Africa. He felt that his greatest contribution, knowing that he had leukemia, knowing that he would die, would be to wage an ideological struggle that would serve to live on and that was the essence of *The Wretched of the Earth*. This ideological struggle that he waged is of particular importance to us as black artists and writers.

We see the black world divided on the question of ideology. Throughout Africa, the lack of ideology does divide people against people and ensures opportunism by certain leaders. Inside the United States, this is a paramount problem where the most technologically advanced group of black people are struggling in various ways for liberation. This advance is being checked through the lack of ideology among other things. The concept of Black Power, for instance, has been diluted to the point where even the most conservative blacks and the most conservative whites, such as [James L.] Buckley, who is running for United States senator on the Conservative Party, are now for Black Power. At the 1968 CORE (Congress of Racial Equality) convention, Whitney Young, the director of the Urban League, preaches for black pride and claims that Black Power is realizable through black capitalism. Floyd McKissick, former director of CORE, who once argued for Black Power, maintains that black people now need black capitalism. The United States government is in the process of giving tax incentives to those who start black businesses and invest in black areas, and the unlimited Ford Foundation, which is funding everything from black television programs, such as *Soul,* to experiments in school decentralization, such as [in] the Ocean Hill-Brownsville area and [in] IS 201, has recently declared that it will place some of its investment portfolio, not its returns, but some of its capital, which is unlimited, in developing black capitalism in the ghetto.

Number three: We cannot stress too much the pitfalls of the bourgeois nationalists. On this subject Fanon was adamant and correctly so. It behooves all those considering revolutionary work, which must be the paramount concern of all intellectuals, black writers, and artists, to be aware of these pitfalls: to study how revolutions are aborted, how independence movements are stifled, how people are cheated [of] the fruits of their efforts, how the foot soldier of the Mau Mau gets betrayed by the bourgeois nationalists is a subject that all writers, artists, and intellectuals must ponder if we are to move forward the clock of time and truly appropriate the wealth of the world for all the people.

Number four: Fanon understood very well the existence of the lumpenproletariat in a colonized country. It is here that the artist, the writer, the intellectual must make the backward thrust and perform its most valuable role by speaking to and working against this unemployed, underfed, ready-to-rebel class of an industrialized society. If it was true of the emerging countries in Africa in 1960, it is even more true of the United States and other countries throughout the world today.

Number five: While Fanon did not write much on military strategy, nevertheless his activities in the Algerian War and those of many other advanced socialists demonstrate quite vividly that the political leaders and the military must be one, must be integrated, and the political objectives must be dominant over the military operators, and that political leaders must not be separated from the base of the fighting. The separation of the military from the political leads to a dualism that is unhealthy, costly, and detrimental to the abolition of private property. The negotiations that led to a settlement in the Algerian War are very complex, it's a very complex matter, but it is a fact of history that the absence of a strong political party integrated with the lumpenproletariat and the peasantry, constantly stressing political education as well as military victories, has proven costly to masses of the Algerian people, and this comes from the separation of the political from the military and the lack of a revolutionary political party. [*Applause*]

Number six: Racism and colonialism were the realities of Fanon's life. They are the realities of all the Caribbean; they are the realities of all black people throughout the world. In his speech before the First Congress of Negro Writers and Artists he stated:

> Racism stares one in the face for it so happens that it belongs in a characteristic whole: that of the shameless exploitation of one group of men by another which has reached a higher stage of technical development. This is why military and economic oppression generally precedes, makes possible, and legitimizes racism.
>
> The habit of considering racism as a mental quirk, as a psychological flaw, must be abandoned.[3]

Harry Edwards has said the same thing in different words. There is an aspect of racism, however, that is often misunderstood, namely, the legacy and unconscious manifestations of racism. In a speech before the Western Regional Youth Conference, "Liberation Will Come From a Black Thing," held in Los Angeles, in November 1967,[4] based primarily upon my reflections of what Fanon meant when he said we must extend a Marxian analysis when we deal with colonialism, [I made] a major theoretical distinction that all colonized people are victims of racism and exploitation, [*sporadic applause*] but that all exploited people are not colonized. For instance, inside the United States we see whites who are oppressed and who are exploited, many of them, but they do not suffer directly from the racism that is inflicted upon blacks by whites. They are not a colonized people but a part of the exploiting group of people. They, in fact, form a part of the colonizing race. But I stress again that one cannot eliminate racism unless one controls the state power necessary to end all exploitation.

Number seven: Violence. Fanon understood that every village in Africa was colonized through violence. The process of decolonization, as he stated, is always a violent phenomenon and must be called for. In calling for violence as the method to end colonialism, Fanon was running against opposition that preached decolonization but stopped at the use of violence. His words were the forerun of the OLAS conference (the Organization of Latin American States, held in Havana, Cuba, in 1967), where peaceful co-existence versus armed struggle was debated. Some of the same opposition that opposed OLAS opposed the use of violence by the FLN in Algeria. Violence had to be legitimized in the Algerian War and in the international context, which is why we see *The Wretched of the Earth* opening up with violence in the phenomenon of decolonization. Let us remember also that in 1956 and up until 1961 and 1962, in the international context, ideas of non-violence were also widespread in those days, and the colonial powers, as they still do, employed violence upon the colonized but preached non-violence. Racism, capitalism, colonialism, imperialism dominate the lives of the people of the Third World. Violence by the oppressors and the military-industrial complex of the United States undergirds this domination.

Fanon, a man of action, was no different from Che Guevara, who was a man of action in Latin America, and brother Malcolm X in the United States. Although he died from leukemia, his death was no less tragic, and I would like to quote parts of a letter that he wrote on his deathbed:

> . . . if I had left Tunis four days later I would now be dead. There is not a single doctor who concealed that from me. In what shape am I now. I am in the difficult period following severe hemorrhages in which the still active leukemic process multiplies its assaults. And thus I am watched day and night, given injections of the types of the blood elements that I so badly lack, and massive transfusions to keep me in shape—that is, to keep me alive.
>
> . . . what I want to say to you is that death is always with us, and the important thing is not to know whether one can avoid it, but whether one does his utmost for the ideas he holds. What shocked me here in my bed as I felt my strength flagging was not to die, but to die of leukemia in Washington when I could have died face to face with the enemy three months previously since I knew I was suffering from this disease. We are nothing on earth if we are not first the slaves of a cause—of the cause of the world's people, the cause of the justice and freedom. I want you to know that even when the doctors gave up hope for me, I was still thinking . . . of the Algerian people, of the peoples of the Third world, and if I have held on it was because of them. . . .[5]

[*Long applause*]

I would like to conclude what I have to say by reading a statement of objectives that SNCC [Student Nonviolent Coordinating Committee] adopted at its annual meeting in June 1968 and that embodies the essence of what Fanon and other Third World figures were talking about:

> We the Africans who live in the United States are the descendants of those ripped from the shores of Africa, transplanted in an alien land, enslaved, forced to develop under political servitude the resources of

the United States. We are merely one part of the dispersed African population that the white Western slavers have scattered throughout the world. During our forced exile away from the continent of Africa, every attempt has been made to rupture our ancestral ties with Africa and to so brainwash us as to make us feel we have no relationship with the continent of Africa.

We assert today that we are part of the African continent.

We are overseas Africans living in the United States.

We are committed to the liberation of the African continent.

We are committed to the liberation of African people wherever they exist and are the victims of racism, exploitation, and oppression.

We make these assertions in the spirit of revolutionary Pan-Africanism. The concept of revolutionary Pan-Africanism makes it imperative that all Africans unite, wage a fight against racism, capitalism, and imperialism, those intertwined triple hyenas that have dispersed our people throughout the world, that keep us in bondage, and that oppress mankind.

We the people of Africa living in the United States must be extremely conscious of our need to cooperate, especially in the liberation of Southern Africa where the white Western powers have decided to maintain colonialism in its most brutal and savage forms. At the same time, we must redouble our efforts to unite all oppressed people suffering from imperialist domination led by the United States.

Concerning our internal situation in the United States, we form a colony within the United States. We are a colonized people. We suffer from racism, political domination, and economic exploitation, as well as cultural degradation.

The struggle of our people has been one of resistance to the colonizing process in the United States. We resisted on the high seas during our so-called enslavement, we resisted throughout the period of our enslavement and we fought with weapons in the United States Civil War for our so-called emancipation from status of slaves to neo-slaves.

We resist today and we shall continue to resist!

Within the brief span of history of our own organization we have seen efforts of the United States government and the white power people and press to further explain away the spirits of our resistance.

On February 1, 1964, students sat at a lunch counter in Greensborough, North Carolina. They were engaged in a new wave of rebellious activity by black college students that has mounted and raised the consciousness of our people to new heights of resistance in the streets of Watts, Newark, Detroit, and many other cities throughout the United States. The armed rebellions of black people in the so-called ghettos are just another manifestation of the resistance spirit of our people.

We are not unaware that the United States government, through its vast propaganda network in Atlanta, in Africa, in Asia, and Latin America, has tried to deceive our brothers overseas that the sit-ins were merely attempts to integrate into the mainstream of American life. This is a lie.

Our struggle during the early sixties was struggle against white supremacy and its racist, exploitative manifestations in the areas of public accommodations and lack of political representation. Even as we struggled then we were committed to fundamentally changing the political and economic framework of this country in which racism and white supremacy run rampant.

We see today on many fronts efforts to explain away and to remove the fire from the concept Black Power. There are those who would like to take the revolutionary sting away from Black Power and make it another American reform movement.

Therefore, it is necessary to state that Black Power is a revolutionary force that seeks the elimination of capitalism and the industrial-military complex which undergirds it. We call upon all our brothers and sisters to intensify the revolutionary consciousness among our people, to unite in the fight against racism, capitalism, and imperialism. It is through our unity and an unrelenting struggle by whatever means necessary that we will help in the liberation of oppressed people throughout the world.

We live in the jaws of the exploiting octopus.

We are a colony in his eye.

Our duty is clear.

Our historical role is evident.[6]

Thank you. [*Extended applause*]

Chapter 10

BLACK POWER
IN THE USA

STOKELY CARMICHAEL

WALTER RODNEY: Exposure to this black question is a tremendous thing for both black people and white people. I know some brothers who argue that if you go to a black man who doesn't know himself, you have to go slow at first. Don't press him too much or else it might be traumatic, it might destroy him. Well, we've had a lot already for the morning. We've had three speakers and we've had Fanon thrown in, too. That's a lot of exposure. I don't think the conference committee can hold themselves responsible for any traumas that are produced, [*laughter from crowd*] but you'll have to cope with brother Stokely coming up next. [*Applause*]

STOKELY CARMICHAEL: Thank you very much. Good afternoon. The trouble with being the last speaker is that either everybody says what you had written down [*crowd laughs*] or some have heard you say it before. [*Carmichael and crowd laugh*] What I think maybe I could do is try to pull together some of the things said this morning and then move on from there. I think it is clear that black people around the world are moving together today to solve the dilemma we face. I agree with brother Forman that we have certain ideological problems. I think we have a lot of ideological problems because we start from different major premises. Before I get into that, I want to regroup where we are now and where we have to go.

Now, there are two types of oppression in the world: There is exploitation and there is colonization. Forman explained that. I want to go into it more deeply because I think when one talks about exploitation, the question of race is not present. One just talks about a group of people who are economically taking advantage of another group. But when one talks about colonization, the question of race comes into play because in colonization it is one race that seeks to dominate an entire other race . . . an entire other race. [*Applause*] And if we begin to understand those concepts, then we will begin to see clearly where our revolutionary ideology must lead us and not into the pitfalls of any other type of ideology . . . any other type of ideology. [*Applause*]

Brother Fanon wrote a book called *The Wretched of the Earth* and he said, in essence, that the Third World was the wretched of the earth. But of the Third World, the most damned happens to be the black man . . . happens to be the black man. [*Applause*] Wherever the black man is found he is on the bottom of the ladder. [*Applause*] And there must be reasons for this other than just economic. I would say the reasons happen to be a deep, ingrained racism produced by white Western society. [*Applause*] And we must understand that and if we try to bluff it over, we will indeed fail where many other black communists and black socialists have failed because they fail to deal with the realities of racism . . . of racism. [*Applause*]

It is indeed a fact that not one Western power today achieved its power without raping Africa. You name it and I'll claim it. [*Applause*] Not one. Portugal, Spain, the Netherlands, Belgium, France, England, the United States, Canada, an extension of the United States, [*applause and laughter*] except for the French Canadians. [*Applause and laughter*] But they are still part of white Western . . . [*words drowned out by laughter*] and they did rape West Africa because my friends in Guinea speak fluent French. [*Applause*]

I want, then, for us to begin to deal clearly with the question of colonization. Wherever the black man is, he is colonized. What, then, in concrete terms, is the difference between exploitation and colonization? There are in fact poor white people in the United States. They are exploited, that is to say they are economically deprived of some wealth in the United States. But those white people have their culture, their history, their language, and their value system. These things have not been stripped from them. But that is not true for black people living in the United States. We have been stripped of our culture, our language, our history, our value system, our way of life. We are in fact what Fanon called dehumanized. We are dehumanized . . . we are dehumanized. [*Applause*] And that is the effect of the process of colonization. It seeks to dehumanize its victims. Exploitation does not . . . exploitation does not. So, we are fighting for our humanity. Fanon says that very clearly at the end of *The Wretched of the Earth*. It is our humanity that we are fighting for. White people are just fighting for more money. Poor white people. [*Applause*]

And we have to understand, we have to understand precisely what that means, what the fight of humanity is all about, because it means then that we will proceed differently.

Number one, it is necessary for Africans (and I make no distinctions between Africans living on the continent or Africans living abroad), there is a necessity for Africans to begin to understand the culture that has been plundered, purposely and maliciously, by white Western society, and it is a necessity for us to pick up that culture and begin to use it as a unifying tool because a culture is a cohesive force for a people . . . it is a cohesive force for a people. [*Applause*] And that culture has been taken from us because we were never meant to be a united people, because, in the unity, there will we alone begin to amass a way for us to make an assault against our aggressor . . . our aggressor.

Now, I want to keep hammering on that point because I think too many times people, especially Africans, just over-gloss it as if it doesn't mean any-thing, as if racism was just nothing. But there must be something to it, we must question, why us? Why did they go to Africa and just scatter us all over the earth? They had the Indians. Why us? Why the black man? Why is it that they saw fit to split us up, put us in Trinidad, in Jamaica, in St. Thomas, in Brazil, in Cuba, in Panama, in Santo Domingo, in Guatemala, in the United States—eh, even in Canada. Why us? Why us? [*Applause*] And to say that it is for economic reasons is to delude one's self . . . it is to delude one's self [*applause*] because they could have just as easily found white slaves; they could have just as easily gotten red slaves; they had Indian slaves (I'm talking from East India); they had Chinese. Why the black man? And unless we begin to deal consciously with that ingrained racism, our ideology will come to nil. We must understand that . . . must understand. [*Applause*]

Now then, in understanding the effects of colonization we must ask ourselves, what is it that they do that dehumanizes us? The main effect that I've found of colonization is that it makes the victim hate himself . . . hate himself . . . hate himself. [*Applause*] And by allowing the victim to hate him-self, he seeks to identify with the master whom he assumes has the values that he himself hates because he hates the values that he produces . . . that he produces. [*Applause*] And that is precisely what white Western society has done wherever it has gone. It has destroyed and created hatred among its victims of each other and of themselves. Therefore, they never want to unite with each other because they hate each other and themselves and they seek to unite with the master whom they love and adore . . . whom they love and adore. [*Applause*] And we must begin to speak to that.

So, colonized people, when we begin to move for a real struggle of liberation, we move on two phases. I call them, for lack of a better word, entertainment and educational. I think that brother Harry spoke of the entertainment. The entertainment is a necessity. That is where you call the oppressor names. You have to call him names because prior to that stage you can't even speak out loud against the oppressor. Let us take, point in case, Africans living in the United States. Until a couple of years ago, they were afraid to say what they really felt about white people out loud. They had to whisper it to each other. So, there becomes a stage where they begin to, as they define themselves, speak out against the oppressor, sort of a warming up session for a fight. You know, like you say, "I can take 'em, I can whoop 'em anytime." [*Applause*] And it's a feel-good session, it's a necessity. It is, as Cortland Cox says, insufficient. We need something else to go with it, but we must recognize the necessity of the stages of our struggle. We cannot let white people interpret it for us because they will always degrade it and if we accept that degradation of ourselves, we are back in the colonial state . . . back in the colonial state. [*Applause*]

Now, once a people who are colonized begin to move against entertaining themselves, then comes the point of education, the point where they begin to speak concretely to the things that must be done. In the United States particularly, Africans have begun to reach that level. That is the most dangerous level for the oppressor . . . the most dangerous level. And that is why there is so much friction among the movements inside the United States that are again caused by the oppressor. Fanon says that. Fanon says very clearly that when—I can't remember what page it is, and I don't think I got the quote correctly—can you get it for me, brother Forman? [*Carmichael laughs*]—but he says, the colonized begin to move, the oppressor tries a number of tricks. Number one is the good trick: they try to be nice, kind to you. They let you [have] poverty programs, grants, they try to pacify you. Once the process of pacification is not working, then they begin to send agent provocateurs inside your movement to stir up and cause fraction within the different branches of your liberation movement . . . liberation movement. [*Applause*] When, finally, that stage itself does not work, they come in, as they always come in, with the armed forces.

All right then. We said the United States, particularly, moves in three ways. We call it the three Ms: missionaries, the money, and the marines. [*Applause and laughter*] Now, let us go back to the hatred because I don't think we can really dig deep into that enough because to cleanse ourselves of this self-hatred is a process that Fanon recognized and said that sometimes that cleansing period comes out in violence against the oppressor . . . against the oppressor. We must begin to direct and channel that violence so that it is a decisive blow against the oppressor. I don't think . . . [*Feedback from the microphone and Carmichael says, "CIA," followed by laughter and applause from the audience*].

Now, if we're going to begin to counteract the hatred that we have had for ourselves and for each other, and it's clearly manifested in black people—I mean the running away from the identity of ourselves, the trying to seek to identify with the oppressor, with his symbols of beauty, his symbols of success, etcetera—we today should come to grips with most of those things. But in order to really counteract it we must begin to develop, since we live in a dialectical world where opposites prevail—we must begin to develop an undying love for ourselves to counteract the hatred that we have for ourselves. And in developing that undying love, which is not in fact contradictory to revolution because it's the same type of love that Che Guevara speaks about—the love the revolutionary has—but for the colonized it must be concrete; it must be the love of ourselves that we have to get and the love of our people, especially for the African, because geographically we have been scattered all over the world . . . all over the world. [*Applause*] And while we can look to Africa as the mother continent, we have many of our people abroad who do not have any geographical area. So the nationalism, which is usually based in land, is going to be lacking for a certain time. While that is lacking, we must give our people at least a type of ideology that they can hold on to. [*Applause*] And that philosophy must be based in the concept of the African wherever he is scattered around the world.

What is the history of the African? In Brazil, 50 percent of the population is African. All over the northern section of South America—Africans. We don't even know where we are. We have never asked to be sent there. In each of these countries we do not own or control anything. In each of these countries we're at the bottom; in each of these countries, at this time, we're not strong enough to seize power; and in each of these countries, at this time, it is the white people who keep running and deciding while we are left on the bottom as puppets; in each of these countries . . . in each of these countries. We've got to understand the roots of racism . . . got to understand that. [*Applause and shouts of "Yes, sir, yes, sir" from the audience*]

Then, we have to state clearly what our fight is. Our fight is against racism and capitalism, and certainly imperialism, which is the highest stage of capitalism. [*Applause and cheering from the crowd*] I do not think any of us sitting on this platform are deluded by the black power pimps in the United States. If they were not there, we would not be doing a good job. The fact that they have to try and co-opt Black Power means that we are doing our job . . . it means that we are doing our . . . . [*Applause drowns out words*] And if we follow correctly, it means that we are heading for the right struggle because that is precisely what they're supposed to do—try and co-opt it. Then when co-option fails, then the real confrontation will begin to take place. And we have to know that in our minds if we say we're revolutionary.

Now then, if we fight against racism and capitalism and imperialism, our question is, what is our goal? Clearly our goal would be a society free of racism and a society free of capitalism or imperialism. When talking about capitalism, there are three dominating economic systems in the world: capitalism, socialism, or communism. It means that if one is anti-capitalism and if one is going to seek, within the conventional framework, to redress one's problems, one must look to socialism and to communism. But just to say socialism or communism today is not enough, because there are many types of socialism and communism in the world today. Tito calls himself a communist, Mao Tse-tung calls himself a communist, Fidel Castro calls himself a communist, and the Russians say that they are communist. [*Applause and laughter*] So, just to throw those words loosely around just won't make it. I certainly don't think that one could go along with the Russian form of communism and also go along with the Chinese form of communism because they are clearly different. They're clearly different ideological areas where people must take sides. And what is happening is that the African, who doesn't have a land to talk about, is caught up in an ideological fight between whether we should be Mao Tse-tungites or whether we should be Russianites, and we don't even have a country to call our own . . . not a country to call our own. [*Applause*] And so the first thing that we must seek is to begin to talk about ourselves and how we get that ideology together, move to seize some land, build a base, and begin to liberate our people and, of course, the Motherland.

Okay. We ought to understand, though, in dealing with communism, especially Russian communism, that we have to gather from the history of our people. There was a black man from Trinidad by the name of George Padmore. He served on the Comintern under Stalin and he left because he said the Russians were racist, essentially. On the question of colonialism in Africa, the Russians compromised clearly, clearly, clearly. Any African student who's been to Russia will tell you clearly that the Russians are racist, period. [*Applause*] And we must begin to understand—we must, we must, we must—because there are too many tricks being played on us today; because the black man is going to be pivotal in the coming years. We know it and they know it.

Our goal of society is one free of racism and free of imperialism. The question is, can we achieve a society free of racism where both races can live together? That is the question that we must really address ourselves to, and not just quote words and say niceties about all human beings because that's Western; they have said that and, as Fanon says, they have proved themselves incapable of bringing it about. [*Applause*] And the question that we must now be asking is, whether or not you can? Brother Harry says that it's clear that inside a society you cannot have two political and economic systems. Can it also be true that you can't have, inside a society, two races that can in fact coexist without one dominating the other? And I'm just not talking about physical domination, I'm also talking about cultural domination.

We have to begin to define some terms that are being thrown around very loosely, such as revolutions, black revolutionaries, militants, black militants, armed struggle, etcetera. I think we ought to understand what a revolutionary is, when a revolution is, and how it comes about. A revolution is the total destruction of the old system, total destruction, the replacement of a new system that speaks for the masses of the people of a given country. That's when you have revolution. You have the changing of hands of governments, you have coup d'états—you don't have revolutions. I think that Forman went into this quite lengthily, so I can just brush over it, but [we must] keep reminding [ourselves] that you don't have a revolution until you have taken power. A revolution does not begin until you take power. To talk about revolution before you take power is to be, at best, politically naïve, at worst, stupid. [*Applause and laughter*]

For example, Fidel Castro fought in the Sierra Maestra for several years. But while he was fighting, the Cuban revolution was not going on. The Cuban revolution did not start until Fidel walked into Havana with guns in his hand, Che on his side, and said, "This day I claim this country for the masses of Cuban people." Then the revolution began . . . then the revolution began. [*Applause*] Now, the period that precedes a revolution is called armed struggle. So what Fidel was waging before he walked into Havana was armed struggle, not revolution. Armed struggle. Armed struggle because you can't have revolution until you have the power. You can't give people jobs if you don't control 'em. You can't distribute the wealth unless you've got the wealth. [*Someone in the crowd says*, "That's right."] So, you can't talk about revolution until you have seized power.

Now for me it is clear, there are only three ways you get things: [*laughter*] You ask, you beg, or you take. [*Applause*] You work for it, you beg for it, or you take it. No, you don't steal it, you take it. You only steal it when you don't have power. If you have power, you take. [*Applause*] I don't think that white Canadians would say that they stole Canada from the Indians. [*Laughter*] They said they took it—and they did. [*Applause and laughter*] Well then, it's clear that we can't work for these lands, we can't beg for them, so we must take them. Then it's clear that we must take them through revolutionary violence. Now, violence is neither good nor bad. There is no moral judgment to violence. Violence is only he who has the power to legitimatize. Oh, yes. Oh, yes. In the United States, if I were in the United States army, I would be in Vietnam. If I killed thirty yellow people with slanted eyes, I would get medals. Yes. In the United States of America, if I shot two white cops in Harlem, I would get the electric chair. So, murder is neither right nor wrong, it is he who has the power to legitimatize it. [*Applause*] And the major dilemma that Africans face is that we have never legitimatized. White Western society has legitimatized everything for us. We have never been able to legitimatize. They legitimatized religion; they legitimatized wars; they legitimatized education; they legitimatized beauty; they legitimatized everything. We must now seek to legitimatize for ourselves. We must say to people in the United States it is more honourable to kill honky cops than to kill Vietnamese. They have done nothing to us. [*Applause*] We have to seek to legitimatize because they will not let us legitimatize. If I were in power and you were arming against me, I wouldn't let you arm against me. Destroy you. Have to if I'm going to stay in power and we have to recognize that. That's our struggle. The struggle is that much harder, the victory is going to be that much sweeter. [*Sporadic applause*]

Now then, what do we mean by revolutionary violence? I think we ought to understand because the line is very thin. It's a line that the late Dr. King used to play with. He said, "I'm against self-defense because in self-defense the line of aggressive violence and defensive violence is very thin." He's correct. It is very thin. But we must understand that self-defense never changes the status quo. It maintains the status quo, it just keeps the victim alive. [*Short applause*] Let me give you an example. If every black man in the United States was armed today and they sat in the boundaries of the communities we're confined to and every time a white cop came after us we shot him, the system of the United States would never change. It would remain the same. We would live longer if they would just isolate us. Self-defense never changes the situation. Che Guevara said that. It maintains the status quo. Aggressive violence is what is needed to change the status quo—clearly, clearly, clearly. [*Applause*] But that is because Africans get caught up in the questions of violence. We think that violence is just shooting or murder. We do not see that poverty is violence; we do not see that race is violence; we do not see that cultural degradation is violence. We have allowed white society to define violence as only the man with the gun. How stupid. It is violent for white society to rape Africa of copper, gold, aluminum, everything. It is violent . . . it is violent . . . it is violent. . . . [*Long applause*] It is violent to have little black children get up and feel that they are ugly. It is violent, it is violent. [*Applause*]

And we have to define violence and redefine how we meet that violence. You meet violence with violence. It's just a degree, that's all it is. And once we begin to define it, then we legitimatize the right to move. We should not think that violence is just the gun or death. As a matter of fact, I would much rather die at twenty-six than live to seventy-six and die of malnutrition and see my children hungry, starving, my daughters prostitutes, and my wife sitting in a corner, and my children with big stomachs. I would rather die at twenty-six. [*Applause*] So, then, what the African has to do is to, for himself, define and no longer allow white society to define. We must define . . . we must define . . . we must define.

I want to say one thing about the period in which black revolutionary movements around the world find themselves. Or maybe I should talk about black militants versus black revolutionaries first. Now, in the United States there are a lot of black militants. There are few black revolutionaries because we said a revolutionary is for the total overthrow of the old order. A black militant is someone in the United States who is an angry black man. But he is angry that he, individually, is kept out of the system. A black revolutionary is someone who wants to overthrow, destroy, turn up, tear up, burn down, and start all over again . . . all over again . . . all over again. . . . [*Applause*] A black militant is someone who yells and screams about the degradation of black men, and as soon as he gets a $20,000 a year poverty job, jumps up and yells, "Cool it brothers, everything's gonna be all right." [*Applause and laughter*]

And we have to make clear that distinction. There are a lot of black militants in the United States. That's why you can have somebody who is for Black Power and black capitalism. He's a black militant. Militant in that he's moving hard against the system because he wants to be part of it. He has been kept out of it. He wants to be in it. A black revolutionary does not want to be any part of it. He wants to completely destroy it.

Now, if there are black revolutionaries in the United States, it's clear that we cannot just look inside the United States, but we must begin to look internationally. To talk about Black Power in the United States is absurd and self-defeating. We must talk about Black Power in the world . . . in the world . . . in the world. [*Applause*] The Congress invited Rap Brown, LeRoi Jones, Eldridge Cleaver, and several other people. They cannot leave the United States because the one thing the United States does not want is the black man making international ties. [*Applause*] Had my passport took from me and I didn't do anything but go where I wanted to go. And they told me I was free to go so I went to China, Vietnam, Cuba. See the world. Why not? I'm an American. [*Laughter*] Took my passport. They take those passports because the most vulnerable spot of capitalism today—because it is no longer domestic capitalism but world imperialism—is the struggle on the international level. Must be. And that's why we cannot seek to just talk about local problems as an entity unto themselves. We must begin to internationalize our thinking, therefore it is our responsibility to know about the struggles in the world, not only of black people, but of other oppressed people and to know which side we're on, who we must begin to support, at this point morally, to a point where we can then move materially. We must begin to do that . . . must begin to . . . . [*Applause*]

Because the United States is aware of this, what they're going to do is create more fractions inside the black movements. You will have divisions. For example, in one country in Africa you have five guerilla groups. Yes! Each of them has the message, each of them has the correct ideology, and each of them is going to lead the masses to revolution. Each of them with their cadres of twenty-five each, they're going to lead the revolution. Now, it seems to me it is the role of anyone who calls himself a revolutionary to, rather than emphasize, de-emphasize the divisions within his own group. We must present a united front . . . we must present a united front. [*Applause*] Because to emphasize those conditions only leads our people, who still hate themselves, to an excuse to wipe out each other, because our people are still colonized in the mind. All of us . . . all of us. The first thing we do when we become revolutionary is to want to attack another black man. It is true that the Vietnamese killed South Vietnamese, but they do not seek to kill South Vietnamese. They run from fights with the South Vietnamese and only when they have to fight the South Vietnamese do they fight the South Vietnamese. They know who their major enemy is. Their major enemy is the United States of America, the aggressors . . . the aggressors. [*Applause*] They understand that in their minds very clearly and that is very revolutionary. When Mao Tse-tung broke from the Comintern in 1929, he didn't go around fighting Chiang Kai-shek. They kept running from the Chinese, pleading with the Chinese saying, "We're brothers. We're the same people. Let's not fight each other. Let's unite. Let's take care of the Japanese invaders." They were always consciously attacking the major enemy. The major enemy is never your own people who have developed and come out of the same environment that you come out of. It is the man who has worked and controlled those environments who produces your people to turn against you. Certainly, the people in South Vietnam—[Nguyen Cao] Ky and [Nguyen Van] Thieu, and there is another one—are just puppets. If you shoot them, the man is going to get another puppet. But if you shoot the man controlling the puppets, then they're gonna do like you want them to do . . . do like you want them to do. [*Applause*]

Our major enemy first—because also, speaking revolutionary, you cannot wage two fights at the same time, especially if you're trying to organize and develop an army. You can't do it. You have to wage only one front. Fidel Castro told the Cuban bourgeoisie, "Let's get rid of Batista, brothers." And then when he got rid of Batista he said, "Dig, this is a Leninist-Marxian state. Pick your sides. Either you're with me or get against the wall." [*Laughter*] He did not fight the bourgeoisie while he was fighting Batista and the American lackeys. It's impossible to do that. He had to first get rid of the external threat and then begin to talk about the internal threat. You can't talk about an internal threat when you have nothing to talk about. You certainly are cautious, but you don't begin to make an onslaught against your own people. That's just what the enemy wants you to do. When you hear the tallies of the South Vietnamese in the Vietnam War, you never hear 500 South Vietnamese killed. You hear 500 Americans killed this week. You very rarely see South Vietnamese because the Vietnamese consciously try to get to their people and to correct them and say to them, "You have no business fighting with the Americans." They try to convert them. They try to get people working inside the lines with America. And unless they have to defend themselves, that's the only time they fight South Vietnamese. And we have to understand that principle.

We have to ask ourselves, how, then, do Africans move against white Western society? Because we cannot see it as an isolated fight—black people in the United States against white America or black Trinidadians against whomever controls them. [*Laughter and applause. Carmichael responds to a comment from the audience:* "They were intellectuals, they went to Oxford. [*Laughter*] That's why we have to redefine education."]

Another member of the audience asks: "Will we get 'em?" *to which Carmichael responds:* "Yeah, we gonna get 'em. No doubt about it."] We have to understand that in Guinea-Bissau, in Angola, in Mozambique, it's not just gonna be black people against the Portuguese. The Portuguese are supported by the United States of America. [*Applause*] Yes. When Portugal bombs Guinea-Bissau, Portugal doesn't manufacture any planes. It's an American plane bombing Guinea-Bissau. But what the Americans say is that we don't give them planes to bomb Africa. They are part of NATO and we have to give them planes for NATO. [*Carmichael laughs and the crowd applauds*] If South Africa were to revolt today, do you believe that the United States of America would sit idly by and let the blacks take their country? You are absolutely deluding yourself. It is going to be an international fight. Do you think that Nkrumah was dethroned merely by some simple black man named Ankrah. No, he was dethroned by the forces of Britain, the United States, and France. [*Applause*] What of the fight in Nigeria today? Do you think the fight in Nigeria is really a black man's fight, or is it white people who are waiting to gain the oil in Biafra because the Arabs have closed their oil ports. [*Applause*] We have to understand precisely what is going on in the world because the African is going to play a key role in World War Three and it's right around the corner.

Now then, when you move as a colonized people, you move culturally, you move politically, you move economically, and you move militarily. Now, obviously, the United States of America is not going to allow black people to move politically in any way that's going to endanger their political system. Clearly, they're not going to allow black people to move economically in any way that's going to—at least if they see it—going to endanger their economic system. They're not gonna let black people move in any way, culturally or militarily, that's going to allow black people to endanger their system. Any way they see it, they will break it up in any way. And finally, of course, there's always force and with force, at this time, they can win. So then, we must begin to instill in our mind something that will balance out the question of force.

Now Mao Tse-tung said, and the Vietnamese prove, that technological power does not win a war. It is the will of the people to fight that wins a war. It is always the will of the people to fight that decides which war is won. The United States should be able to defeat Vietnam. They cannot because Ho Chi Minh has instilled in the people of Vietnam a faith that, no matter what, they die. The only way America can have Vietnam is when the last Vietnamese is wiped out, if he is six months or 106 years. Only way . . . only way. [*Applause*]

We have to begin, then, to do that to our people. That is the job of writers. They must instill in our people a will to fight to the death. It is a question of either we win or we die. Nothing else . . . nothing else. We win or we die. [*Applause*] Either we control the resources of our mother continent or no one controls the resources of our mother continent. [*Applause*] Either we control the destinies of our lives or nobody controls any lives where we live . . . no lives where we live. [*Applause*] The paradoxes must be clear and the contradictions must be heightened, because in heightening contradictions you prepare the ground for revolutionary warfare. We must heighten the contradictions. It is the job, then, of the black writer to work to heighten the contradictions. Let us not waste our time mish-mashing. Let's polarize the forces. Let's polarize them so that the contradictions are clear, so that there is a choice: either you fight with us or you fight with them. There is no middle ground. We must heighten the contradictions. We must consciously work to heighten the contradictions. That is the job of the artist. It must be his job, because he, at this time, is allowed to move where other people are not. And he must seek now to break the ground and to prepare the movement for the political-economic 'cause the military will continue to go on, but not in the onslaught that is needed at this time.

He must begin, the black writer must begin to redefine for the African whom our heroes are. We no longer need white cowboys. We need Kwame Nkrumahs, Sekou Toures, Du Bois, Marcus Garvey, Malcolm X, LeRoi Jones, Rap Brown. [*Applause*] It is the job, then, of the black writer to do this. It is the job of the black writer to do this. And the black writer must begin to redefine it and not in a concept of Western society but in an African concept that means it is not wholly intellectual but rather quite emotional. [*Applause*] Because Africans are an emotional people. [*Applause and laughter and a* "That's right" *from the audience.*] I know we've been taught to be ashamed of it 'cause white society says, "You just can't do something, you got to sit down and think about it." [*Laughter*] And we sit down and think about it and think about it and then still go out and do the wrong thing. [*Laughter*] Even one of their philosophers, Pascal, says the mind has a heart of its own. Of its own. And we do not have to just think all the time that you can't move until you analyze certain situations. Of course there is need for scientific analyzation but the period of analyzation has always been used by white society to delude and forestall our movement . . . always has been used. [*Applause*]

All we have to do is look at Dr. W. E. B. Du Bois. They allowed him to play back and forth with their intellectual nonsense and forestall our movement. Yes. And if we continue to play intellectual games with them, we do a disservice to the masses of our people. We are not responsible to answering Western society. We are responsible only to fulfilling the needs of the masses of Africans in the world today. Nothing else . . . nothing else. [*Short applause*] And clearly, that is the job of the black writer. And if he wants to do that, he must just ignore—do not even waste time answering or contradicting. They are not worth our time. In most of the places, only the black writer who has been to a white college knows of them. [*Someone on the panel says*, "Shakespeare." *Stokely asks:* "What's that cat who wrote the *Canterbury Tales*?" *and someone says*, "Never heard of him," *followed by laughter from the audience. Then Carmichael says*, "Come on there, Joans," *likely referring to poet Ted Joans.*] We don't have to waste our time even contradicting the arguments that they give because that means we are on the defensive. We have always to be on the offensive because we are fighting a just struggle. They have to be on the defensive. If we allow them to put us on the defensive, we never wage a war. We are just caught up defending them.

For example, a black man gets up and a white man says, "You're racist," and he spends twenty-five minutes explaining that he is not a racist to white people . . . to white people. [*Applause*] Later, you can call him racist. They tell you, "Yeah, I'm a racist and if you get smart, I'm gonna kill you and there ain't nothing you can do about it." [*Applause and laughter*] Because they do not waste their time arguing. Black man says that black people must arm themselves and white people say that's violence, you have to be non-violent, and a black man is gonna argue for years and years on the need for violence. When they came to get slaves from Africa they didn't come non-violently. [*Applause and laughter*]

When they took South America, when they took the United States, when they took Canada, they didn't take it non-violently. They took it with a pioneering spirit. [*Applause and laughter*] And it is with a pioneering spirit that we must move forward. [*Applause and laughter*] Then that becomes the main task and the main responsibility of the black writer, because too many black writers are involved in contradicting and proving white society incorrect. The fact that you pay attention to them means that you give their arguments validity. Assume your major presumption is that they are invalid. Let us create our own and move on. Move on . . . move on. [*Applause*]. Forman said that it is the job of the black writer to become involved. Certainly, he is not a writer first. He is black first. [*Applause*] The writings that he produces are the writings from an environment that he is from because he is black, not because he has writer's skills—because he is black . . . because he is black. Yes. That's his first task. Not to talk about the literary skills of writing and blah, blah. Who defines the literary skills of writing? [*In response to a statement from the crowd Carmichael says* "Shakespeare," *which is followed by laughter.*]

Now then, before I conclude I want to touch on the subject of where we must move, and that's the international arena. And this becomes the most important task of the writer because he can begin to create heroes through the poems, through the rhymes, through the short stories. For example, he can write a book called *Our Comrade in Arms the Vietnamese—the North Vietnamese.* And we could just pass it around because the Vietnamese are our comrades in arms. [*Applause*] Then let the white writers try to tell us why they are not our comrades in arms. He could write *Our Friends the Arabs* 'cause we must understand the conflicts in the Middle East if we are to be international. And we must understand why it is imperative that black people side with the Arabs because theirs is a just war . . . a just war. [*Applause*] But most of the black writers get caught up in defending the so-called state of Israel and justifying the fact that six million Jews got killed therefore they should have Israel. What nonsense is that? All of us are sorry that six million Jews got killed but that doesn't mean therefore Israel. Therefore East Germany. Therefore East Germany. [*Applause*] The Arabs did not kill the Jews, Hitler killed the Jews. You want, take it from Hitler . . . take it from Hitler. [*Applause*]

The black writer today is caught in a period where he's afraid to open his mouth, because as soon as he says Arabs, they say anti-Semitic, and he crawls back into his shell. They're anti-black. Later for them. Let's move on. We must understand the implications of the Middle East war and we must understand why the Arabs. Emotionally, Egypt is in Africa. [*Applause*] It has been in Africa for over four thousand years. If we say we come from Africa, then we fight for Africa. Can we let people who just developed a state in 1948 cling to that any more than we cling to over four thousand years of history? No, we must be clear, we must be precise, and we can never be afraid of not moving. We may be afraid, but we can never let fear immobilize us. We've got to move on. [*Applause*] We've got to move on . . . got to move on. We have to understand the implications of Cuba and we have to say, yeah, the Cubans are doing it and we are with them. Go on Fidel, work with it, work with it, work with it. [*Applause*] And we have to prepare ourselves for the Sino-Soviet dispute, which is going to grow, and understand whose side we're on and why we're on their side. Check Mao Tse-tung out, check Mao. [*Scattered applause*]

We have to understand the implications of the Organization of American States in South America and the hold that it has on our territories, our territories in the Caribbean. We must understand that, have to understand that, got to understand that. [*Applause*] We have to understand the French interventionist forces that Forman talked about. So, De Gaulle can preach his junk, but he moves in with force any time somebody threatens one of his territories in our motherland. Got to understand that . . . got to understand that. [*Applause*]

There is little time for us to do anything but to consciously think, read, communicate, prepare, and get guns, and get guns, and get guns. [*Applause*] Get 'em. Get all the guns you can get. We believe in equality. [*Applause and laughter*] White people got guns, black people should have guns. [*Applause*] Don't get caught up with that new pro-liberation nuclear madness. That's junk. Russia, the United States, France, England, and now Israel got the atomic bomb and now they're going to say to everybody "Don't develop it. You all don't need it, we got it." [*Applause and laughter*] If they got an atomic bomb, every country needs an atomic bomb. If they got a hydrogen, cobalt, whatever bomb they have, every country has to have it, because we must understand, equality is not this political nonsense about one man, one vote. It is economic and military equality that counts in the world today. [*Applause*] It is must be political, it must be economical, it must be militarily. When you have those three, then you have real equality. Can't have one without the other; can't have the vote and no gun if the white man got the gun; can't have the vote and no money if the white man got the money. I can have the vote and he can have the vote; I can have the gun, he can have the gun; I can have the money, he can have the money. Then when he gets smart, we can go to it. [*Laughter*]

But if I don't have anything and he has everything, I have to take from him what he gives to me. We've got to get guns. Got to get guns. Because if you talk about revolutionary, you cannot be revolutionary until you pick up the gun and you are willing to kill for your people. Notice I didn't say die. Anybody can do that. [*Laughter*] I am serious. It is much easier to die for one's people than it is to kill for one's people. Dr. Martin Luther King is a living testament to that. Yes, it is much easier to die for one's people than to kill for one's people, especially if you are the oppressed.

Now, once one picks up the gun, it doesn't necessarily mean that you are revolutionary. Then you need to develop that political direction that we have been discussing. But that political direction develops as we move. Fanon is correct. There is lacking an ideology for the Africans, but the

Chinese didn't have their ideology in a blueprint of revolution. They struggled, they fought, the contradictions arose, they resolved. If they didn't resolve the contradictions, the contradictions resolved them. It was not until they conquered that they began to develop a real revolutionary ideology. [*Applause*] The same then is true of Cuba and the same must be true for us. We must work, struggle, develop that ideology, but we must be conscious of what we're against—racism, capitalism, and imperialism. That is our fight.

Thank you. [*Massive applause*]

RODNEY: I have a few bureaucratic functions to perform. The first is to ask people if they can just hold tight until we are quite through, until the speakers have a chance to leave the platform. Apart from that, it is important to notice that the white press attempted to play up certain family differences that black people had at this conference, that are necessary and do not break up the family in any way. And one positive thing that those of us have come here to participate would like to do is to express our appreciation to the congress organizers, to the West Indian Student Society [*applause*] for having undertaken what is a major operation, and hope that this, in itself, will be a form of development within the Montreal and Canadian community, as far as the blacks are concerned and, indeed, the whites.

And as I said, this is our testimonial, as it were, to our own solidarity with those black brothers who went to the trouble of preparing this conference. There is very little else to say. Initially, if those of you who might not have heard, the conference, of course, is over, because we've had everything we should have had this afternoon. But for those delegates and other participants who are still around, at 2:30 p.m. those delegations will meet again in another family discussion from, I think, 2:30 p.m. Three o'clock is the time that is announced. I think we'll meet here. And I don't think anybody need misunderstand when we say family discussion. [*Applause and cheering*]

SOMEONE FROM THE AUDIENCE: Make them stand in respect to the prime minister of the black nation.[1] Yes, sir.

RODNEY: Well, we'll have a standing ovation while the brothers leave. [*Applause*]

Chapter 11

"A BLACK WOMAN SPEAKS OUT"

BARBARA JONES

McGill Reporter, November 4, 1968

BLACK PEOPLE living in Canada are afflicted by all the problems that confront the French Canadian, the Indian, and the Eskimo in the so-called "Just Society." Black people came to Canada in the early part of the 18th century after the slave trade and slavery were abolished in the colonies. The importation of slaves *per se* was outlawed in Quebec by a law including a clause that children of slaves would become free at the age of twenty-five. In Upper Canada slavery was outlawed later, and in Nova Scotia runaway slaves settled near Halifax to give an estimated thirty thousand slaves in Canada.

Today, over 100 years later, the 100,000 resident blacks in Canada are asking themselves and Canadian society whether blatant and open discriminatory practices will be allowed to continue. Perhaps it is at this point it should be mentioned that within the past two months two major conferences concerning black people have been held in Montreal, and these conferences will in large measure indicate the steps that black Canadians are willing to take at the national and international levels to right the wrongs meted out to them in Canada.

The conference held at Sir George Williams University, October 4, 5, and 6, sponsored by the Caribbean Committee, for the first time broadened the base of the annual conference on West [Indian] Affairs to the theme of "The Involvement of the Black Community in Canadian Society." Speakers were included from all the representative groups from British Columbia to the Maritimes, and included Dr. Howard McCurdy; Mr. Frank Collins, president of the National Association for the Advancement of Colored People (NAACP), Vancouver; Dr. Daniel Hill, director of [the] Human Rights Commission, Ontario; Mr. Rafeek Ali, a student from Sir George Williams University; Prof. John Shingler, McGill; Mr. Ray W. Traversy, Fair Employment Practices of [the] Canadian Department of Labor, Ottawa; Mr. H.A.J. Wedderburn, president of the NS [Nova Scotia] NAACP; Mr. Richard Lord, English-speaking VP, Quebec Liberal Party. The main problems discussed were those of employment, mobility, and advancement in the labor force, and the problems of social, political, and cultural alienation within the society.

It was discovered that Ontario is the only province to have any housing legislation (see Ontario Human Rights Code—1961–1962—where it states: "No person . . . shall . . . deny to any person or class of person occupancy of any commercial unit or any self-contained dwelling unit.). Legislation in Nova Scotia cannot afford such housing. The beginnings of black ghettoes in the major cities of Nova Scotia, Ontario, Quebec, and British Columbia should serve as a warning to any political party which envisages a Canada different to the urban northern United States. Black Canadian ghettoes are formed as a measure of protection from a white society which has sat back smugly and decried its neighbor to the south.

Also included in the conference discussion were the psychological, sociological, and political aspects of the black man's alienation from Canadian society. The fear of acceptance in society, dehumanization of blacks, and discriminatory practices in job training and hiring all reinforce the feelings of inferiority which the North American slave-earned capitalist society has instilled in the black man. The black man in Canadian society wants only a fair share in the multi-ethnic society that is Canada.

The three-day conference ended with a series of resolutions from the workshops and open debates. They are as follows:

1) Be it resolved that in the interest of achieving the goals and objectives of the black population of Canada in a coordinated way, a National Organization be established to gather and periodically disperse for effective use by regional groups, information about events, programs, and activities of particular interest to black people in Canada; that the chairman of this organization be Dr. Howard McCurdy, with Mrs. Dorothy Wills as secretary.

2) Be it resolved that the National Organization explore the possibility of encouraging governments to have firms employ graduates of job

training and retraining programs or to provide on-the-job training for those unemployable because of their lack of skills.

3) Be it resolved that the educated blacks become more involved in the employment education and job training problems of the less fortunate members of the black community.

4) Be it resolved that an open telegram be sent to the Minister of Justice and the Canadian Press, informing them of the formation of a National Organization and asking that a Royal Commission be appointed to look into the question of Civil Rights and that a similar telegram be sent to the appropriate branches of the provincial legislature.

In effect, with the right legal backing, and the full co-operation of all the local groups, the problem of the black man at the national level is going to be brought to the forefront of Canadian thought.

The Congress of Black Writers, which took place at McGill, featured the opinions of black men from Africa, the Americas, Asia, and Europe, and put the question of black liberation in a world context. They feel that the racist, capitalist, and imperialist white Western world, which emasculated and humiliated the black man, can only be a comfortable place for black men after a complete social and violent revolution takes place. In the public lectures, but more importantly in the all-black caucuses, there were efforts to define the problem of the black man and construct a world-wide strategy for his liberation. This unifying ideology, it is felt, must precede the arms struggle and the final violent revolution.

The speakers at the Conference varied in opinion as to the extent of the need for violence and the white liberal. At one point, it appeared that the inhibiting presence of white observers, sympathizers, empathizers, the CIA, RCMP, and the press might cause a rupture in the participating groups, but such a fracture was averted.

However, the most important issues of the congress were debated in all-black caucuses because it was felt that black people, having always feared white oppression, are not prepared to share the strategy for action with the white man.

It must be understood that the separation does not always involve a lack of confidence in the validity of the empathy which the white liberal claims to have. It is rather a realistic approach. The danger of this kind of separation does not escape the black leaders and writers. As Harry Edwards pointed out, it is worse to have a black cobra within the house than a white wolf outside the door.

At this session Robert Hill, an historian at the University of the West Indies, informed the 400 blacks present of the Jamaican Government ban on the re-entry of Dr. Walter Rodney, a professor of African history at UWI.

Mr. Hill also talked about repressive measures being taken against all racial intellectuals, such as George Beckford, whose passport was revoked after he gave a lecture at the University of Havana, and against members of Rastafari cult of West Kingston, who long ago rejected the values of the colonial system and look to Africa as their home.

The main point of conflict, Mr. Hill said, is that the Shearer government [in Jamaica] has come out in the open, to the point of using militia against the poor blacks, with their backing from the small black bourgeoisie, the Middle East merchants, and the large British and American sugar and bauxite companies. The present situation is that underground movements are actively trying to unseat the two puppet reactionary parties of Jamaica.

Some very significant resolutions were passed in these caucuses and were later brought to the house where they were passed unanimously:

I) Jamaica Delegation:
    That the congress affirm and align itself with the struggle of the black people in Jamaica to expose the puppet government in Jamaica and those of Africans all over the world, with the aim toward the lifting of the ban on all persons and literature involved in that struggle.

II) French West Indies and Haitian Delegation:
    That the people of the Antilles under colonial and neo-colonial regimes identify with the black peoples of the world to fight and if necessary destroy the social and economic oppression which Western civilization has used to destroy them and to invest in the struggle all their physical and intellectual resources.

III) Trinidad and Tobago Delegation:
    That the government of Trinidad and Tobago be condemned for the banning of the native, Stokely Carmichael, from the country of his birth.

IV) Nigeria/Biafra Delegation:
    That the continuing process of selling arms to both warring parties be condemned; that there be a cease-fire; that all relief supplies be examined; that the Nigerian writers in jail be released; that a plebiscite be held about the political status of Biafra; and that an international body investigate whether there is a genocide in Biafra.

V) Angola Delegation:
    That the armed struggle of all black men for their freedom, especially those on the African continent, be recognized, and that a day be set aside for honoring the brotherhood of all black people.

VI) Ethiopian Delegation:

That institutions of CUSO, the Peace Corps, and such organizations which serve as training ground for agents of the CIA, etc., be replaced with a corps of educated blacks, who would go out to Africa to counteract the forces which are sent out by imperialistic countries under the guise of aid, but which in fact paralyze the society and prevent future development.

VII) Communications Workshop:

That an international communications centre be formed, founded on the principle of the need for international unity and that the centre be represented by members of groups of black people all over the world.

At this stage in the Congress, the writers made the point that the role of black woman in the progress of black peoples must be emphasized, even though slavery cruelly disrupted the extended family and the honored place of the woman in the black society.

The meeting concluded with a word of wisdom from Mr. Carmichael, who said that black people must not attack themselves, must not condemn themselves; that although colonialization effected this negative syndrome, black men and women should spend more time helping each other culturally, economically, politically, and militarily, so that the contradictions in and the struggle against the system can be heightened.

For the black man in Canada, it was a stimulating and edifying experience. His only hope now lies in a new era of black militance and a new humanism. To quote Frantz Fanon, ". . . man is a *yes* . . . *Yes* to life. *Yes* to love. *Yes* to generosity. But man is also a *no*. *No* to scorn of man. *No* to degradation of man. *No* to the exploitation of man. *No* to the butchery of what is most human in man: freedom."

Chapter 12

"YOU DON'T PLAY WITH REVOLUTION"

C. L. R. JAMES
interviewed by **MICHAEL SMITH**
McGill Reporter, November 4, 1968

REPORTER: I've noticed that, although this is a Congress of Black Writers, many of the writers that have come and some of the ones scheduled to speak seem to be writers only incidentally to their work in the black liberation movement.

JAMES: For instance, who?

REPORTER: I was thinking of Stokely Carmichael, and I was thinking of Eldridge Cleaver and H. Rap Brown. They are writers, but they seem to have been selected because of their importance in the movement.

JAMES: I think that was precisely why they should have been selected.

REPORTER: Yes, I agree with that. The question that I wanted to pose to you is, "What do you think is the role of the artist or the writer in the black liberation movement?"

JAMES: I can't say what the role of the artist should be because THE artist is always a PARTICULAR artist. He does his work in terms of his own ability and his responses to the world around him. He may not write about politics at all. But he may be giving a picture of the situation as it is. He may be on one side or the other. One of the finest West Indian writers I know (I don't know what his politics are, except that, by and large, he is on the correct side!) is a man called Wilson Harris. I call him an existentialist writer, but his existentialism is based upon a firm grasp of the local situation in Guyana. Well, I think he is an artist who is contributing to the situation. He is making our minds clearer on the issue.

REPORTER: Do you think it is possible for an artist to remove himself from the struggle, to do art for art's sake; to write a novel for the sake of writing a novel? Or must he be continually immersed in the movement?

JAMES: He may not necessarily be immersed in the movement. An artist is immersed in what makes him an artist: his needs, his interests, his desire to express himself—and today, however you write is an expression of the stage in which we are. If you manage to write something which is not connected with the struggles that are going on, you are then stating quite clearly in your writing that you are not interested in them. So, whatever the artist does today, it is part of the world in which we live. He cannot escape that.

REPORTER: I would like to read a small section of Ralph Ellison's book *Invisible Man*.

JAMES: Yes. I know that book well.

REPORTER: "Stephen's problem, like ours, was not actually one of creating the uncreated conscience of his race, but in creating the *uncreated features of his face*. Our task is that of making ourselves individuals. The conscience of a race is the gift of its individuals who see, evaluate, record. We create the race by creating ourselves and then to our great astonishment we have created something that is far more important: We will have created a culture."[1] Would you agree with that?

JAMES: I believe that an artist, a first-class artist, who creates an individual—it will be himself or another individual—cannot be abstracted from the social environment in which he works. And the greater the artist, the more of the social environment he embraces. So, a number of artists expressing individual responses in that way ultimately result in a broad and total view of the society being expressed, I think.

He is quite right and particularly right in telling the artist to do what he wants to do to create this individual. He cannot settle to create a culture; he probably will not be successful. But if he does this, an artist will reflect, in one way or another, the life that is being lived around him.

REPORTER: I have noticed that the black delegates at the Congress come from an extremely wide range of backgrounds—generally perhaps from three broad areas: from Africa, the West Indies, and the US and Canada. I wonder if you would comment on the links which hold these various groups of delegates together at a conference like this?

JAMES: The link is very obvious and very simple. We are black people. And therefore, in our various ways, we are conscious of being subjected to all sorts of degradation and humiliation. I think it is less in Canada than elsewhere—very strong in the United States. We are all conscious of our past, because we are students, and our present can only be understood by our past. All that links us together, however different the individual experiences in the particular country may be.

REPORTER: In one of your first talks you mentioned something about West Indians who were looking for their cultural heritage in Africa, and at the same time rejecting their cultural heritage from the West Indies or from the Americas. And you said that in some instances these individuals have a tendency to ignore the best of their own culture and to take the worst from the African culture. I wonder if you could explain.

JAMES: Let me express myself. I was saying that they were not opposed to the West Indian culture. What they were opposed to was the domination of European culture. And they were rejecting that by going toward Africa. But, unfortunately, the grasping and understanding of African culture is not a simple business to a man brought up in Western civilization. And they put on some jacket and all sorts of African robes and that was the end of their getting hold of African culture. So they were rejecting European culture, which they were objecting to because it dominated them, but they weren't making any serious attempt to penetrate into the African culture. They were losing both sides.

REPORTER: In your book, *Party Politics in the West Indies*, you made a comment that I would like to read a small section of. You made this comment when you went to Ghana and were there during the independence celebrations: "Day in and day out, Nkrumah sings on the need for developing the 'African personality.' It is a grand phrase." The important part is the next section. You say, "He has here the inestimable advantage of an African background, language, religion, law, institutions, culture. We have to make our own way, dominated by language, institutions, culture, which are in essence similar to Britain and the still more powerful United States." [2] What I would like to know is, when someone does make a serious effort to get into the African culture, what are the valuable aspects of it which he might bring to the West Indies or to America?

JAMES: I don't know that people should go into African culture with the idea of bringing elements of the African culture to the West Indies and America. First of all, the West Indies and America are two very different places. America has a culture of its own. It has an attitude to the world—social, political, and otherwise. To bring African culture to that is quite a problem. I don't see it as something realistic.

But you go to study the African culture because, first of all, there are an immense number of people who are very sick of the state of European culture. They feel that it has reached a stage of degradation. And the man of African descent can go toward Africa, looking for African culture in the sense that he can find something to which he is organically connected, but which is offering him something European culture is not offering anymore. That he can do. But I don't know that he is going there to bring something back to affect the American culture. That is not the view that I have of why these people act.

Maybe a social group may do something of the kind. (I can say here that Picasso and Braque used the African mask for [their] work, and Picasso has always objected to a period of his work being called "the African period." And I think I know why he has objected to it. He objected because he was working on some things. The African mask gave him a certain concreteness and method of finding out what he was already working at. That you can do.) But what I think one can learn is a sense of nationalist politics. The West Indian is very backward in regard to that, and the African has no trouble in being an African nationalist. That I believe he can learn. But I don't know that that is a part of culture in the sense in which we are using the term.

REPORTER: Isn't negritude something that West Indians and black Americans already have in common with Africa?

JAMES: My concept of negritude is essentially a concept put forward by Aimé Césaire. A lot of other people have different views about what negritude is. Aimé Césaire looks upon negritude as an essential contribution to human civilization of something which the African environment has developed and which is valuable. I insist that it is a poetic sentiment. I don't think that Césaire is telling Europeans, "go and do that."

But he is aware of the breakdown of European civilization. And he is pointing out the fact that the African has something which if you look at it you will see is a valid contribution to what he calls "the rendezvous of victory"—where all of us are meeting. And he is not merely a despised, degraded person. His ideals and the things that he thinks have a natural and important validity. That's what Césaire, the poet, is saying. I don't think it is correct for *me* to go further. I know many other people take it and make it a sort of demonstration of the validity of the African culture against European domination. That, I think, is quite justified. But I take it more as a poem that Césaire wrote. Other people can make use of it.

I have seen where Nkrumah has launched a ferocious attack on it, and *he* has been talking a great deal about African personality. I begin and insist that what Césaire wrote is something that is a poetic contribution to the concept of race. And I think it has validity. When you think about what he says about what is real to the African, you can then see African civilization and the civilization of people of underdeveloped countries in a way different from what you did before you saw Césaire's poetic work. I hope that means something to you.

REPORTER: It does. I would like to quote once more from your book, *Party Politics in the West Indies*. You say here that "Political power, a dynamic population which knows its political power, a backward economy. That is a potentially explosive situation . . ." And you have a footnote here which says, "Marxism equals 'communist' equals r-r-revolution. That is the fashionable logic. I am a Marxist, I have studied revolution for many years, and among other things you learn not to play with it."[3] Could you elaborate on this?

JAMES: I am saying that in the West Indies today—I say it now still more than then—you have a situation which is potentially revolutionary. The economic basis and social structure of those islands are in a certain situation where most of the wealth is owned and controlled by people abroad; you have a small concentrated population. It is an explosive situation. And therefore, we must look out and be prepared for a revolutionary development. At the same time, I was talking to people who, when you ask for some simple human democratic right, [they] immediately call you "communist." So I say, you don't play with it.

But I am aware of the important revolutionary character of the situation, and at the same time I am not calling everybody who asks for a human democratic right, or protests against some autocracy by the government—neither is he a communist nor does he claim to be. Immediately [when] you call him "communist," you are playing with it. I use the term "revolutionary situation" in a very serious way. That is why I put that in the footnote. The moment you demand something: "We need the sugar estates, we are working on the sugar estates to get so and so and so and so," they shout, "Communist!"

REPORTER: Then you believe that there is an alternative to a revolution, to a revolutionary situation.

JAMES: In the Caribbean? I believe there is an alternative. A desperate authoritarian regime, essentially fascist as far as they can impose it—that, I have written, is what the Caribbean faces. The particular situation which they have at the present time cannot continue. And either the governments move forward with a revolution essentially social in content, or they are going to be struck down and made to submit to a very autocratic regime.

By the way, let me say that I do not believe it will be easy for any autocratic regime to impose autocracy on the Caribbean population. I say those are the two alternatives and I would like to say the domination, the forced domination and submission of West Indians by an autocratic government, would be very difficult. It would be wrong for me to go further, speculating as to what will happen . . . but I pose the two alternatives.

REPORTER: This morning, Stokely Carmichael made a differentiation between two types of oppression—exploitation, which was essentially economic in character, and colonization, where one race subjugated another, completely stripping the colonized race of its culture and dehumanizing it. Would you make the same distinction?

JAMES: The distinction that he makes can be a valid distinction. The only thing is, when colonialism is carried down to its roots, it is a form of economic exploitation, as well as racial, because it is the mass of the population that is being exploited economically under the colonialist's regimes. If he wishes to insist that the colonialist regime is a little bit different because it always has racial overtones, he is entitled to.

But his idea that poor people (he talks about poor people; I speak about the proletariat), the mass of the population in an advanced country, has got the same culture and values and so forth as those people who are exploiting them, I don't accept that. I don't believe that the culture and the values of De Gaulle are the culture and values of the mass of the population in France. I don't believe that the culture and values of Franco are the culture and values of the mass of the population in Spain.

So, his unification and consolidation of culture in an advanced country as being the same values and culture of all people there, while in the colonial regime it is different, I don't accept that completely at all. There is a difference, but it isn't as great a difference as he seems to make it out to be.

REPORTER: Do you think the battle that must go on in the United States, for example, is essentially one of restructuring the system, or one of restructuring mental attitudes toward people in the system?

JAMES: You cannot reconstruct a system without restructuring mental attitudes. And I was extremely pleased today to hear the talk of Harry Edwards, and then James Forman. Those fellows have a firm grasp of the way that racism could seriously be removed from the United States by a total revolutionary change in the social system.

REPORTER: One of the dilemmas I find myself in . . .

JAMES: You are an American citizen?

REPORTER: I am a Canadian citizen, but I have very close ties with the United States and I find it is becoming increasingly difficult not to take sides. As Stokely Carmichael said, the job today for him and his people is to *make* it increasingly difficult not to be committed: that is, not to pick up a gun and go into the streets.

JAMES: If a man talks about picking up a gun and going into the streets, I am not going to oppose him, because that is the revolution, and we may come to that. But I don't think that in 1968 in the United States it is correct to talk about the revolutionary struggle in terms of picking up a gun and going into the streets. I don't quite see that people in Harlem should pick up guns and go into the streets. There *are* times when you have to use violence and many of the American Negroes have been using violence under certain circumstances. I don't oppose anybody doing that. That means he is on the correct side. But there is a lot more to the social revolution than merely picking up a gun and going into the streets.

REPORTER: Could you elaborate on that perhaps?

JAMES: The social revolution means that the great mass of the population has come to the conclusion that the life they are living cannot continue and they want to change it. That happened in Britain in the seventeenth century, and that was the basis of the support of Oliver Cromwell and the rest of them. They broke up the old regime. It is true that what they thought they would substitute [for it] didn't come exactly, but the thing you must remember is that, as Mr. Hilaire Belloc says, "Royalty returned when Charles II came back; monarchy did not." The Cromwellians had finished the old monarchical regime, and that can only be broken up when the mass of the population feels the time has come to finish up with it. What may take its place depends on what the mass of the population feels that it requires.

People talk about leaders, but leaders can only lead a developed people who have an instinct in a certain direction and that is a thing that takes time. A great revolution took place in the United States in 1776. They wanted to finish up with the imperialist regime of Britain, and they wanted to substitute something new. That they did, and were highly successful in doing so because, by and large, the population either was sympathetic to them or it was neutral: it didn't see any cause to fight for the British, although it might not have plunged into the revolutionary struggle.

The finest example I know of social revolution today is what took place in Hungary, where a mass of the population rose and broke up the Stalinist regime. And the only way that regime could be restored was by Russian tanks coming in and physically destroying it. But that was a social revolution in which the population wanted to finish with what there was and to create something new.

In Cuba there is one. They are creating something new in Cuba. Immense difficulties, but they finished with Batista and then found that in order to finish completely with what Batista represents, they had to make certain new creative social and political forces. And that they are doing, and doing, in my opinion, extremely well, despite immense difficulties.

And I should say a socialist revolution in the United States—nobody will be in any doubt as to what it really is. That will be something that will write itself across the sky. No, there's no problem.

REPORTER: What do you think is the significance of the events which have taken place in Africa over the last eleven years, since Ghana became independent, for people in the West Indies and in the Americas?

JAMES: The significance of those events is this: I was in Ghana in 1957, talking at times to Nkrumah and Padmore. We had been very much involved in the struggle for political emancipation of the African people, and Ghana was the first of them. And if we had heard anybody preaching to people saying "In ten years there will be thirty new African states; there will be over a hundred million Africans who will gain political independence," we would have got together and said, "We have got to attack that fellow and expose him as an adventurer; a man who is ready to carry the African people into all sorts of dangerous policies, putsches, and so forth. Because that is *nonsense*." We couldn't believe that in ten years there would be over thirty new African states and over 100 million people free, politically free. Because that is all that political emancipation means: politically free.

What that means to us is this: the enormous revolutionary potential that is contained even in all sorts of elements in the population where you didn't expect it. We didn't expect that there would have been such a terrific force that would have swept over Africa with the tremendous rage with which it has done. What it means to me and what I say it would mean to other people is this: those people are on the move. They have moved in ten years in a manner that *nobody* expected. And over the next few years we must expect them to move in the way that the black people, and particularly those in the Americas, [have moved,] in harmony with tremendous social and political developments that are taking place in Western civilization itself. The slave revolt in San Domingo was an inextricable part of the French Revolution and the change from feudalism to modern bourgeois society.

And what is taking place in Africa today and what the people in other parts of Western civilization—the Africans—must know, is that the struggle they are carrying on is part of an immense change in the whole social structure that exists in the world at the present time. It may be Black Power here, another thing there, independence here, freedom, democratic rights there. But it is part of this tremendous change that is taking place in the whole social structure that exists in the world at the present time.

And the African revolt is part of that. And we, black people in America and in the Caribbean, must look upon the African revolt as symbolic of what is likely to take place everywhere and to which we are very closely allied.

Chapter 13

ON THE BANNING OF WALTER RODNEY FROM JAMAICA

C. L. R. JAMES
at Montreal Rally
Sir George Williams University, October 18, 1968

YOU WILL ALLOW ME to be somewhat individual in the approach that I take to this question. Most of all, I want to speak of Walter Rodney, not only as a person persecuted and the subject, the necessary subject, for a protest. I want to let you know that in West Africa, in East Africa recently, and in London among circles interested in Africa, Mr. Walter Rodney is already noted as a distinguished scholar in African affairs. He has not written much but what he has done shows an invasion of a field that has either been neglected or spoken about without sufficient knowledge—the state of Africa before the slave trade began.[1] That has been recognized as of tremendous importance to us who are concerned with our own origins and the impact of the African race upon ancient and modern civilizations.

Already he has made his impact in that sphere and, as I say, on two sides of the African continent. And in London, I hear his work spoken about by people who understand it and its importance. It is a scandal that the University of the West Indies has seen fit to carry out its political activity against him. That is the first point I want to make.

The second point I want to make is a negative point. I hear people speaking about things in the Caribbean and elsewhere and I repeatedly hear the remarkable initials the CIA. Now, it is not for me to say what the CIA has done or what it will do. What I want to say here tonight [is] I do not see the slightest reason for detaching the full responsibility of what has taken place in the Caribbean as a whole and passing it on to the United States. The persons responsible for this are the political rulers of the Caribbean territories. And what I want to do this evening is to show you that what has taken place has been anticipated.

I have here a book, *Party Politics in the West Indies*. (This is not an advertisement because I don't think that they are still for sale.) I will read certain passages from it to show you the reasons why I left the Caribbean. I knew what was going to happen and this was no surprise. It is not the erratic behavior of some individual. It is characteristic of a whole tribe and race of people who are now misgoverning the West Indies. Now, I will read this passage:

> Politics is not an activity. Not merely to support something or somebody. It is to discuss and plan and to carry out some programme and perspective of our own and then to judge how far you have succeeded or failed, and why. It does not limit a government. The more of this the people do, the bolder and more comprehensive the plans of a Government can be, the more it can defy its enemies. Otherwise as sure as day you find you have to shoot them down.[2]

In other words, this shooting down of the population is not an accident. It is not some method of government of the present rulers of the Caribbean countries. Here it is: "Otherwise," if you don't govern properly, if you do not develop a democratic of the people, if you do not let a new people, formerly slaves, realize that independence must mean something to them then, "as sure as day you find you have to shoot them down."

I am going to read another passage:

> Some readers may remember seeing the movie of the night of the independence of Ghana, and hearing Nkrumah choose at that moment to talk about the African Personality. This was to be the aim of the Ghanaian people with independence. Is there a West Indian personality? Is there a West Indian nation? What is it? What does it lack? What must it have? The West Indian middle classes keep far from these questions. The job, the car, the fridge, the trip abroad, preferably under government auspices and at government expense, these seem to be the beginning and end of their preoccupations. What foreign forces, social classes, ideas, do they feel themselves allied with or attached to? Noth-

ing. What in their own history do they look back to as a beginning of which they are the continuation? I listen to them, I read their speeches and their writings. "Massa Day Done" seems to be the extreme limit of their imaginative concepts of West Indian nationalism. [*James:* Massa day done and they have become "massa."] Today nationalism is under fire and every people has to consider to what extent its nationalism has to be mitigated by international considerations. Of this as of so much else the West Indian middle class is innocent. What happens after independence? For all you can hear from them, independence is a dead end. Apart from the extended opportunities of jobs with the government, independence is as great an abstraction as was Federation. We achieve independence and they continue to govern.[3]

But it is not going to stop there—they continue to misgovern the country—and already we see in Jamaica, and I am saying this is going to happen all over the Caribbean, a violent confrontation between the backward reactionary government that still is living in the seventeenth century with a population that is part of the twentieth century. That is the problem that is going to explode all over the Caribbean; we must be ready for it.

Before I sit down I want to bring one more point before you, and this is something that I was told by a man for whom I have the greatest personal respect and affection—George Lamming. He told me this story, and he told it to me with a significant purpose in mind. George was in Barbados, his home country, and Walcott,[4] head of the trade union movement, asked him to come and speak to the trade union movement. All the trade unionists heard Mr. Lamming, a great writer, was going to speak. There were thousands of them and they had to put loud speakers outside the place.

And George spoke. He spoke about the Conference in Berlin. He was speaking about black people and how in Berlin, Bismarck [and European governments] divided up Africa—"That is for me and that is for you, and you take that." And he [George Lamming] drew the development from these days up to 1958 when there took place the First Conference of the Independent African States. George spoke about the development of the Negro people, of the Barbadian people, of African Independence, etcetera. There was tremendous applause, a great deal of excitement and enthusiasm. George went back home.

George never made any sort of reference to any Barbadian politicians. He did not say he wished to stay in Barbados to make politics. But after that speech, the next day, the question from Barbadian politicians and their friends was "George, when are you leaving?" They did not want anybody to tell the Barbadian that they had an important history.

The mere fact that George had spoken to them about the history of black people and the strife that we had met during the previous seventy or eighty years was enough to get them frightened and ask, "George, when are you leaving Barbados?" So, Rodney is in difficulties because he is telling the people something about the history of Africa, history that has been much neglected. I think it is not only important, but it is highly significant that we not only say what we think but, by resolutions and other ways, register our disapproval, not only of what has happened to Rodney, but the [way that the] educated classes in the Caribbean are misgoverning our poor countrymen.

Thank you very much.

Chapter 14

LETTER TO C. L. R. JAMES FROM ROSIE DOUGLAS

Congress of Black Writers
2052 Close, Suite 10
Montreal, Quebec

<u>Standing Committee</u>
Financial Secretary – Marguerite Alfred
Fund Raising – Raymond Watts
Public Relations & Propaganda – Bertram Boldon

June 9, 1968

Dear Mr. James,

The Congress of Black Writers Committee was formed in Montreal by a group of West Indians (English- and French-speaking) for the specific purpose of organizing a Conference of black writers, scholars, and politicians in the coming October, in which an attempt will be made to trace the whole history of the black liberation struggle in a series of popular lectures. One of the crying necessities at the present stage of the struggle, we feel, is the need for the black masses to develop a sense of their own history, of the role which their own people have played in the whole history of black-white confrontation. Such a total conception of the development of the black struggle seems to us absolutely vital as a means of giving moral strength to the concrete political struggle now being waged. Black people must begin to see themselves as the subjects, rather than the objects, of history; the active creators, rather than the passive sufferers, of historical events.

The conference will be held on the weekend of October 11th to 14th, and the program, which we hope to publish and make available to a wider audience eventually, will be as follows:

Theme: Towards the Second Emancipation:
The Dynamics of Black Liberation.

Topics:
A. The Origin and Consequences of the Black-White Confrontation
     1) The History and Economics of Slavery in the New World
     2) The Psychology of Subjection: Race Relations in the USA
B. The Germs of Modern Black Awareness
     3. The Haitian Revolution and the History of Slave Revolt
     4. The Fathers of the Modern Revolt: Garvey, DuBois, etc.
C. The Re-evaluation of the Past
     5. The Origins and Significance of Negritude
     6. The Civilizations of Ancient Africa
     7. The Contributions of the Afro-American to American History and
        Civilization
D. Perspectives for the Future
     8. Racial Discrimination in Britain and the Way Out
     9. Black Power in the USA
     10. The Black Revolution, the Third World, and Capitalism

On behalf of the Congress Committee, I would like to take this opportunity to invite you to be one of our guest speakers at the Conference, and to address us on the first and third topics of the program: "The History and Economics of Slavery" and "The Haitian Revolution and the History of Slave Revolt." We hope you will be able to accept our invitation, and we shall be grateful for any advice, suggestions, opinions you may have to give us on the program. Looking forward to hearing from you as early as possible.

Yours sincerely,
Rosie Douglas, Chairman.

PS: We would like to invite a prominent member of the black community in England to address us on the eighth topic, but we would like your advice as to who you think would be best in a position to satisfy our requirements. Ideally, he should be actively involved in some organization or union. Could you let us have an early answer on this?

Chapter 15

LETTER TO ROSIE DOUGLAS FROM C. L. R. JAMES

20 Staverton Road
London NW2

27 June 1968

Miss (sic) Rosie Douglas, Chairman
Congress of Black Writers
2052 Close, Suite 10
Montreal, Quebec
Canada

Dear Miss (sic) Douglas,

I believe your proposal to be one of extreme important (sic) and timeliness, and I will be glad to take part of it.

First of all, however, I want to be absolutely certain not only that the Congress will take place, but that arrangement would be made without difficulty for my transport there and [the] journey back home. I say this because on the last occasion that I came to Canada I had no personal trouble but was told that BOAC or some company had promised a free passage for someone like myself, but then they heard that the person involved was C. L. R. James, they hastily said that they would not be able to give the passage and some money had to be found. I mention this to prevent any misunderstanding or embarrassment on either side. That being in order, I will be glad to come. And wish the conference every success.

May I suggest that the subject on which I am to speak be phrased a little differently; for example, A1) Slavery in the New World, and B3) The Haitian Revolution and Slave Revolt in the New World. I hope that your committee will approve of this suggestion for their consideration.

Hoping to hear from you soon so that I can rearrange my affairs and have everything in order.

Very truly yours,
C. L. R. James

NOTES

Introduction: The Dialect of Liberation

1 Kristin Ross, *May '68 and Its Afterlives* (Chicago: University of Chicago Press, 2002), 39, 90–94.

2 Pierre Vallières, "Quebec: Nationalism and the Working Class," *Monthly Review*, 16,1 (February 1965), 597. For an historical account of this unique period in Quebec history and the impact of anti-colonial thinkers, particularly Frantz Fanon, see Sean Mills, *The Empire Within: Postcolonial Thought and Political Activism in Sixties Montreal* (Montreal and Kingston: McGill-Queen's Press, 2010).

3 Dennis Forsythe, "By Way of Introduction," in *Let the Niggers Burn! The Sir George Williams Affair and Its Caribbean Aftermath*, ed. Dennis Forsythe (Montreal: Black Rose Books, Our Generation Press, 1971),10; and Pierre Vallières, *Nègres blancs d'Amérique* (Montréal: Parti pris, 1968), 453.

4 Manning Marable, *Malcolm X: A Life of Reinvention* (New York: Viking, 2011), 404. See www.youtube.com/watch?v=C7IJ7npTYrU.

5 Vallières, *Nègres blancs*, 454.

6 Vallières, *Nègres blancs*, 454.

7 Constantin Baillargeon, *Pierre Vallièrres: vu par son professeur de philosophie* (Montréal: Médiaspaul, 2002), 66.

8 Vallières, *Nègres blancs*, 454–55.

9 David Austin, *Fear of a Black Nation: Race, Sex, and Security in Sixties Montreal* (Toronto: Between the Lines, 2013), 45–46, 54–72.

10 Elder Thébaud, "Black Writers Congress: The Organizers Talk. . ." *The Review: McGill Daily Supplement*, October 11, 1968, 4–5.

11 Pierre Vallières, *White Niggers of America* (New York: Oxford, 1969), 21.

12 Vallières, *Nègres blancs*, 62.

13 Dennis Forsythe, "By Way of Introduction," 10.

14 Rosie Douglas and Elder Thébaud, "Black Writers Congress: The Organizers Talk. . ." *The Review: McGill Daily Supplement*, October 11, 1968, 5.

15 For more on the demographics of Montreal's black population during this period, see Dorothy W. Williams, *Blacks in Montreal, 1628–1986: An Urban Demography* (Cowansville: Les Éditions Yvon Blais Inc., 1989) and *The Road to Now: A History of Blacks in Montreal* (Montreal: Véhicule Press, 1998).

16 Marable, *Malcolm X*, 16.

17 Marable, *Malcolm X*, 16.

18 Jan Carew, *Ghosts in Our Blood: With Malcolm X in Africa, England, and the Caribbean* (Chicago: Lawrence Hill Books, 1994), 131.

19 Max Elbaum, *Revolution in the Air: Sixties Radicals Turn to Lenin, Mao and Che* (London: Verso, 2002), 21.

20 For a detailed history of blacks in Montreal during this period, see Paul C. Hébert, "'A Microcosm of the General Struggle': Black Thought and Activism in Montreal, 1960–1969" (Ph.D. dissertation, University of Michigan, 2015). "'In the Belly of the Beast': Black Power, Anti-imperialism, and the African Liberation Solidarity Movement, 1968–1975" (Ph.D. dissertation, New York University, May 2001), 41, 42.

21 Yvonne Greer, interview by Samah Affan, Montreal, March 29, 2011.

22 Burnley "Rocky" Jones, interview by author, Montreal, June 21, 2012.

23 George Lamming, "The West Indian People," *New World Quarterly* 2, 2, (1966): 63; and in the October 1967 publication of the Conference Committee.

24 Lamming, "The West Indian People," 63. Between 1965 and 1967, the CCC had organized three major annual conferences on the Caribbean with Caribbean writers George Lamming, C. L. R. James, and Orlando Patterson as keynote speakers: "Shaping the Future of the West Indies," "The Making of the Caribbean Peoples," and "The West Indian Nation in Exile." These meetings brought some of the most important Caribbean intellectuals and artists to Montreal. And, given the CCC's representatives in Toronto, Ottawa, Nova Scotia, Alberta, New York, the group's connection to Facing Reality in Detroit, as well as representatives overseas—England, Jamaica, Guyana, St. Vincent, St. Lucia, and in East Africa—the work of the CCC and the smaller C. L. R. James Study Circle reverberated well beyond its singular events and well beyond Montreal. It is also important to situate the congress alongside Expo '67, the international fair that brought people to Montreal from across the globe. Caribbean pavilions displayed the art and culture of the Caribbean to the world in Montreal at a time when Canada's Caribbean population was growing significantly. Despite the absence of any formal Caribbean-wide political structure, with the collapse of the West Indian Federation in 1962, there remained a strong sense of Caribbean nationhood and West Indians rallied in support of the region's participation in the fair. But as the title of the CCC's last conference suggests, exile and the presence and conditions of West Indians, if not blacks in general in Canada, assumed increasing importance by 1967.

25 See Austin, *Fear of a Black Nation*, 73–93; and David Austin, "In Search of a National Identity: C. L. R. James and the Promise of the Caribbean," in *You Don't Play with Revolution: The Montreal Lectures of C. L. R. James*, ed. David Austin (Oakland: AK Press, 2009), 1–26.

26 W. F. Santiago-Valles, "The Caribbean Intellectual Tradition that Produced James and Rodney," *Race and Class*, 42(2), (2000): 53.

27 Cedric J. Robinson, *Black Marxism: The Making of the Black Radical Tradition* (1983; reprinted Chapel Hill, NC: 2000), xxx.

28 Robinson, *Black Marxism*, 313.

29 David Scott suggests that the term "black" is not a fixed entity but is open to interpretation over time, as are the terms "radical" and "tradition" and that the joining of the terms radical and tradition are counterintuitive, as radical suggests a break or a breach, whereas tradition suggests sameness and continuity shaped by the desire to be framed by a particular set of experiences. See David Scott, "On the Very Idea of a Black Radical Tradition," *Small Axe*, 17,1 (March 2013), 1–3. See also Nijah Cunningham, "A Queer Pier: Roundtable on the Black Radical Tradition," *Small Axe*, 17,1 (March 2013), 84–95.

30 Alfie Roberts, *A View for Freedom: Alfie Roberts Speaks on the Caribbean, Cricket, Montreal and C. L. R. James* (Montreal: Alfie Roberts Institute, 2005), 74.

31 See Austin, *Fear of a Black Nation*, 73, 79–80, 87, 91.

32 Roberts, *A View for Freedom*, 76.

33 Franklyn Harvey to Alfie Roberts, January 31, 1969.

34 See "The Conference Committee, MTL (Caribbean and Other Black Organizations), 4th Annual Conference on October 4, 5, and 6, 1968" (program).

35 "Conference Committee, MTL."

36 Forsythe, "The Black Writers Conference," 58–59.

37 Barbara Jones, "A Black Woman Speaks Out," *McGill Reporter*, 1(7), November 4, 1968, 1.

38 Leo Bertley, *Canada and Its People of African Descent* (Montreal: Bilongo Publishers, 1977), 272–73; Williams, *The Road to Now*, 119.

39 See Austin, *Fear of a Black Nation*, 157–76.

40 Raymond Watts, interview by author, Montreal, January 25, 2007.

41 For analyses of the Black Power movement in the US, see Jefferey O. G. Ogbar, *Black Power: Radical Politics and African American Identity* (Baltimore: John Hopkins University Press, 2004) and Peniel E. Joseph's popular history, *Waiting 'Til the Midnight Hour: A Narrative History of Black Power in America* (New York: Henry Holt and Company, 2006).

42 Austin Clarke, "The Confessed Bewilderment of Martin Luther King and the Idea of Non-Violence as a Political Tactic," in *The Austin Clarke Reader*, ed. Barry Callaghan (Toronto: Exile Editions, 1996), 277–85.

43 Richard Iton, *In Search of the Black Fantastic: Politics and Popular Culture in the Post-Civil War Era* (Oxford and New York: Oxford University Press, 2008), 202.

44 Austin, *Fear of a Black Nation*, 157–176, and Michael O. West, "Seeing Darkly: Guyana, Black Power, and Walter Rodney's Expulsion from Jamaica," *Small Axe* 12,1 (February 2008), 93–104.

45 Austin, *Fear of a Black Nation*, 11.

46 Austin, *Fear of a Black Nation*, 103, 124, 153–76.

47 Giorgio Agamben, *Means Without End: Notes on Politics* (Minneapolis: University of Minneapolis Press, 2000), 4–6 and *Homo Sacer: Sovereign Power and Bare Life* (Stanford: Stanford University Press), 119.

48 Austin, *Fear of a Black Nation*, 157–76, and West, "Seeing Darkly: Guyana, Black Power, and Walter Rodney's Expulsion from Jamaica," 93–104.

49 Greer, interview.

50 RCMP, Congress of Black Writers Conference, October 11, 12, 13, 1968, vol. 2, 84.

51 Dr. François Elder Thébaud lived in New York where he practised psychiatry as one of the leading experts of transcultural psychiatry and was the author of *West African*

Mental Health Practitioner's Guide (Montreal: Les Éditions du CIDIHCA, 2008).

52 Elder Thébaud and Rosie Douglas, "Editorial," *Souvenir Program of The Congress of Black Writers: Towards the Second Emancipation, The Dynamics of Black Liberation*, October 1968.

53 Thébaud and Douglas, "Editorial."

54 Dennis Forsythe, "The Black Writers Conference," in *Let the Niggers Burn! The Sir George Williams Affair and Its Caribbean Aftermath*, ed. Dennis Forsythe (Montreal: Black Rose Books, Our Generation Press, 1971), 61.

55 Magloire Chancy, unpublished reflections that were shared with David Austin on the Congress of Black Writers and other events, 145.

56 See "Cemetery Refused to Bury Negro," *The Gazette*, October 12, 1968.

57 Robin Bunce and Paul Field, *Darcus Howe: A Political Biography* (London: Bloomsbury, 2013), 61.

58 Bunce and Field, *Darcus Howe*, 60.

59 Bunce and Field, *Darcus Howe*, 61.

60 Bunce and Field, *Darcus Howe*, 60.

61 Robert Hill, (unpublished), 1966. This title was in turn borrowed from a Swiss traveler who visited Saint Domingue prior to the Haitian Revolution. See C. L. R. James, *The Black Jacobins: Toussaint L'Ouverture and the San Domingo Revolution* (New York: Vintage Books, 1989), 10.

62 Ed Horka, "Black Nationalism Has White Roots," *McGill Daily*, October 17, 1968, 7.

63 Horka, "Black Nationalism Has White Roots," 7.

64 Rosie Douglas, "Black Writers Congress: The Organizers Talk. . ." *The Review: McGill Daily Supplement*, October 11, 1968, 7.

65 Walter Rodney, *The Groundings with My Brothers* (London: Bogle and L'Ouverture Publications, 1990 [1969]).

66 Rodney, *The Groundings with My Brothers*, 12–13.

67 Rodney, *The Groundings with My Brothers*, 13.

68 Rodney, *The Groundings with My Brothers*, 13.

69 Rodney, *The Groundings with My Brothers*, 14–15.

70 Rodney, *The Groundings with My Brothers*, 15.

71 Rodney, *The Groundings with My Brothers*, 60.

72 Rodney, *The Groundings with My Brothers*, 61.

73 Rodney, *The Groundings with My Brothers*, 62.

74 Rodney, *The Groundings with My Brothers*, 63.

75 Rodney, *The Groundings with My Brothers*, 64.

76 Rodney, *The Groundings with My Brothers*, 67–68.

77 Rodney, *The Groundings with My Brothers*, 68.

78 Walter Rodney, "African History in the Service of Black Revolution," October 12, 1968.

79 Robert Hill in Clairmont Chung (ed.), *Walter A. Rodney: A Promise of Revolution* (New York: Monthly Review Press, 2012), 65–66.

80 Hill in *Walter A. Rodney*, 66.

81 For an insightful account of Rodney's impact in Jamaica see Rupert Lewis, "Jamaican Black Power in the 1960s," in ed. Kate Quinn, *Black Power in the Caribbean* (Gainesville: University Press of Florida, 2015), 61–71. As Lewis points out, "Jamaica's *Abeng* newspaper, founded in 1969, was part of a regional awakening that included new pub-

lications, such as *Moko, Pivot,* and *East Dry River Speaks* (Trinidad), *Black Star* (Barbados), *Outlet* (Antigua), and *YULIMO* (St. Vincent), that appeared alongside existing publications, such as Jamaica's *Impact* (1967–1968) and *Bongo-Man* (1968–1972), Trinidad's *Tapia,* and Guyana's *Ratoon,*" Lewis, "Jamaican Black Power in the 1960s," 70. For an overview of this period in Jamaica and across the Caribbean see Brian Meeks, "Conclusion: Black Power Forty Years On—An Introspection," in ed. Kate Quinn, *Black Power in the Caribbean* (Gainesville: University Press of Florida, 2015), 261–74.

82 George Lewinski, Radio McGill, Montreal, circa October 1968.

83 Both of James' presentations on slavery might be seen as precursors to his long essay, C. L. R. James, "The Atlantic Slave Trade and Slavery: Some Interpretations on Their Significance in the Development of the United States and the Western World," in *Amistad: Writings on Black History and Culture* (New York: Vintage Books, 1970), 119–64.

84 Ian Urquhart, "Socialize Bourgeois Knowledge: James," *McGill Daily,* October 15, 1968, 3. But as James wrote in "The Atlantic Slave Trade and Slavery," the slave regime in Ancient Greece "did not help to build the social order of the Greece that laid the foundations of Western civilization in so many spheres. Rather, it was the growth of slavery which ruined ancient Greece," although he did not support the claim in the essay. James, "The Atlantic Slave Trade and Slavery," 121.

85 Urquhart, "Socialize Bourgeois Knowledge: James," 3.

86 C. L. R. James, *The Black Jacobins: Toussaint L'Ouverture and the San Domingo Revolution* (London: Allison & Busby, 1980 [1938]), 47–48.

87 James, *The Black Jacobins,* 86; James, "The Haitian Revolution in the Making of the Modern World," in *You Don't Play with Revolution,* ed. David Austin, 54.

88 Jordan T. Camp and Christina Heatherton, "The World We Want: An Interview with Cedric and Elizabeth Robinson," in Gaye Theresa Johnson and Alex Lubin, *Futures of Black Radicalism* (London: Verso, 2017), 102.

89 For an in-depth analysis of the presence and political and cultural impact of Haitian exiles in Montreal in general, see Sean Mills, *A Place in the Sun: Haiti, Haitians, and the Remaking of Quebec* (Montreal and Kingston: McGill-Queen's University Press, 2015). The work of Adeline Magloire Chancy is briefly discussed on page 179. Her husband, Max Chancy, was an important Haitian-Marxist intellectual who played an active role within the Haitian exile community. See Adeline Magloire Chancy, *Profil: Max Chancy* (Pétion-Ville: Fondation Gérard Pierre-Charles, n.d.).

90 Elder Thébaud, "Black Writers Congress: The Organizers Talk. . . ."

91 Mills, *A Place in the Sun,* 179.

92 Adeline Magloire Chancy email communication with David Austin, March 21, 2018.

93 Magloire Chancy, unpublished reflections that were shared with David Austin on the Congress of Black Writers and other events, 145.

94 Magloire Chancy, unpublished reflections, 145.

95 Moïse Kapenda Tshombe was president of the seccessionist Katanga state of the Democratic Republic of the Congo from 1960–1963. He also served as prime minister of the Congo from 1964 to 1965 and was seen by many as an illegitimate leader of a government that was buttressed by the support of the US and Belgium when the democratically elected prime minister, Patrice Lumumba, was overthrown and eventually executed in a military coup in 1960.

96 François Duvalier served as the president of Haiti from 1957 to 1971. His dictatorship used repressive measures against opponents to maintain his totalitarian rule, including violent force carried out by his infamous paramilitary force, the Tonton Macoutes.

97 George Lewinski, Radio McGill, Montreal, circa October 1968. In the surviving clip from James' presentation on Negritude, a Haitian member of the audience commented on Negritude, after which James responded:

> COMMENT: *Je me permets d'apporter mon point de vue à ce problème de négritude et je suis parfaitement d'accord au point de vue historique avec Mr. James. Il y a une chose qu'on ignore: c'est que l'africain n'a jamais été esclave. Nous autres, nord-américains, nous avons été esclaves, nous avons perdu notre culture, et par conséquent nous avons accepté malgré nous d'autres cultures. Donc le premier mouvement de négritude est parti de l'Amérique du nord, c'est Du Bois qui a été à l'origine. Ce mouvement a été repris par un anthropologue haïtien, le docteur Price-Mars et par conséquence Césaire, lui aussi dans le domaine après a exalté les vertus africaines. On peut dire que la négritude n'est d'autre qu'une opposition à l'assimilation que nous a imposée l'impérialisme occidental. Merci* (applause).

> JAMES: *Je suis très heureux d'offrir mes compliments à les remarques très élevées de celui qui a parlé récemment.* (I'm very pleased to hear what the gentleman has said, I agree with him entirely and I'm glad to find someone who knows the subject obviously and who agrees with me so wholeheartedly and spontaneously.) Thank you very much.

98 *Les jacobins noirs: Toussaint L'Ouverture et la révolution de Saint Domingue* (1949; Paris: Editions Caribéennes, 1983).

99 For an account of Stokely Carmichael's activities during this period, see Peniel E. Joseph, *Waiting 'Till the Midnight Hour: A Narrative History of Black Power in America* (New York: Henry Holt and Company, 2006), 191–97.

100 Peniel E. Joseph, *Stokely: A Life* (New York: Basic Civitas, 2016), 164–68.

101 Frantz Fanon, quoted in Stokely Carmichael, "Black Power," in *The Dialectics of Liberation*, ed. David Cooper (London: Penguin Books, 1968), 150.

102 Carmichael, "Black Power," 151–52.

103 Carmichael, "Black Power," 153.

104 Carmichael, "Black Power," 158.

105 Carmichael, "Black Power," 160–61.

106 Carmichael, "Black Power," 164–65.

107 Carmichael, "Black Power," 167–68.

108 Carmichael, "Black Power," 161.

109 Carmichael, "Black Power," 168.

110 Carmichael, "Black Power," 168.

111 Tariq Ali, *Street Fighting Year: An Autobiography of the Sixties* (London: Verso, 2005), 198–99.

112 David Scott, "The Re-Enchantment of Humanism: An Interview with Sylvia Wynter," *Small Axe*, 4,2 (2000), 159.

113 Richard Gott, *Cuba: A New History* (New Haven: Yale Nota Bene, Yale University Press, [2004] 2005), 228.

114 Elbaum, *Revolution in the Air*, 23.

115 For a detailed analysis of Carmichael's Cuba visit, see Joseph, *Stokely*, 168–74.

116 Stokely Carmichael, *OLAS Conference: Black Power and the Third World* (Montreal: Caribbean Nation, N.D.), 4.

117 Carmichael, *OLAS Conference: Black Power and the Third World*, 1.

118 Carmichael, *OLAS Conference: Black Power and the Third World*, 1.

119 Toni Morrison, *Playing in the Dark: Whiteness and the Literary Imagination* (Cambridge: Harvard University Press, 1992), 12.

120 Frantz Fanon, *Black Skin, White Masks* (New York: Grove Press, 1967), 138. For Sartre, race is "concrete and particular," class is "universal and abstract," and Negritude as the antithesis to white supremacy. But "this negative moment is insufficient by itself" and "the Negroes who employ it know this very well; they know that it is intended to prepare the synthesis or realization of the human in a society without races. Thus, negritude is the root of its own destruction, it is a transition and not a conclusion, a means and not an ultimate end." Jean-Paul Sartre quoted in Fanon, *Black Skin, White Masks* (New York: Grove Press, 1967 [1952]), 133. For Fanon, Sartre reduces the black colonial's experience to "a minor term of a dialectical progression" within an undifferentiated putative universal. As he argued, "black consciousness is immanent in its own eyes. I am not a potentiality of something, I am wholly what I am. I do not have to look for the universal. No probability has any place inside me. My Negro consciousness does not hold itself as lack. It is. It is its own follower," Fanon, *Black Skin, White Masks*, 135.

121 Carmichael, *OLAS Conference: Black Power and the Third World*, 7.

122 Carmichael, *OLAS Conference: Black Power and the Third World*, 8.

123 Carmichael, *OLAS Conference: Black Power and the Third World*, 3.

124 Carmichael, *OLAS Conference: Black Power and the Third World*, 4.

125 Carmichael, *OLAS Conference: Black Power and the Third World*, 7.

126 Carmichael, *OLAS Conference: Black Power and the Third World*, 3.

127 Carmichael, *OLAS Conference: Black Power and the Third World*, 4.

128 Frantz Fanon, *The Wretched of the Earth* (New York: Grove Press, 1961), 316.

129 Carmichael, *OLAS Conference: Black Power and the Third World*, 12.

130 James Forman, *The Making of Black Revolutionaries* (New York: The Macmillan Company, 1972), 521.

131 Forman, *The Making of Black Revolutionaries*, 519.

132 Forman, *The Making of Black Revolutionaries*, 520.

133 Forman, *The Making of Black Revolutionaries*, 520.

134 C. L. R. James, "Black Power," in *The C. L. R. James Reader*, ed. Anna Grimshaw (Oxford: Blackwell Publishers, 1992), 363.

135 James, "Black Power," 364.

136 James, "Black Power," 364.

137 Ethel N. Minor, *Stokely Carmichael Speaks: Black Power Back to Pan-Africanism* (New York: Vintage Books, 1971), xv.

138 Stokely Carmichael with Ekwueme Michael Thelwell, *Ready for Revolution: The Life and Struggles of Stokely Carmichael (Kwame Ture)* (New York: Scribner, 2003), 544.

139 Magloire Chancy, unpublished reflections, 138–39.

140 L. R. Butcher, "The Congress of Black Writers," in *Let the Niggers Burn! The Sir George Williams Affair and Its Caribbean Aftermath*, ed. Dennis Forsythe (Montreal: Black Rose Books, Our Generation Press, 1971), 71.

141 Carmichael with Thelwell, *Ready for Revolution*, 546.

142 Carmichael with Thelwell, *Ready for Revolution*, 546.

143 Gott, *Cuba*, 229.

144 Elbaum, *Revolution in the Air*, 83.

145 This is a point that Rupert Lewis would make many years later after reflecting on his experience in the Workers Party of Jamaica (WPJ), the country's communist party. In the 1970s and 1980s, the WPJ was closely allied with the Soviet Union at the height of the Cold War, and this had an important influence of the course of the Grenada Revolution. Lewis argued that had both Jamaica and Grenada learned from the Caribbean's historical experience, and particularly from Padmore and C. L. R. James' critiques of the Soviet Union, perhaps they would have avoided some of the pitfalls that beset the Caribbean left in the 1980s. David Scott, "The Dialectic of Defeat: An Interview with Rupert Lewis," in *Small Axe*, 5(2) (2001): 119.

146 Carmichael's notion of revolution was at odds with that of Cabral, for whom Carmichael had profound respect. During the protracted struggle in Guinea-Bissau against the Portuguese, areas that were liberated were immediately set into motion. Schools and a basic social and political infrastructure were established, the result being that the practice of revolution was an ongoing, continuous process in the making.

147 Robert F. Williams, quoted in Timothy B. Tyson, *Radio Free Dixie: Robert F. Williams and the Roots of Black Power* (Chapel Hill: University of North Carolina Press, 1999), 198.

148 Carmichael with Thelwell, *Ready for Revolution*, 234.

149 Austin Clarke, "The Confessed Bewilderment of Martin Luther King and the Idea of Non-Violence as a Political Tactic," in *The Austin Clarke Reader*, ed. Barry Callaghan (Toronto: Exile Editions, 1996), 277–85.

150 Cornel West, in *The Radical King*, ed. Cornel West (Boston: Beacon Press, 2015), 221.

151 Charles Johnson, *Being and Race: Black Writing Since 1970* (Bloomington and Indianapolis: Indiana University Press, 1990), 21.

152 For a brief analysis of the exchange, see Austin, *Fear of a Black Nation*, 118–19.

153 Carmichael with Thelwell, *Ready for Revolution*, 105, 95.

154 Walter Rodney, *Walter Rodney Speaks: The Making of a Caribbean Intellectual*, ed. Robert Hill (Trenton, NJ: Africa World Press, 1990), 16.

155 James, "Black Power," 370.

156 James, "Black Power," 364.

157 James, "Black Power," 364.

158 James, "Black Power," 364.

159 James, "Black Power," 374.

160 Michael Smith, Interview: C. L. R. James, "You Don't Play with Revolution," *McGill Reporter* 4, (7), (November 4, 1968), 7.

161 According to Cabral,

"In societies with a horizontal structure, like the Balanta society . . . the distribution of cultural levels is more or less uniform, variations being linked solely to individual characteristics and to age groups. In the societies with a vertical structure," Cabral informs, "like that of the Fula . . . there are important variations from the top to the bottom of the social pyramid. This shows . . . the close connections between the cultural factor and the economic factor, and also explains the differences in the overall or sectoral behaviour of these two ethnic groups towards the liberation movement." Moreover, the "class character is still more noticeable in the behaviour of privileged groups in the rural environment, notably where ethnic groups with a vertical structure are concerned, where nevertheless the influences of assimilation or cultural alienation are nil or virtually nil. This is the case of the Fula ruling class, for example. Under colonial domination," adds Cabral, "the political authority of this class (traditional chiefs, noble families, religious leaders) is purely nominal, and the mass of the people are aware of the fact that the real authority lies with and is wielded by the colonial administrators. However, the ruling class retains in essence its cultural authority over the mass of the people in the group, with very important political implications." The colonial authority, knowing this reality, "installs chiefs whom it trusts and who are more or less accepted by the population, gives them various material privileges including education for their eldest children, creates chiefdoms where they did not exist, establishes and develops cordial relations with religious leaders. . . ." This system, we are told, "by means of the repressive organs of colonial administration . . . ensures the economic and social privileges of the ruling class in relation to the mass of the people," though "this does not remove the possibility that, among these ruling classes, there may be individuals or groups of individuals who join the liberation movement. . . ." Amilcar Cabral, "National Liberation and Culture," in *Unity and Struggle* (London: Heinemann Educational Books, 1980), 144–46.

162   See James et al., "Facing Reality."

163   Austin, *Fear of a Black Nation*, 1–2.

164   For more on Richard B. Moore, see W. Burghardt Turner and Joyce Moore Turner, *Richard B. Moore, Caribbean Militant in Harlem* (Bloomington and Indianapolis: Indiana University Press, 1992).

165   David Austin, "Introduction to Walter Rodney," *Small Axe* 5,2 (September 2001), 64.

166   See Frances Henry, "Black Power in Montreal: The Ideas, Leaders and Pain Behind the Sir George Williams Riot," *Literary Review of Canada*, July-August 2013, http://reviewcanada.ca/magazine/2013/07/black-power-in-montreal/, and David Austin, Re: "Black Power in Montreal," by Frances Henry, http://reviewcanada.ca/magazine/2013/07/letters/.

167   David Austin, *Fear of a Black Nation*, 81–84, 120–28.

168   David Austin, Re: "Black Power in Montreal," by Frances Henry, http://reviewcanada.ca/magazine/2013/07/letters/.

169   See Michael O. West, "Rosie Douglas, Black Power on Campus, and the Canadian Color Conceit," *Palimpsest*, 6(2), 190–91.

170   "Ramabai Espinet," in Kwame Dawes, ed. *Talk Yuh Talk: Interviews with Anglophone Caribbean Poets* (Charlottesville and London: University Press of Virginia, 2001), 121.

171   B. A. Jones, "Mixed Emotions," *Among the Potatoes: A Collection of Modern Verse* (Ilfracrombe: Arthur H. Stockwell Limited, 1967), 81.

172   Jones, "Viet Nam," 76.

173   Jones, "Mixed Emotions," 82.

174   Jones, "Le Roi Jones," 79.

175   Jones, "Mixed Emotions," 7.

176   Jones, "The Bridges," *Among the Potatoes*, 6.

177   "Espinet," in Kwame Dawes, ed. *Talk Yuh Talk*, 121.

178   Jones, "Life I," *Among the Potatoes*, 23.

179   Jones, "Depression," *Among the Potatoes*, 22.

180   Jones, "A Black Woman Speaks Out," 5.

181   James St. G. Walker and Burnley "Rocky" Jones, *Burnley "Rocky" Jones Revolutionary* (Black Point, NS: Roseway, 2016), 52–53.

182 RCMP, "Hemispheric Conference to End the Vietnam War, November 28 to December 1, 1968 – Montreal, Quebec," Congress of Black Writers Conference, October 11, 12, 13, 1968, Montreal, Quebec, January 29, 1969, vol. 5, 000485.

183 Norman Cook, interview by author, Ottawa, June 30, 2004.

184 See David Austin, "Anne Cools: Radical Feminist Trailblazer," *MaComère*, 12, 2 (2010), 68–76. For a brief reference to Anne Cools' influence as a member of the women's movement, see Judy Rebick, *Ten Thousand Roses: The Making of a Feminist Revolution* (Toronto: Penguin Canada, 2005), 9–10. Cools' relationship to feminism is complicated and conflicted, but it deserves considerably more attention than it has thus far been given.

185 Patricia Hill Collins, *Black Feminist Thought: Knowledge, Consciousness, and the Politics of Empowerment* (New York: Routledge, 1991), 140–41.

186 Sarah Evans, *Personal Politics: The Roots of Women's Liberation in the Civil Rights Movement and the New Left* (New York: Vintage Books, 1980), 193–94.

187 Anne Cools, "Womanhood," in Black Spark Edition of the *McGill Free Press*, February 1971, 8.

188 Kathleen Cleaver, "Women, Power, and Revolution," in *Liberation, Imagination, and the Black Panther Party: A New Look at the Panthers and Their Legacy*, eds. Kathleen Cleaver and George Katsiaficas (New York: Routledge, 2001), 124, 126.

189 Njoki Nathani Wane, "Black Canadian Feminist Thought: Drawing on the Experiences of My Sisters," in *Back to the Drawing Board: African Canadian Feminisms*, eds. Njoki Nathani Wane, Katerina Deliovsky, and Erica Lawson (Toronto: Sumach Press, 2002), 47. See also Carole Boyce Davies, *Black Women, Writing and Identity: Migrations of the Subject* (London: Routledge, 1994), 36, 39, 41, 43.

190 Audre Lorde, "Learning from the Sixties," in *Sister Outsider: Essays and Speeches by Audre Lorde* (Freedom, CA: The Crossing Press Feminist Series, 1984), 135–36.

191 Lorde, "Learning from the Sixties," 137.

192 Carole Boyce Davies, *Left of Karl Marx: The Political Life of Black Communist Claudia Jones* (Durham: Duke University Press, 2008).

193 Adrienne Katherine Wing, "Brief Reflections Towards a Multiplicative Theory and Praxis of Being," in Njoki Nathani Wane, Katerina Deliovsky, and Erica Lawson (eds.), *Back to the Drawing Board: African Canadian Feminisms* (Toronto: Sumach Press, 2002), 269.

194 Richard Wright, "Traditional and Industrialization" in *Presence Africaine: The First International Conference of Negro Writers and Artists*, Nos. 8, 9, 10 (June-November 1956): 356.

195 Jones, "A Black Woman Speaks Out," 5.

196 See Rosalind Hampton, *Racialized Social Relations in the Higher Education: Black Student and Faculty Experiences of a Canadian University*, in partial fulfillment of the requirements for the degree of Doctor of Philosophy, Department of Integrated Studies in Education, Faculty Education, McGill University, September 2016.

197 Stephen E. Henderson, "'Survival Motion': A Study of the Black Writer and the Black Revolution in America" in *The Militant Black Writer in Africa and the United States* (Madison: University of Wisconsin Press, 1969), 65.

198 An editorial in the *McGill Reporter* described the congress as "an upsetting experience" for whites who were "distrusted, excluded, ignored, because someone looked at us and saw faceless, de-humanized white ('Your own back, Honkey.')." The editorial referred

to what it called the "over-simplification of complex situations. Black was equated with good, white with evil: 'racist . . . imperialist . . . liberal bigot'." It is obvious that, in addition to the personal sense of alienation that many whites must have felt, the issue was one of politics. According to the editorial, it was not simply that whites felt degraded and excluded, but that, with few exceptions (C. L. R. James and James Forman, according to the editorial), the speakers failed to "put the question of race in wider context, that of a broad socialist revolution," or to "talk about the socially-concerned against the forces of inhumanity," The Editors, "Youth in Revolt: Black Militants and Red Guards," *McGill Reporter*, November 4, 1968, 1. The editors' assessment was by and large correct, but they failed to recognize that this was precisely the point: Blacks were not only resisting systematic and institutional anti-black racial oppression, but also the tendency of the left to universalize struggle in ways that bypassed the lived experiences of blacks. Again, this is precisely the point that Frantz Fanon makes in relation to Jean-Paul Sartre's description of Negritude. But despite its criticisms, the editorial concluded that the congress provided Canadians with a "first-hand experience of a subject widely discussed as 'an American problem'" and described the "black experience" as "a subject which must be of concern if Canada is to avoid the political and emotional polarization so evident in the United States today." The Editors, "Youth in Revolt," 1. They were seemingly unaware that this emotional polarization already existed in Canada and that the congress (as would the Sir George Williams University protest that began in April 1968 and ended in February 1969 with the destruction of the university's computer centre) served to reveal what had long lay dormant, simmering beneath the surface.

199   Watts, interview and Rennie, interview.
200   Barbara Jones, "A Black Woman Speaks Out," 1, 5.
201   Depradine, interview.
202   Jones, "A Black Woman Speaks Out," 5.
203   Jones, "A Black Woman Speaks Out," 5.
204   Many of those involved in the protest had been involved in both the Congress of Black Writers and the Sir George Williams protest. They, along with members of the African Studies Association led by African American historian John Henrik Clarke, former editor of *Freedomways*, demanded the inclusion and greater participation of Africans and people of African descent within the ASA. In disrupting the meeting and raising the question of academic inclusion, their actions helped put the question of academic racism in African studies on the agenda in North America. See Austin, *Fear of a Black Nation*, 27, and David Austin, "All Roads Led to Montreal: Black Power, the Caribbean and the Black Radical Tradition in Canada," *The Journal of African American History*, 92,4 (Fall 2007), 532.
205   Stephen E. Henderson, "'Survival Motion': A Study of the Black Writer and the Black Revolution in America," in Mercer Cook and Stephen E. Henderson, *The Militant Black Writer in Africa and the United States* (Madison: University of Wisconsin Press, 1969), 65, 67, 72, 79. More recently in the US, Anna Stubblefield has argued in favour of understanding race in terms of family. Instead of simply dismissing race as a social construct, Stubblefield suggests we should understand how this construction directly impacts lives. Families care for, nurture, protect, and sustain one another with the understanding that difference within families (age, gender, sexual orientation, disabilities, etc.) is normal. Race as family according to Stubblefield does not mean a descent into parochialism. For blacks, this notion of family is a way of confronting the

stigmatism and the impact of anti-black racism that constricts black life chances. Race as family also permits whites to work toward confronting the privileges that racism and white supremacy have afforded them as both families work toward a common humanity. Anna Stubblefield, *Ethics Along the Color Line* (Ithica, NY: Cornell University Press, 2005), 3, 166, 173–74.

206 Phillip Winslow, "Split over Whites Threatens Black Congress," *The Gazette*, October 13, 1968.

207 This speech was first published as "African History in the Service of Black Revolution," *Small Axe*, 5,7 (September 2001), 66–80.

208 Forsythe, "The Black Writers Conference," 64.

209 Best, interview.

210 Watts, interview.

211 Watts, interview and Rennie, interview.

212 Boyd, interview.

213 Lloyd Best, interview by the author, Port of Spain, Trinidad & Tobago., October 14, 2003.

214 West, "Rosie Douglas, Black Power on Campus, and the Canadian Color Conceit," 90–91.

215 Harry Edwards, untitled presentation delivered at the Congress of Blacks Writers, October 14, 1968.

216 A version of James Forman's speech was published in *The Guardian*, November 23, 1968, 21.

217 Fanon Che Wilkins, "'*In the Belly of the Beast*': *Black Power, Anti-imperialism, and the African Liberation Solidarity Movement, 1968–1975*," (Ph.D. dissertation, New York University, May 2001), 41, 42.

218 James Forman, "The Black Revolution: The Third World and Capitalism," October 14, 1968.

219 Forman, "The Black Revolution."

220 Robert Hill, "The Fathers of Modern Revolt: Garvey, etc.," October 12, 1968.

221 Robert Hill, interview by author, Los Angeles, CA, May 15–16, 2003.

222 Phillip Winslow, *The Gazette*, October 13, 1968.

223 Watts, interview.

224 Watts, interview.

225 Bukka Rennie, interview. According to Robert Hill, James wrote the letter to Carmichael in 1966 after hearing him speak in Montreal (Hill, interview), but it is evident that the date was 1967.

226 Austin, *Fear of a Black Nation*, 118.

227 Hill, interview, Watts, interview, and Leroy Butcher, interview by author. Toronto, Canada, February 3, 2007.

228 Forman, *The Making of Black Revolutionaries*, 522–523. See also Ward Churchill, "'To Disrupt, Discredit, and Destroy': The FBI's Secret War Against the Black Panther Party," in Cleaver and Katsiaficas, eds. *Liberation, Imagination, and the Black Panther Party*, 89.

229 Carmichael with Thelwell, *Ready for Revolution*, 671–72. See also Joseph, *Waiting 'Till the Midnight Hour*, 233.

230 Forman, *The Making of Black Revolutionaries*, 519–522, 529, 530.

231 Forman, *The Making of Black Revolutionaries*, 531.

232 See Austin, *Fear of a Black Nation*.

233 Austin, "All Roads Led to Montreal," 535–36.

234 Michel-Rolph Trouillot, *Silencing the Past: Power and the Production of History* (Boston: Beacon Press, 1995), 53.

235 Katherine McKittrick refers to the element of "erasure, surprise and wonder" in Canadian historical narratives. See Katherine McKittrick, *Demonic Grounds: Black Women and the Cartographies of Struggle* (Minneapolis: University of Minnesota, 2006), 33, 54, 96.

236 Here I recall a student in Cape Town who recounted a story about his attempt to show solidarity with Marikana miners in the aftermath of the 2012 police massacre of thirty-four strikers, only to be chastised for his attempt to "save" them with Marxism. The miners were fighting for their lives and not for what must have appeared to be a misplaced attempt to impress an ideology on them when they were clear and resolute about their demands for a living wage.

237 Tony Martin, *Race First: The Ideological and Organizational Struggles of Marcus Garvey and the Universal Negro Improvement Association* (Westport, CT: Greenwood Press, 1976), 55. The quote is republished from *Negro World*, December 15, 1923.

238 Martin, *Race First*, 240.

239 Martin, *Race First*, 225.

240 Robert A. Hill, ed. *The Marcus Garvey and Universal Negro Improvement Association Papers*, Volume V, September 1922–August 1924, 551.

241 Hill, *The Marcus Garvey and Universal Negro Improvement Association Papers*, 551.

242 Hill, *The Marcus Garvey and Universal Negro Improvement Association Papers*, 555.

243 For a detailed account of Du Bois' engagement with socialism, Marxism, and communism, see Bill V. Mullen, *W. E. B. Du Bois: A Revolutionary Across the Colour Line* (London: Pluto Press, 2016), 57–72.

244 Martin Luther King Jr., "Honoring Dr. Du Bois," in *The Radical King*, ed. Cornel West (Boston: Beacon Press, 2015), 119.

245 Cornel West in *The Radical King*, ed. Cornel West (Boston: Beacon Press, 2015), 221.

246 Martin Luther King Jr., "Where Do We Go from Here?" in *The Radical King*, ed. Cornel West (Boston: Beacon Press, 2015), 177.

247 King Jr., "Where Do We Go from Here?" 177.

248 Svetlana Alexievich, *Second Hand Time: The Last of the Soviets* (London: Fitzcarraldo Editions, 2016).

249 Martin Luther King Jr., "Beyond Vietnam: A Time to Break Silence," in *The Radical King*, ed. Cornel West (Boston: Beacon Press, 2015), 203–5.

250 Malcolm X, *Malcolm X Talks to Young People* (New York: Pathfinder Press, 1991), 40.

251 Malcolm X, *Malcolm X Talks to Young People*, 59–60, 75–78.

252 Malcolm X, *Malcolm X Talks to Young People*, 87, and Malcolm X, *Malcolm X: The Last Speeches* (New York: Pathfinder Press, 1990), 162–63, 164–65.

253 A. B. Spellman, "Interview with Malcolm X," *Monthly Review*, 56,9 (February 2005), https://monthlyreview.org/2005/02/01/interview-with-malcolm-x/.

254 *Leon Trotsky On Black Nationalism and Self-Determination* (New York: Pathfinder Press, 1978).

255 Marable, *Malcolm X*, 302, 304.

256 Marable, *Malcolm X*, 304, 305–6, 336, 337, 340, 355, 395, 399, 400, 404, 405, 406, 407. Malcolm had also developed ties with the Revolutionary Action Movement (RAM), a

black radical social organization, and there was talk of a merger between RAM and the OAAU, 353–54; and also developed a friendship with Shirley Graham Du Bois. And while Malcolm's position on socialism and anti-capitalism was not wholly consistent (369–70), the weight of the evidence clearly demonstrates that he was heading in this direction.

257 Marable, *Malcolm X*, 399.

258 Malcolm X, *Malcolm X Talks to Young People*, 88.

259 Malcolm X, *Malcolm X Talks to Young People*, 91.

260 Karl Marx, *Capital: A Critique of Political Economy*, Vol. 1 (New York: International Publishers, 1967), 233.

261 Malcolm X, *Malcolm X Talks to Young People*, 91.

262 Malcolm X, *Malcolm X Speaks* (New York: Grove Press, 1966), 120–21.

263 Malcolm X, *Malcolm X Speaks*, 69. Also cited in Keeanga-Yamahtta Taylor, *From #Black Lives Matter to Black Liberation* (Chicago: Haymarket Books, 2016), 197.

264 Richard Iton, *Solidarity Blues: Race, Culture and the American Left* (Chapel Hill: University of North Carolina Press, 2000).

265 Malcolm X, *Malcolm X Speaks*, 102, and Marable, *Malcolm X*, 396.

266 Taylor, *From #Black Lives Matter to Black Liberation*,166–67.

267 Toni Morrison, *Playing in the Dark: Whiteness and the Literary Imagination* (Cambridge: Harvard University Press, 1992), 63, 64.

268 Morrison, *Playing in the Dark*, 63.

269 Morrison, *Playing in the Dark*, 64.

270 For a detailed analysis of the history of racial oppression in Canada, see Robin Maynard, *Policing Black Lives: State Violence in Canada from Slavery to the Present* (Halifax and Winnipeg: Fernwood Publishing, 2017).

271 Taylor, *From #Black Lives Matter to Black Liberation*, 194.

272 Marable, *Malcolm X*, 403

273 Marable, *Malcolm X*, 261, 262.

274 The FBI fear that Malcolm X might be a communist dates back to the early 1950s. Clayborne Carson (edited by David Gallen), *Malcolm X: The FBI File* (New York: Carroll & Graf Publishers, 1991), 65, 100, 103, 203.

275 James Boggs, "The Influence of Malcolm X on the Political Consciousness of Black Americans," in *Malcolm X: The Man and His Time*, ed. John Henrik Clarke (New York: Collier Books, 1969), 52.

276 Boggs, "The Influence of Malcolm X on the Political Consciousness of Black Americans," 53.

277 Boggs, "The Influence of Malcolm X on the Political Consciousness of Black Americans," 54.

278 Boggs, "The Influence of Malcolm X on the Political Consciousness of Black Americans," 54–55.

279 Stefano Harney and Fred Moten, "Improvement and Preservation, or Usufruct and Use," in Gaye Theresa Johnson and Alex Lubin, *Futures of Black Radicalism* (London: Verso, 2017), 84.

Chapter 1: The Psychology of Subjection

1 Robert Gover, *The One Hundred Dollar Misunderstanding* (New York: Grove Press, 1961).

Chapter 2: The Haitian Revolution and the History of Slave Revolt

1 See Hilaire Belloc and Cecil Chesterton, *The Party System* (London: Stephen Swift, 1911).

2 James is referring to the speech he delivered at the congress on the morning of October 12, entitled, "The History and Economics of Slavery in the New World." No record of the speech has been found.

3 James is referring to Robert A. Hill.

4 C. L. R. James, *The Black Jacobins: Toussaint L'Ouverture and the San Domingo Revolution* (1938; New York: Vintage Books, 1989), 265.

5 The person credited with originating the Pan-African movement was Henry Sylvester Williams of Trinidad.

6 James, *The Black Jacobins*, 265.

7 James, *The Black Jacobins*, 265.

8 James, *The Black Jacobins*, 343.

9 James, *The Black Jacobins*, 346.

10 James, *The Black Jacobins*, 350.

11 James, *The Black Jacobins*, 353.

12 James, *The Black Jacobins*, 368–369.

13 W. E. B. Du Bois, *Black Reconstruction* (1935; New York: Touchstone, 1992), 100.

14 The exact speech reads:

> Four score and seven years ago our fathers brought forth on this continent a new nation, conceived in liberty and dedicated to the proposition that all men are created equal. Now we are engaged in a great civil war, testing whether that nation or any nation so conceived and so dedicated can long endure. We are met on a great battlefield of that war. We have come to dedicate a portion of that field as a final resting-place for those who here gave their lives that that nation might live. It is altogether fitting and proper that we should do this. But in a larger sense, we cannot dedicate, we cannot consecrate, we cannot hallow this ground. The brave men, living and dead, who struggled here have consecrated it far above our poor power to add or detract. The world will little note nor long remember what we say here, but it can never forget what they did here. It is for us the living rather to be dedicated here to the unfinished work which they who fought here have thus far so nobly advanced. It is rather for us to be here dedicated to the great task remaining before us—that from these honored dead we take increased devotion to that cause for which they gave the last full measure of devotion—that we here highly resolve that these dead shall not have died in vain, that this nation under God shall have a new birth of freedom, and that government of the people, by the people, for the people shall not perish from the earth.

15 Referring to Robert Hill. This would suggest that Hill spoke before James, although in the conference program, James is listed as having spoken first.

16 *Les jacobins noirs: Toussaint L'Ouverture et la révolution de Saint Domingue* (1949; Paris: Éditions Caribéennes, 1983).

17 In a fragment of James' other speech that has survived from the Congress of Black Writers, he also had the following to say about Haiti:

> I know very well that Black Power can be, today, a very oppressive power. So that the slogan Black Power is a general slogan against colonialism, neo-colonialism,

and against what Frantz Fanon was so clear about, native local governments that are merely continuators of the imperialist government that has been overthrown. We must be quite clear about that. So that Stokely used to say, for him, Tshombe was not a Black man *[Applause]*. He says Tshombe served the interests of imperialism. And we are very clear about that—I from personal experience. A Black government does not necessarily mean a government that does not feel the power that we mean when we say Black Power. So that Doc Duvalier is Black, that does not matter at all. I myself am waiting, and a lot of other people are waiting, for the day when the Haitian people are going to overthrow him. That is certain to come. *[Applause]* Maybe not as quickly as some of you Haitians might like but you must understand and take it for certain, he cannot continue indefinitely. Many of them have tried and he is certain to go. The population everywhere is aware of that. The other day I saw in the paper that he said he was going away. He was ill and he wanted to go to the United States for medical attention. And some of his friends told him no, you don't go to the United States for medical attention. All the medical attention you need, we will give you here. *[Laughter]* So he's still there. But he had reached the stage where he wanted to get out. I read that in the French paper *Le Monde* which tells less lies than the other bourgeois papers *[Laughter and applause]*. So that, a few months ago, Duvalier thought it was best to seek medical advice abroad. We don't know when he will need to go abroad for medical advice again, but we can hope for the best.

Chapter 3: The Fathers of the Modern Revolt

1 C. L. R. James, *The Black Jacobins* (1938; New York: Vintage Books, 1989), 10.
2 Hill is referring to de Wimpffen, whom James describes in *The Black Jacobins* as "an exceptionally observant and able traveller." James, *The Black Jacobins*, 18.
3 James, *The Black Jacobins*, 87.
4 Orlando Patterson, *The Sociology of Slavery: An Analysis of the Origins, Development, and Structure of Negro Slave Society in Jamaica* (London: MacGibbon and Kee, 1967), 70.
5 Hill is referring to Duse Mohamed Ali, a prominent member of England Islamic community and editor of the *Africa Times and Orient Review*. Ali employed Garvey as a writer of the paper and Ali himself was later associated with the UNIA.
6 William E. Bittle and Gilbert Geis, *The Longest Way Home: Chief Alfred C. Sam and the Back-to-Africa Movement* (Detroit: Wayne State University Press, 1964), 211.
7 Marcus Garvey, compiled by Amy Jacques Garvey, *The Philosophy and Opinions of Marcus Garvey or Africa for the Africans* (1923; Dover: The Majority Press: 1986), 37.
8 E. David Cronon, *Black Moses: Marcus Garvey and the Universal Negro Improvement Association* (Madison: The University of Wisconsin Press, 1955/1969), 21, and Garvey, *The Philosophy and Opinions of Marcus Garvey*, 2.
9 Cronon, *Black Moses*, 65.
10 Cronon, *Black Moses*, 66.
11 Hill is quoting directly from Cronon, *Black Moses*, 119, and Garvey, *The Philosophy and Opinions of Marcus Garvey*, 180–183.
12 *The Black Jacobins*, 396.
13 *The Black Jacobins*, 397.

14 Hill takes some poetic license with the conversation between Fanon and Sartre. For an account of their encounters, see Simone de Beauvoir's *Force of Circumstance* (Harmondsworth: Penguin Books, 1968), 597, 605–611, 620–622.

Chapter 4: African History in the Service of the Black Liberation

1 Richard B. Moore was born in Barbados. Described in the Congress brochure as a "deep student of African and Afro-American history," and as someone who "played a significant part in founding the Barbados Labour Party," Moore is the author of *The Name "Negro": Its Origins and Evil Use* (New York: Afro-American Publishers, 1960), among other books. Moore, who spoke directly after Rodney, presented a paper titled "The Civilizations of Ancient Africa."

2 Esteban Montejo, *The Autobiography of a Runaway Slave* (Cleveland: World Publishing Company, 1968).

3 The reference is to Hugh Shearer, who was prime minister of Jamaica between 1967 and 1972.

4 Aspects of this important debate were recently precipitated by the publication of Martin Bernal's *Black Athena: The Afroasiatic Roots of Classical Civilization* (New Brunswick: Rutgers University Press, 1987). See the debate assembled in *Black Athena Revisited*, ed. M. R. Lefkowitz and G. M. Rogers (Chapel Hill: University of North Carolina Press, 1996).

5 Rodney is perhaps referring to the negative response of some members of the audience to James' comment that Greek civilization represented humanity's highest achievement. Reference to this can be found in the October 15, 1968 issue of the *McGill Daily*, 3.

6 Rodney is referring to poet LeRoi Jones, otherwise known as Amiri Baraka, the renowned African-American poet, playwright, and politico whose work helped to define the Black Power period of the sixties and seventies.

7 Mungo Park, *Travels in the Interior Districts of Africa in the Years 1795, 1796, and 1797* (London: Printed by W. Bulmer and Co. for the author; and sold by G. and W. Nicol, 1799).

8 Julius K. Nyerere, "Socialism and Rural Development," *Uhuru na Ujamaa/Freedom and Socialism* (Oxford: Oxford University Press, 1968).

Chapter 5: The Civilizations of Ancient Africa

1 The actual title is "Basic Views on Image of the Afro-American in Literature, Related Thoughts on Image and Independence and the Independence in Guyana." Mimeograph (New York: Afroamerican Publishers, 1966).

2 The actual titles are "Caribbean Unity and Freedom," *Freedomways*, 4(3), Summer 1964, 295–311, and "Du Bois and Pan-Africa," *Freedomways*, 5(1), Winter 1965, 166–187.

3 All references to "my younger brother," "our young friend," or "young collaborator" are made in reference to Walter Rodney who spoke prior to Moore on "African History in the Service of Black Liberation."

4 Lewis H. Morgan, *Ancient Society* (Chicago: Charles H. Kerr and Company, 1877).

5 Arnold Toynbee, *A Study of History* (London: Oxford University Press: 1934-1961).

6 L. S. B. Leakey, *The Progress and Evolution of Man in Africa* (London: Oxford University Press, 1961), 3.

7 Leakey, *The Progress and Evolution of Man*, 6–7.

8 Leakey, *The Progress and Evolution of Man*, 7–8.

9 Leakey, *The Progress and Evolution of Man*, 8–9.

10 Desmond Clarke, "The Prehistoric Origins of African Culture," in *The Journal of African History*, 5(2), 164.

11 Clarke, "The Prehistoric Origins," 168.

12 Clarke, "The Prehistoric Origins," 177.

13 "Africa proper, as far as History goes back, has remained—for all purposes of connection with the rest of the World—shut up . . . the land of childhood, which lying beyond the day of self-conscious history, is enveloped in the dark mantle of Night?" Georg Wilhelm Friedrich Hegel, *The Philosophy of History* (New York: Dover Publications, Inc., 1956), 91. Relying on biased and ethnocentric missionary accounts for information, for Hegel, "The Negro . . . exhibits the natural man in his completely wild and untamed state" and "all thought of reverence and morality—all that we call feeling" must be cast aside if Africans are to be understood. (93) Any trace of culture that might merit Africans assuming their place around the table of humanity, according to Hegel, stems from the influence of Islam. For Hegel, Africa "is no historical part of the World; it has no movement or development to exhibit" and, to the extent that it does, this movement belongs "to the Asiatic or European World" as Egypt "does not belong to the African Spirit." (99) Lastly: "What we properly understand by Africa, is the Unhistorical, Undeveloped Spirit, still involved in the conditions of mere nature, and which had to be presented here only as on the threshold of the World's History." (99)

14 Paul Lewinson, *Race, Class, and Party: A History of the Negro in the South* (1932; New York: Russell and Russell, 1963).

15 *The Name "Negro": Its Origins and Evil Use* (New York: Afro-American Publishers, 1960).

16 Referring to Walter Rodney.

17 Basil Davison in collaboration with F. K. Buah and with Advice from J. F. Ade Ajay, *A History of West Africa* (1965; London: Longman, 1977).

18 Georges Balandier, *Daily Life in the Kingdom of the Kongo: From the Sixteenth to the Eighteenth Century* (London: Allen and Unwin, 1968).

19 Leo Frobenius, *Histoire de la civilisation Africaine* (Paris: Gallimard, 1952).

20 W. E. B. DuBois, *The World and Africa: An Inquiry into the Part which Africa played in World History* (1946; New York: International Publishers, 1990), 79.

21 Moore is referring to the student protests that gripped Columbia University in 1968. Cordier was brought in to quell the protest and restore order on the campus.

22 Sir Allan Henderson Gardiner, *Egypt of the Pharaohs: An Introduction* (London: Oxford University Press, 1961).

23 William Foxwell Albright, *The Proto-Sinaitic Inscriptions and their Decipherment* (Cambridge: Harvard University Press, 1966).

24 Marcel Grioule, *Conversations with Ogotemmeli: An Introduction to Dogon Religious Ideas* (1965; London: Oxford University Press, 1970).

25 Father Placide Tempel, *Bantu Philosophy* (Paris: Presence Africaine, 1959).

26 Rodney is referring to Richard Moore.

27 Arvida is a city in the Saguenay region of Quebec. The city was established in 1926 to accommodate Alcan factory workers. Alcan is one of the world's largest producers of aluminum.

Chapter 6: Black History in the Americas

1 Moore is likely referring to the presentation given by C. L. R. James on "The Haitian Revolution and the History of Slave Revolt." See Chapter 2.

Chapter 7: Race in Britain and the Way Out

1 Powellism refers to the phenomenon of Enoch Powell, the conservative anti-immigration English politician.

2 Chaguaramas, a deep-water harbour in Trinidad, was the site of a US military base. The United States obtained a ninety-nine-year lease on Chaguaramas, as well as several other military bases throughout the West Indies, from the British in exchange for several dozen antiquated warships in 1940. The base became a strong point of contention between the PNM and the United States government once Williams' PNM came into office in 1956 and demanded that the base be returned to the West Indies for use as a capital site for the West Indian Federation.

3 Enoch Powell was a Conservative MP who, in his now infamous April 1968 "Rivers of Blood" speech, outlined his fears concerning the inflow of Caribbean and Third World immigrants to Britain. Cyril Osborne was a Conservative MP who attempted to introduce a bill in British Parliament in 1965 limiting the flow of immigrants to Britain and was generally viewed as having extreme views on immigration.

4 The Notting Hill Riots began in August 1958 in response to a series of attacks on blacks in the Notting Hill district of London.

5 The pardner is a popular savings scheme involving people, primarily women, of Caribbean descent. Money is collected, usually on a weekly basis, and distributed to one of the participants. The recipient of the money pot is rotated until every member receives their share. At this point, people can decide to drop out or continue through to the next cycle. Many find the pardner a useful tool for saving money for emergencies or unexpected expenses.

6 Small is referring to Darcus Howe of the Race Today Collective, who later went on to establish the Race Today Collective in England and edit its eponymous magazine. Howe was also C. L. R. James' nephew.

Chapter 9: Frantz Fanon and the Third World

1 See James Forman, *Sammy Young, Jr.: The First Black College Student to Die in the Black Liberation Movement* (New York: Grove Press, 1968).

2 Forman was originally scheduled to share the podium with Eldridge Cleaver on "The Black Revolution: The Third World and Capitalism."

3 Frantz Fanon, "Racism and Culture," in *Toward the African Revolution* (New York: Grove Press, 1967), 37–38

4 See https://omeka.library.kent.edu/special-collections/items/show/3179.

5 It is not certain whose translation of Fanon Forman is drawing on, and it is perhaps his own. Another partial translation of the letter was published in Peter Geismar's *Fanon: The Revolutionary as Prophet* (New York: Grove Press, 1969), 185.

6 See http://www.crmvet.org/docs/6806_sncc_objectives.pdf.

Chapter 10: Black Power in the USA

1 Referring to Carmichael, who was then honourary prime minister of the Black Panther Party.

Chapter 12: "You Don't Play with Revolution"

1 Ralph Ellison, *Invisible Man* (1952; New York: Second Vintage International Edition, 1995), 354.
2 C. L. R. James, *Party Politics in the West Indies* (San Juan, Trinidad: Vedic Enterprises Ltd., 1962), 100.
3 James, *Party Politics in the West Indies*, 89.

Chapter 13: On the Banning of Walter Rodney from Jamaica

1 At the time of James' talk, Rodney had published scholarly articles, such as "Portuguese Attempts at Monopoly on the Upper Guinea Coast, 1580–1650," *The Journal of African History*, 6(3), 1965 and "African Slavery and Other Forms of Social Oppression on the Upper Guinea Coast in the Context of the Atlantic Slave-Trade," *The Journal of African History*, 7(3), 1966. In 1970 he published *A History of the Upper Guinea Coast, 1545–1800* (Oxford: Clarendon Press, 1970).
2 C. L. R. James, *Party Politics in the West Indies* (San Juan, Trinidad: Vedic Enterprises Ltd., 1962), 125.
3 James, *Party Politics in the West Indies*, 135.
4 Frank Walcott (1919–1999) was a central figure in the trade union movement and a politician who served the Barbados Workers' Union for more than forty years.

INDEX

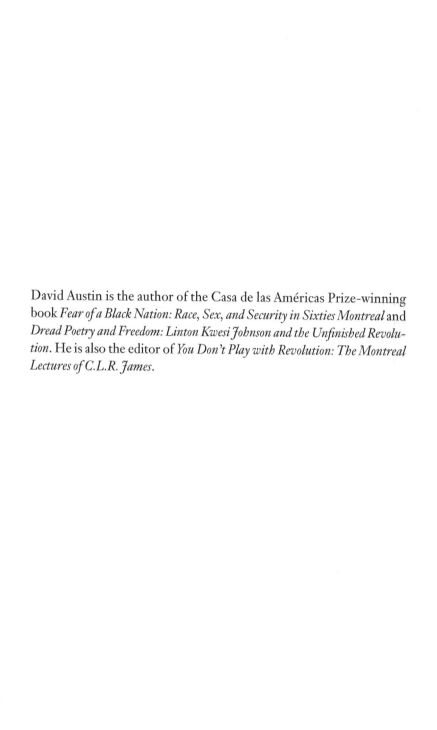

David Austin is the author of the Casa de las Américas Prize-winning book *Fear of a Black Nation: Race, Sex, and Security in Sixties Montreal* and *Dread Poetry and Freedom: Linton Kwesi Johnson and the Unfinished Revolution*. He is also the editor of *You Don't Play with Revolution: The Montreal Lectures of C.L.R. James*.

Printed and bound by CPI Group (UK) Ltd, Croydon, CR0 4YY

13/04/2025

14656488-0002